POLITICS AND SOCIETY IN WALES

Religion, Secularization and Social Change in Wales

POLITICS AND SOCIETY IN WALES SERIES
Series editor: Ralph Fevre

Previous volumes in the series:

Paul Chaney, Tom Hall and Andrew Pithouse (eds), *New Governance – New Democracy? Post-Devolution Wales*

Neil Selwyn and Stephen Gorard, *The Information Age: Technology, Learning and Exclusion in Wales*

Graham Day, *Making Sense of Wales: A Sociological Perspective*

Richard Rawlings, *Delineating Wales: Constitutional, Legal and Administrative Aspects of National Devolution*

Molly Scott Cato, *The Pit and the Pendulum: A Cooperative Future for Work in the Welsh Valleys*

The Politics and Society in Wales Series examines issues of politics and government, and particularly the effects of devolution on policy-making and implementation, and the way in which Wales is governed as the National Assembly gains in maturity. It will also increase our knowledge and understanding of Welsh society and analyse the most important aspects of social and economic change in Wales. Where necessary, studies in the series will incorporate strong comparative elements which will allow a more fully informed appraisal of the condition of Wales.

Religion, Secularization and Social Change in Wales

CONGREGATIONAL STUDIES IN A POST-CHRISTIAN SOCIETY

By

PAUL CHAMBERS

*Published on behalf of the Social Science Committee
of the Board of Celtic Studies of the University of Wales*

UNIVERSITY OF WALES PRESS
CARDIFF
2005

British Library Cataloguing-in-Publication Data.
A catalogue record for this book is available from the British Library.

ISBN 0–7083–1884–3

Printed in Great Britain by MPG Books Limited, Bodmin, Cornwall

Contents

Foreword

It is always a pleasure to see a doctoral thesis turn into a book, the more so when the task of external examiner has been a particularly rewarding one. Such is the case with Paul Chambers's careful analysis of *Religion, Secularization and Social Change in Wales* – a study which brings to life the ongoing process of religious change in Swansea.

Chambers works at two levels. First, he maps the religious scene in Swansea. Secondly, he looks in detail at four different case studies (bearing in mind that one of these is a composite story) in order to understand the precise mechanisms that take place in the lives of churches as they grow and decline. Both the initial mapping and the case studies themselves are set against the wider economic and social changes occurring in south Wales, a part of the world in which industrialization and urbanization led initially to religious growth as both the free church traditions and Catholicism catered – in many ways very effectively – for a newly urbanized population. The south Wales story is distinctive, a history that Chambers knows from the inside and understands well.

Secularization may have come late to south Wales, but it came fast. Post-industrialization has not been kind to the free churches in Swansea. As the communities, of which the chapels were a part, have collapsed, so too have the chapels themselves – as indeed have the associated political and industrial institutions that were part of the same evolution. A whole way of life has come to an end, leaving its last survivors bewildered and bereft. Parish-based churches have withstood the shock a little better, but many of these are communities of the old rather than the young, posing inevitable questions about the future.

This is not the whole story however. Life, including church life, goes on, but in different ways. In my own work, I have become increasingly aware of a shift taking place in the churches of northern Europe, right across the denominations. This is a shift from a culture of obligation in the religious field to one of choice or consumption. No church or chapel that relies on a sense of duty to bring people to church is likely to prosper in the new millennium; such an approach no longer resonates. Conversely, if a church or chapel can make it worthwhile for people to come, as a matter of choice or conviction rather than duty or obligation, that congregation can flourish. One of the most interesting aspects of Chambers's work is explaining in some detail how this is done.

Modern Europeans are increasingly opting into their churches instead of opting out. The fact that this shift has taken place unusually fast in south Wales, including Swansea, is one of the reasons that makes this case study, or more precisely, this set of case studies, particularly fascinating. Swansea becomes a laboratory in which we see a speeded-up version of the shifts taking place in a late modern European society. On one hand, Chambers documents a process of relentless and rapid decline; on the other, he shows how particular congregations can, despite everything, move forwards and the factors that must be taken into account if this is to happen.

With this in mind, I commend this book warmly both to academics who are interested in the field, but also to those whose responsibility it is to plan carefully for the future of the churches in this part of Wales. Both groups will benefit from a careful reading of Chambers's exemplary text.

Grace Davie
August 2004

Series Editor's Foreword

We are extremely fortunate that Professor Grace Davie has agreed to write the foreword to this new volume in the Politics and Society in Wales series. Grace is the foremost sociologist of religion in the UK and is a past president of the Association for the Sociology of Religion. One aspect of her work that has attracted a great deal of attention throughout the world is her idea that, when it comes to religion, Europe is exceptional. She argues, for example, that the low religiosity of Europe is actually a part of being European. From this point of view, finding out what kind of religion, if any, can survive in the relatively hostile European environment becomes a particularly interesting, and indeed vital, question. This new book by Paul Chambers helps to give us some answers to this question.

There is no need for me to say more about the latest addition to the Politics and Society in Wales series except, briefly, to make some general remarks about the place of books like this one in the series. As Grace Davie notes, this book began life as a Ph.D. thesis. It has always been one of the objectives of the series to publish the very best doctoral research in social science in Wales. In sociology, at least, there is a long and glorious history of turning Ph.D.s into books; some of the most enduring texts in the discipline began life in this way.

While this tradition carries on (in the US as well as in the UK), publishers do not always look as favourably on this enterprise as they once did. This is a matter of profound regret because brilliant Ph.D.s are potentially a much more promising source of academic books than many of the proposals that publishers and authors pitch to each other. Work that is produced in this way tends to be more detailed and, perhaps, has stronger foundations and a greater respect for the accurate representation of its subject matter. In other words, Ph.D.s are made to last.

Good Ph.D.s are written with great care and a rare kind of commitment but working fulltime on a Ph.D. is a singular opportunity to take some time to think according to your own lights. At no other time in an academic writer's career can the main items on their agenda be set solely by their imagination and conscience. In more normal times they may well find that their minds are tamed and constrained by the agencies that fund research, publishers (or series editors) and the demands of the academic job market.

So, Ph.D.s ought to be about obsessions and passions – indeed why else would men and women devote so many years of their lives to them? They really have to care about getting their subject exactly right and this care is evident in every page of this welcome addition to our series. We hope to feature more books that share this heritage in the years to come.

1

Introduction

St Helens Road lies in the centre of the city of Swansea. For the casual observer, its nondescript mixture of takeaway food shops, restaurants, charity shops, mosques and churches, with many of the latter abandoned and derelict, is an unremarkable vista. Built in the nineteenth century, a product of the evolution of an urban and industrial landscape and sharing many of the characteristics of industrial communities in south-west Wales, it represents a microcosm of the social, cultural and economic changes that have swept Wales in the twentieth century. In a space of 1,000 metres, the sheer number of buildings that are or have been devoted to religious purposes attests to both the rich religious heritage of Wales and the effects of social and cultural change on institutional religion. Each building has a different story to tell, some are now occupied by non-Christian faith groups, others are devoted to secular uses and a few still house small and dwindling congregations. Most are merely abandoned and derelict, mute monuments to the secularization of Welsh society.

This book seeks to address one of the most significant recent transformations in Welsh society, the dislocation of its people from their religious institutions and the struggle of those institutions to retain any continuing relevance in contemporary Welsh society. Wales is a singular country. Situated on the western margins of Europe, it is a region that is both economically deprived and politically subservient to England, and that also retains a distinctive culture, originally demarcated by language. Historically, the Welsh language has always served to differentiate Wales from her neighbours and the same can be said for religion (G. H. Jenkins, 1978; P. Jenkins, 1992, G. A. Williams, 1985). Religion has, in the past, functioned as a key carrier of Welsh social, cultural and 'national' identity (Davie, 1994) and traditionally the Welsh have been characterized as a 'religion shaped people'. This picture of Welsh religiosity is largely derived from the nineteenth-century triumph of Nonconformism and its hangover into the early twentieth century, a time period marked by intense religious enthusiasm and rigid public morality. While this picture was never entirely accurate (G. A. Williams, 1985; R. Davies, 1996) we can say with rather more certainty that the pervasive influence of institutional religion on Welsh society is now a thing of the past. Organized religion is declining there at a faster rate than anywhere else in the United Kingdom (Bible Society, 1997) and this represents a crucial change in the life of a people who, not so long ago, could properly be described as 'wedded to the chapel'.

A BRIEF HISTORY OF RELIGION IN WALES

In order to understand the place of religion in contemporary Wales, we must know something of its past and how it came to be such a significant source of Welsh identity. Identity, and a sense of identity, is not an arbitrary phenomenon but draws its strength from and is characterized by the multiplicity of experiences and the sense of continuity which inform the self-definitions of populations. People, places, events, situations and institutions, filtered through the prism of social interaction, all form the basic building blocks of identities. Identity is also both a species of categorization and the product of meanings applied to categories, whether they be categories of status, class, gender, ethnicity, language, 'nationality' or even religion. These meanings, and their production and reproduction, shift with time and context, and are constantly being reformulated and developed, or even abandoned in the light of new experiences. In the brief discussion that follows,[1] the question of identity, specifically the story of how the Welsh came to have such a close identification with religion and then came to lose it will be central.

   This Welsh reputation for piety has been something of a movable feast and owes much to the age of religious revivals spanning the eighteenth and nineteenth centuries. Prior to this the Welsh were generally seen by their contemporaries as an irreligious people, addicted to superstition and magic, and of questionable moral fibre (Thomas, 1971; G. H. Jenkins, 1978; G. Williams, 1994). In terms of institutional religion, the period spanning the Anglo-Norman conquest of Wales and the Tudor settlement saw the imposition of new ecclesiastical structures and the progressive marginalization of vernacular religious practices. The Reformation in Wales was merely a continuation of this process, marking the replacement of one alien liturgical language, Latin, with another, English (Harris, 1990). Unsurprisingly, the religious reforms stemming from the Tudor settlement were met with general indifference among the majority of the Welsh population. This indifference persisted throughout the Tudor and Stuart periods and it was the perceived irreligiosity of the Welsh that provided the impetus for a period of concerted activity by reformers in Wales that laid the foundations for the re-emergence of a truly vernacular form of religion.

Initially, reforming energies were directed towards creating a vernacular religious literature, culminating in the translation of the Bible into the Welsh language and its publication in 1588. While this event had profound implications for the future development of the language, the Protestant reformers found Wales to be stony ground in terms of the propagation of the Christian gospel. The Propagation Act of 1650 sought to redress this situation by organizing evangelism on a national scale, but the effects were muted. Received with indifference by the indigenous population and using as its vehicle an impoverished and moribund established church that represented little more than the dominance of the landowning gentry, it manifestly did not lead to the type of social and moral revolution that the puritan reformers envisaged. What it did do, however, was to establish the impassioned preaching of the gospel in the vernacular language of the people as a crucial medium of salvation (G. H. Jenkins, 1978).

Language and in particular the written word was to prove a crucial element in the formulation of what would in time become a distinctive national identification with religion. After 1588, Protestant reformers sponsored a steady stream of printed religious texts in the Welsh language, mainly translations of European works. This publishing activity was primarily a short-term expedient aimed at revitalizing religious life and incorporating the Welsh into the Protestant community, although it was also to have some unforeseen consequences. What the reformers bequeathed to the Welsh people was a body of printed texts in a uniform fixed version of their vernacular language, something which Benedict Anderson (1991) has identified as a prerequisite for the emergence of collective identification, first as a reading public and eventually at the level of national identity. Initially, this reading public was largely restricted to that interstitial section of the population, lesser gentry, yeomen, tradesmen and craftsmen and their families, who were later to become the bedrock of religious dissent. In later years, the peasantry would be added to this readership who, in Gwyn Alf Williams's words, 'learned to read in terms of the Bible and Protestant sectarianism' (1988: 121). In doing so this readership became a new form of imagined community, where literary consciousness, religious consciousness and 'national' consciousness became fused together.

If Puritanism in Wales was at the time a largely failed experiment, its methods – the propagation of the gospel through the written word and preaching – established the template for future religious activity. The period following the Restoration in 1660 saw the gradual establishment of dissenting congregations in parts of Wales. This was to have far-reaching ramifications for the future development of a truly indigenous form of religion. As Wales emerged into the eighteenth century, a new generation of dissenters built upon these foundations. In geographical terms, the spread of dissent had been patchy. Largely restricted to the rural upland areas, it thrived best in local conditions where the established Church was stretched for resources and weak. All this was to change with the arrival of Methodism in Wales. What Methodism initially brought was something that had been signally lacking before, namely mass enthusiasm for religion and, from this, Nonconformist Wales was to emerge (G. H. Jenkins, 1988).

From the lofty vantage point of the late nineteenth century, this period was viewed by contemporary religious commentators as a 'Great Awakening', the beginning of the age of revivals and proof positive of Methodism's impact on the Welsh psyche. In this narrative, charismatic young preachers emerged, passionate in their desire to spread the gospel. New congregations were established, dissenting academies created and the gospel was preached with powerful force to eager listeners. However, the new enthusiasm had not emerged from a vacuum. Immediately prior to the arrival of Methodism, a network of circulating schools had been established providing both basic literacy and religious instruction for the common people, and in consequence furnishing fertile ground for the labours of evangelists. Methodism also owed much to the former labours of dissenting preachers and writers and able Anglican clerics. Indeed, at the height of the Great Awakening, only a minority of Welsh men and women heeded the siren call of Methodism. Its greatest successes were in south Wales, under leaders such as Howell Harris. In the north, popular allegiance to Anglicanism, despite its perceived shortcomings, remained strong and the older dissenting traditions had won a new lease of life. Nevertheless, Methodism laid down a social and moral foundation that was to bear its fruit in due time.

By the nineteenth century, the social and moral revolution that the Puritans had dreamed of and which the new enthusiasts had proclaimed with such passion and power had largely come to pass. The impetus for this revolution came from another revolution, industrial in character and accompanied by the mass movement of people within Wales. In much the same way as contemporary globalization has facilitated the growth of religion in the late modern world, this mass movement of people saw the emergence of a genuinely new social movement, working-class Nonconformity (Lambert, 1988). Dominated by the Presbyterians in the north and Congregationalists and Baptists in the south, the Welsh could now properly be called 'the people of the Book' (G. A. Williams, 1985: 131). The Roman Catholic Church, which had been almost extinct prior to industrialization, also benefited from successive waves of immigrants from Catholic Ireland to industrial south Wales. Clearly, while industrialization was to carry the seeds that would eventually challenge and undermine the position of religion in Welsh life, in the short term it did much to promote the cause of religion in Wales (R. Davies, 1996). The 1851 religious census appeared to confirm this picture. On the Sunday that the census took place, over half the population of Wales were recorded as present in the pews, and two out of three were Nonconformists. Even when taking into account the possible inflation of figures (Gill, 1992), it is evident that a major cultural shift had accompanied equally major social and economic changes.

Working-class Nonconformity, transplanted to and rooted in the new industrial communities, touched the lives of everyone in those communities. Even those who chose not to attend a place of worship were nonetheless constrained under the heavy hand of Nonconformist values and attitudes (Lambert, 1988; R. Davies, 1996). From the perspective of the nineteenth century, a new self-understanding was proclaimed from the pulpit and in the press and numerous books. This new understanding characterized the Welsh as a fervently religious people and asserted an unambiguous link between Nonconformity and Welsh identity. This portrait of a people united in their religious faith was true, but only up to a point. Welsh Non-conformity was also characterized by dissension within its ranks, voluntary introversion, schismatic tendencies and organizational problems, not least the inability of national leaderships to impose their will on the largely inde-pendent local congregations of the south. Competition between congregations was fierce, although this was less a question of theological distinctions and more a by-product of the massive over-provision of places of worship (Gill, 1993). Building bigger, better, ever grander chapels, with little regard for either local demand or the crippling debts passed on to future generations, was just one symptom of the underlying problems besetting Welsh Nonconformity.

At the national level, the picture looked somewhat rosier. Nonconformity had replaced the established church as the main religious, social and cultural force, and increasingly Nonconformity was also becoming a political force. Nonconformity was deeply implicated in rural politics, in the Chartist movement and the struggle for greater suffrage, and in moves towards the disestablishment of the Anglican Church. After 1867 and the passing of the Second Reform Bill, which extended the vote to working-class males, the fortunes of Welsh Nonconformity and the new Liberal Party became increasingly interdependent. The first fruits of this combination of influence became visible with the passing of the first legislative Act specific to Wales, the 1891 Sunday Closing Act. Not only was this a triumph for the forces of temperance, it also announced the arrival of Nonconformity as a political force in Wales. The 1906 electoral landslide, which returned 377 Liberal members of parliament to Westminster, also saw the rise of the leading Welsh Nonconformist politician of his day, David Lloyd George, first as President of the Board of Trade, then as Chancellor of the Exchequer and ultimately, in 1916–22, as Prime Minister. However, this Liberal–Nonconformist hegemony was to be short-lived.

In 1915, when the journalist and short-story writer Caradog Evans published *My People* (reprinted, 1987), his scathing portrayal of the widespread venality and hypocrisy underpinning the supposed Nonconformist idyll, he was relentlessly attacked by the Liberal–Nonconformist elite in Wales. Branded a traitor to his people (and worse), Evans's unflattering portrayal merely reflected growing tensions within Welsh society (R. Davies, 1996). The momentum of Nonconformity had only been maintained by periodic religious revivals and, by the turn of the century, in the increasingly anglicized industrial areas, the competing claims of socialism and secularism were already making themselves heard. The last great Welsh Revival of 1904 merely highlighted these tensions and effectively drew a line under the self-understanding of the Welsh people as fervently religious. The disestablishment of the Welsh Church in 1920 proved to be a hollow victory for a Welsh Nonconformity that was becoming increasingly disengaged from the concerns of the people. The Anglicans consolidated their position numerically, as did a Roman Catholic Church that continued to benefit from immigration from Catholic countries. Socialism, trade unionism and the Labour Party effectively replaced the Liberal–Nonconformist axis as the main vehicle for social concerns within the industrial areas. In the rural areas, change was slower and concerns centred more around the politics of culture, culminating in 1925 at the Maesgwyn Temperance Hall, Pwllheli, with the formation of Plaid Genedlaethol Cymru (the Welsh Nationalist Party), with the Reverend Lewis Valentine as its first president (McAllister, 2001).

If Nonconformist influence on the national stage was waning, the hegemonic status of religious institutions at the local level was to prove more resilient. The 1904 Revival had not led to the widespread re-evangelization of the Welsh people and indeed the numerical gains accompanying this movement had largely dissipated by the 1920s. Competing social and cultural attractions, most notably the cinema, and the rise of socialism and the Labour Party, all undermined the position of the chapels, but it was not until the Great Depression in the 1930s that fissures really began to be exposed. The widespread over-provision of places of worship came home to roost as increasingly impoverished congregations attempted to meet the costs of their mortgaged churches and chapels. For poorer families, the financial costs of church and chapel membership became more than they could bear. Numbers began to fall and while numbers rose again during the period of the 1939–45 war, for many younger worshippers called into war work or the armed services, the social and geographical dislocation loosened their ties with their home chapels. The 1950s constituted something of an Indian summer, with numbers up on the inter-war years and many flourishing and vibrant chapels.

Nevertheless, cracks were appearing. Greater social and geographic mobility took many younger members out of the orbit of their home chapels. Congregations were increasingly coming to be numerically dominated by females and there were fewer candidates for the ministry. The progressive erosion of the Welsh language in areas where it had previously been strong led to marked decline in that sector of the religious economy, and almost everywhere the local influence of the chapels on morals and manners was declining. By the 1960s, the Indian summer had passed and winter beckoned. Numbers were falling significantly, many congregations were increasingly ageing and feminized, while ministers were increasingly stretched in their activities as they took on oversight of more and more congregations. From the 1970s onwards the rate of religious decline in Wales was, and continues to be, higher than anywhere else in the United Kingdom (Brierley and Wraight, 1995; Bible Society, 1997), although this process is uneven. Some congregations in urban areas remain fairly buoyant compared to their rural counterparts. Some types of congregation, most notably evangelical congregations, appear to have resisted decline more effectively than their non-evangelical counterparts and in some cases are growing. The Church in Wales and the Roman Catholic Church have not declined numerically to the same extent as the chapels. Moreover, the profile of other non-Christian faith groups, notably Islam, has grown with post-war in-migration and the major urban areas are now home to significant Muslim communities, although these remain a marginal force within the overall Welsh religious economy and represent a tiny proportion of the general population.[2] Nevertheless, despite the ebb and flow of the fortunes of disparate faith groups, it is now fairly obvious to all but the most optimistic observer that, in general, the Welsh are no longer 'a religion shaped people'.

SECULARIZATION AND WALES

Wales is not alone in its experience of rapid and deep secularization, a phenomenon which characterizes much of northern Europe, but this does not in itself tell us very much. While there is a huge sociological literature on secularization, it tends to be rather generalized and abstract. More importantly, general theories of secularization do not address the specific questions of how religion came to be such a socially significant factor in the creation of Welsh identity and why it has collapsed so quickly. Attempts to find answers to these questions have until now largely been the province of historians and rather less has been written about the ongoing processes of religious decline within contemporary Welsh society. Religion in Wales, if not entirely dead, is seen as terminally sick, subject to the secularizing influences common throughout Europe. This picture is less than accurate on two counts.

First, religion in Wales, while generally declining, has also become fragmented, with some growth in parts of the religious economy. The factors underlying this growth need to be explained if we are to understand better how and why religion is declining so rapidly in Wales and what the future of Welsh religion might look like. Secondly, the emergence of a distinctively 'Welsh' form of religion that pervaded all areas of Welsh life was the result of a nationally specific set of social, economic and cultural circumstances, operating mainly at a local community level. Its decline should be seen in the same context. In order to understand the nature of general religious decline in Wales, it is necessary to understand the nature of the changes that have affected local communities and the varied attempts of local churches and chapels to adapt to these changes.

Therefore the focus of this book is, by necessity, local, but this poses problems for any writer who seeks to investigate the general scope of religion in Wales. Wales, like any other country, is not a homogeneous whole and there are wide variations in local conditions and lived experience. South-west Wales has been chosen as the focus for this study for a number of reasons, not least because it encompasses many dimensions of Welsh community life. Situated on the edges of the anglicized south and the Welsh-speaking 'heartland' of west and mid-Wales, it has a unique heritage that is both industrial and agricultural, urban and rural, and in linguistic terms, encompasses Welsh- and English-speaking communities. As such it *approximates* the generalized experience of many varied communities in Wales in a way that other parts of Wales might not.

The methodological rationale of this book is grounded in the idea that the individual practice of the Christian religion is necessarily related to the idea of a community of believers and that this is best realized within the institutional framework of the local congregation. The focus, therefore, is largely ethnographic. This book aims to address issues surrounding contemporary Welsh religion through the examination of the experiences of a number of broadly representative congregations as they seek to come to terms with and adapt to an increasingly secularized environment.[3] Within the narrative framework of these case studies, a number of recurrent issues raised by the secularization thesis and some commonly held assumptions about religion in modern societies will be addressed and in some cases either refuted or modified.

The first is the assumption that mainstream religious institutions must inevitably decline in the face of modernization. Clearly, this is not the case in all modern societies, which suggests that the relationship between modernity, secularization and religion is both complex and better explored through the use of individual national cases (Casanova, 1994). Religion, in common with many other Welsh institutions, has both declined in social significance and become more anglicized. This suggests that what we are seeing is a major fragmentation of those traditional sources of Welsh identity of which religion is a part and concomitant changes within the religious sphere.

Secondly, to suggest that one lead process, secularization, is wholly responsible for the decline of religious institutions is to ignore a number of other possible and more immediate contributory factors. Religious institutions are also social institutions. While 'secularization' may constitute a structural constraint upon religious institutions, we cannot afford to ignore the changing nature of social relations in modern societies, particularly at the local level, and the ways in which these changes might promote as well as inhibit religious affiliations. Clearly, the idea that, in conditions of late modernity, mainstream religion is particularly susceptible to the effects of disembedding and detraditionalization has some salience here, but it is also true of all institutions and not just religion. Moreover, I shall argue that the key to understanding both religious decline and religious growth lies within the sphere of the self-understandings of religious groups as they seek to operate within these transformed social environments and not in terms of broad social processes.

A third commonly held assumption that crops up frequently, in both the literature relating to secularization and among religious professionals, is that sectarian groupings of an evangelical disposition are generally more resistant to processes of decline and more successful in their recruitment strategies among the general population. The evidence presented in this book will suggest that this view is at best over-simplistic and, in terms of successful recruitment among the general population, it is a myth.

THE STRUCTURE OF THE VOLUME

This book is structured with three broad aims in mind: first, to address critically the debate concerning secularization in modern societies; secondly, to describe and account for the general religious situation in south-west Wales and to examine these issues in rather more depth through the medium of four case studies of Christian congregations operating in the city of Swansea; thirdly, to demonstrate how empirical data can aid our understanding of religious decline or growth by identifying those factors most likely to inhibit or promote congregational growth.

Chapter 2 will offer a brief examination of the empirical evidence relating to secularization in Britain and introduce the reader to the theoretical framework known as the 'secularization thesis' and some of the controversies surrounding it. From this theoretical discussion I then shift my focus to Wales and the question of the progressive disengagement of religious institutions from Welsh society and culture. Chapter 3 will concentrate on a discussion of social and religious change in the city of Swansea, based on the results of the author's 1995 survey of 219 congregations and an analysis of interviews with twenty-eight religious professionals and church leaders. Shifting from this broad overview, the book then moves to a more detailed examination of various aspects of congregational life and experience. This will be through the medium of four case studies and it is here that a number of questions relating to the current health of Welsh religious institutions and the effects of secularization will be addressed. Key issues that will be discussed include factors such as mobility, class and culture, the varying institutional characteristics that might inhibit or promote the health of religious groups and the nature and effects of competition between these groups. Chapter 4 examines a number of long-established congregations that have experienced sustained decline and are now facing imminent extinction. Chapter 5 is based on an ethnographic study of an Anglican parish situated in one of the oldest working-class communities in Swansea. In contrast to the preceding chapter, it describes a religious organization that has flourished in recent years, despite its situation in a locale characterized by many declining churches and chapels. Chapters 6 and 7 describe two very contrasting Free Church congregations situated in the same suburban setting, a district where religious organizations are generally buoyant. The concluding chapter 8 returns to the theoretical theme and examines some of the sociological implications of social and religious change. It does this by isolating and integrating various factors drawn from the above data in order to further our understanding of both social and religious change in Wales and, more generally, the processes that inform church growth and decline in modern societies and its implications for religious institutions.

   I am conscious that this book could not have been written without the help of others. I am grateful for the financial aid from the Economic and Social Research Council that allowed me to pursue the postgraduate research that this book is based upon and to my Ph.D. supervisor Professor C. C. Harris who provided invaluable guidance both during the research process and the writing of this book. My thanks are also extended to Professor David Dunkerley and to the Centre for Civil Society Studies, University of Glamorgan, for the research fellowship that allowed me the time and space to complete this book and to those colleagues, notably Dr Sue Hutson and Dr Andrew Thompson, who have supported me in this venture. Mention should also be made of Professor Douglas Davies of Durham University, who kindly agreed to read and comment on the finished work, and to Professor Ralph Fevre of the Board of Celtic Studies and Cardiff University, who encouraged me to write this book. I would also like to express my thanks to the many other folk that helped me along the way. One of the greatest privileges of this research has been the opportunity to talk to some of Swansea's oldest residents and to gain some first-hand knowledge of that lost world of vibrant churches and chapels and a society that was working class in character and religious in tenor. In reporting these voices I hope that I have done them justice. Likewise, this book could not have been written without the great contribution of all those within the religious community who taught me so much about the religious life of Swansea and allowed me to participate in so many aspects of their collective life. It is to this community that this book is offered in a spirit of reciprocity.

Secularization in Western Societies

A few years ago, I attended an interview for a university teaching post. As is often the case on these occasions, my inquisitors were rather less interested in my capabilities as a potential teacher and rather more in what I could add to the institution's research profile. I duly made the type of presentation of future research plans that one would expect of a sociologist with an interest in the study of contemporary religion and awaited responses. These were interesting. They ranged from incredulity that any social scientist would be interested in a subject as marginalized and irrelevant as contemporary mainstream Christianity, through to some humour of the 'Vicar of Dibley' sort, and then on to bored indifference. The general consensus seemed to be that secularization was a fact of life, mainstream religion was on its way out (*and a good thing too*) and were there not *more* important things to investigate and write about?

This vignette neatly sums up current attitudes in much of mainstream academia towards both the Christian religion and heritage (Wilson, 1992: 210). Moreover, it serves to illustrate the way in which religion has become an increasingly peripheral force in modern societies (ibid.). Religion as an institution has always been a central part of human social life. This was patently so in European societies and it is patently not so now in those same societies. The picture is uneven, varying from country to country and religion continues to persist, albeit increasingly on the margins of social, cultural and political life, but there can be little doubt that religion in Europe has declined in general social importance. In the light of these significant changes, it is surprising therefore that contemporary religion attracts so little mainstream sociological interest. It would appear that the jury has already arrived at the verdict that modern industrial societies are unquestionably equated with secular societies. Like a juggernaut, modernity crushes religion and there is nothing much left to say other than to raise a glass to the death of religion in modern societies. Clearly, religion, reflecting its marginal social status, has become peripheral to the concerns of many sociologists.

As one would expect with specialists in the sociological study of religion, approaches to the idea of secularization are rather more complex and nuanced. However, there is little agreement over what secularization might entail or even, in some cases, whether it even exists. As sociologists seek to chart the fortunes of religion and map its changes, some writers interpret the available data as pointing to a continuing trajectory of religious decline, a process that if left unchecked might lead to the total loss of faith in religion as an institution. Others see this in terms of the transformation of religion, leaving its future open. Understandably, then, this can lead to some confusion among those interested readers who might, with some justification, ask how can such differing interpretations be derived from what appear to be the same data?

As a general rule of thumb, those sociologists who focus on the study of religious institutions tend to see decline, whereas those sociologists who focus on individual social agents tend to see plenty of evidence of continued religious belief. For the former, all the evidence unquestionably points to the progressive marginalization of religion and religious institutions within modern societies. For the latter, despite obvious institutional decline in terms of numbers and influence, there remains a significant latent demand for religion, albeit in forms which are not easily quantifiable. As with most things in life, the truth probably lies somewhere in between. However, truth can often be difficult to get at, particularly when the waters are muddied by the emergence of a number of competing theories about secularization. These raise many questions. Whether secularization exists as an identifiable process and, if so, what are its dimensions – what are its likeliest outcomes? The answers are not always clear. As Steve Bruce (2002) has recently commented, the debates surrounding secularization have tended to leave much to be desired in terms of sense and sensibility. A high degree of abstraction, the fudging of evidence, the adoption of inappropriately partisan ideological positions and a tendency for theorists to talk past each other rather than to each other is hardly, in his mind, a recipe for reasoned debate. Bruce has a point, but I would suggest that the controversies surrounding the notion of secularization are not merely so much intellectual gamesmanship, but should be seen for what they are: genuine attempts to account for and capture the changing nature of modern societies. What follows in this chapter is an attempt to cut through some of the conceptual confusion surrounding secularization by introducing the reader to the principal lines of thought in this complex debate. Beginning with a brief examination of the evidence relating to secularization in Britain and an overview of the secularization paradigm, we will then examine the impact of recent social theorizing on thinking about religion in modern societies.

RELIGIOUS DECLINE – THE EVIDENCE FOR BRITAIN

Introduction

There can be little doubt that the span of the twentieth century has seen the visible decline of mainstream religion in Britain. However, there is little agreement as to what this means in terms of social processes and even some denial of this contention. In 1995 at the British Sociological Association Sociology of Religion Conference in Lincoln, Steve Bruce created something of a stir among his critics when he challenged some propositions put forward by Stark and Iannaccone (1994). The latter suggested that there remained considerable latent demand for religion in Britain, that modern societies were not necessarily more secular than they were in the past and that, consequently, secularization was a myth. In contrast, basing his argument on past and present indices of involvement in religious activities and marshalling data from the 1991 British Social Attitudes Survey, Bruce argued that the overall picture was clearly that of the continued decline of mainstream religion.[1]

In terms of institutional religion, Bruce suggested that a decreasing proportion of the general population were church members or attendees. Churchgoers attended less frequently and fewer children attended Sunday school. There were fewer clergy and, in terms of status, the general population held them in lower esteem, and their levels of remuneration were less in real terms. The churches had also suffered a loss of both their social and political significance. As far as religious legitimization of family and community were concerned, fewer women are churched after birth and a decreasing proportion of the general population are baptized or married in church. Funerals have tended to retain a religious character[2] but there has been a slight increase in non-religious services. In the area of traditional religious beliefs, there has been a decline in orthodox Christian beliefs and these beliefs are seen as less salient and binding. Indices of generalized supernaturalism are down and people are less likely to describe themselves as religious. Bruce suggests that we must conclude from this evidence that 'indices of involvement in religious activities . . . [have] . . . declined markedly and . . . indices of religious belief, rather than moving independently of the former are also declining' (quoted from the abstract of the unpublished conference paper, 'God really is Dead: a challenge to the Silver Liningists').

Attitude surveys present their own problems, particularly in the areas of privatized beliefs and latent religiosity, but it is evident that, at the institutional level, there has been a decline in all indices of religious practice and of the legitimating functions of those religious institutions. Elsewhere,

Bruce (2002) notes that Christian church membership in the years 1900–2000 has declined from 27 per cent of the general adult population to 10 per cent. Church attendance in the period 1815–1998 dropped from approximately 50 per cent of the general adult population to 7.5 per cent. Furthermore, the rate of numerical decline is increasing in tempo and this trend has been most apparent among the larger denominations and the historic churches.

Bruce is not alone in his bleak assessment of the current status of institutional religion. The most recent summary of statistics for English church attendance, *The Tide is Running out* (Brierley, 2000), has chapters with such lurid titles as 'Bleeding to death', 'One generation from extinction?' and 'All over bar the shouting?'This all sounds overly apocalyptic, but perhaps less so when one considers that, between 1989 and 1998, more than a million people stopped attending church on Sunday and this at a time when the general population was increasing (Brierley, 2000: 67). Writing as a committed Christian and marshalling an impressive array of statistics on a number of indices, Brierley is deeply pessimistic about the implications for the future health of Christian organizations, particularly within the mainstream denominations and churches. In the same vein of pessimism, these concerns are also expressed in *Challenge to Change*, the results of the Welsh Churches Survey of 1995 (Bible Society, 1997). There seems little room for optimism on the part of religious institutions. Looked at objectively, the data from both England and Wales suggest a significant decline in both churchgoing and in the resources necessary to maintain the institutional wherewithal whereby people have somewhere to worship in the future.

Institutional decline – facts and figures

In terms of specific religious institutions, arguably, it has been the state church that has been most deeply embedded in English culture and the life of the people. As the established church, it has always provided religious services to a wider constituency than its active members, and is therefore a good indicator of levels of religious practice among the general population. Adrian Hastings (1991) notes that, throughout the twentieth century, a number of discernible trends emerged: fewer people chose church marriages, there were fewer baptisms and fewer people chose to send their children to Sunday schools. While the state church was becoming increasingly disengaged from the lives of the general population, the character of Church of England congregations was also changing, becoming predominately middle-class and female. As the number of Anglican ordinations fell, many theological colleges closed and in the period 1969–84, the Church of England declared 1,086 churches redundant. By 1990, infant baptisms, the best indicator of penetration into the community, had fallen to 28 per cent. Hastings suggests that, on all indices, the Church of England had shrunk by 50 per cent in the period 1960 to 1985.

Among the Free Churches, the picture was remarkably similar. The nineteenth century saw Nonconformity becoming a hugely influential social movement in both England and Wales, not only gathering large numbers of adherents under its banner, but also massively influencing social, cultural and political life. At its peak in the years 1905 to 1914, its position seemed unassailable, but from 1919 on, the picture was of a remarkably rapid decline, first in terms of its societal influence and increasingly, then, in terms of numbers (Munson, 1991). Intimations of decline could be felt in the immediate post-war years, and from 1946 to 1960 overall membership declined by 8 per cent, thereafter accelerating to 21 per cent from 1960 to 1970, a decade where church decline became very visibly marked (Currie, Gilbert and Horsley, 1977). Since then, these trends have continued, albeit with some regional and denominational variations. Evangelically orientated groupings proved more resistant to decline, theologically liberal groupings rather less so. For example, in the period 1995–2000 Methodist membership fell by 11 per cent, whereas the more evangelically orientated Baptists experienced only a 3 per cent drop in membership (Brierley, 2002). This picture is even sharper if we compare church attendance figures from 1989–98. Whereas overall aggregated evangelical attendance declined by only 3 per cent, their non-evangelical counterparts experienced a 30 per cent decline in the same period (Brierley, 2000).

The Roman Catholic Church presents a slightly different picture, in that from 1900 to 1970 membership increased by 140 per cent (Currie, Gilbert and Horsley, 1977), reflecting both continued immigration from Catholic countries and higher levels of fertility. From 1970 to 1995, while the total estimated Catholic population in England and Wales rose by a further 8 per cent, adult mass attendance fell by 38 per cent, baptisms fell by 30 per cent and confirmations by 48 per cent. (Brierley and Wraight, 1995). The most recent figures suggest that these trends are slowing somewhat as mass attendance in the period 1995–2000 declined by 11 per cent and baptisms by 13 per cent. It seems, then, that despite the ethno-religious character of Roman Catholicism in Britain and its conservative ideology and distinctive organization, factors that have historically helped to insulate the church from the worst effects of church decline, it is still not immune to the currents of secularization.

And so, in the 1970s and beyond, all the major historic denominations experienced losses. Taking the aggregated figures for the English Christian community, Brierley (1991) recorded a drop in total adult church attendance of 9.4 per cent in the period 1975–89. The decline in attendance by children was even more marked, at 17.6 per cent. Overall church membership declined by 3.8 per cent in the same period. In 1989, active adult churchgoers represented 10 per cent of the general population (Brierley and Wraight, 1995) but by 2000 this figure had dropped to 7.5 per cent and future projections suggest potentially similar rates of continued decline (Brierley, 2000, 2001). On the basis of denominational estimates, Brierley suggests that, by 2005, we will have seen the loss of nearly 2 million churchgoers in the twenty-five-year period 1980–2005, an average decrease of 1,400 people a week. To put this into an even starker context, this loss of churchgoers has happened in the same period as the general population has increased by nearly four million people.

Brierley and Wraight (1995) record that, within the Welsh context, in the years 1970–95 the Presbyterian Church of Wales closed 350 chapels and experienced a 51 per cent drop in membership. The Union of Welsh Independents closed 166 chapels and membership dropped by 49 per cent. The Baptist Union of Wales closed 163 chapels and membership dropped by 58 per cent. These losses are far higher than those of their counterparts elsewhere in Britain. In the same period there was a 37 per cent drop in Easter communicants of the Church in Wales, compared to 14 per cent in England. In contrast, Roman Catholics in Wales experienced only a 14 per cent drop in mass attendance in the years 1970–95 compared to 39 per cent among Catholics in England. Clearly, there is quite a lot of divergence between the English and Welsh experiences. The latest all-Wales survey (Bible Society, 1997) records that Welsh church attendance is now slightly lower than in the rest of the UK and paints a bleak picture of wholesale chapel closures in a religious environment where areas of decline far outstrip areas of growth.

Brierley's figures for Wales (Brierley, 2001) estimate that, in the period 1980–2005, church attendance will have dropped by a record 54 per cent (as opposed to 35 per cent for England and 30 per cent for Scotland), a loss of 213,000 worshippers. He suggests that, by 2005, active Christians will represent a mere 6 per cent of the general population in Wales. To put that figure into some kind of context, we might note that, in the 1851 religious census, almost 50 per cent of the Welsh population were recorded as active church and chapelgoers. Even allowing for some inflation in that figure, it is clear that there has been a massive decline in public religious observance in Wales, and if this is not religious decline, then one could be forgiven for asking what is.

While Wales may, in some respects, represent a special case, the patterns of religious decline (if not the rate of decline) generally reflect those to be found elsewhere in the UK. As far as institutional religion in Britain is concerned, all the statistical indices point to a general trajectory of numerical decline throughout the twentieth century, although the process is uneven and there are exceptions among some groups. For example evangelical groups in England and Wales have, at least in urban areas, generally managed to hold their own in terms of numbers. However, even within this sector the picture is patchy. Pentecostal and particularly charismatic (or 'new') churches represent the only sector where individual congregational growth is still regularly reported, although what these reports mean is somewhat obscure. In terms of where new recruits are drawn from, Brierley (2000) suggests that many of these may well be transfers from other Christian groupings, a theme that will be developed in this book. Furthermore, when we are looking at what appear to be very impressive rates of numerical growth, it is salient to remind ourselves that charismatic Christians constitute a mere 14 per cent of the English churchgoing population (Brierley, 2000) and an even smaller percentage, 6 per cent, of the Welsh churchgoing population (Bible Society, 1997).

As far as the statistical evidence for institutional religion is concerned, the general picture is of unremitting decline. Although this decline has been uneven in distribution and tempo (and it should be noted that membership figures have fallen as the general population has grown, an important factor for those churches not noted for proselytizing), nevertheless numerical decline has quickened in pace since 1960. This is incontrovertible fact and cannot be ignored even if there are signs of continued growth in the evangelical and 'new' church sector.[3]

Religion – believing without belonging?

If the picture painted so far has been of institutional decline, then what of residual religious belief among the general population? Can religious belief persist despite the collapse in churchgoing? If so, does this suggest that what we are seeing is not so much the decline of religion as its continuity, albeit in a transformed way? Certainly, there does appear to be a marked mismatch between indices of church attendance and indices of religious belief among the general population, which consistently remain far higher. Brierley (2001) records that just under 70 per cent of the UK population retain a belief in God and, while this figure has dipped slightly over the past twenty years, it remains remarkably consistent. However, other indices of belief appear to be steadily moving away from orthodox Christian positions. While belief in heaven has also held up well, belief in hell and the divine status of Jesus has diminished. In the same vein, just over 20 per cent of the UK population now express a belief in reincarnation. Clearly, if religious belief persists, it increasingly does so in ways that reflect individual preferences rather than institutional orthodoxy.

Grace Davie (1994) suggests that what we are seeing here is a move towards 'believing without belonging', where religious belief persists among European populations without the benefit of overt institutional support. While attitude surveys suggest there is some evidence to support this view, nevertheless, I would also suggest that institutional factors are important. Brierley (2001: 5.5), drawing from research conducted by Robin Gill, suggests that strong religious beliefs and values are most likely to be shaped and held among the constituency of regular churchgoers. Gill's contention, contra Davie, is that belief grows out of belonging (Gill, 1994), which, if true, suggests that institutional decline must inevitably have a negative impact on religious belief and practice among the general population. More recently, Davie (2000) appears to have modified some of her views, pointing to the importance of collective memory and its corollary, cultural transmission, in the persistence of religion. As the social and cultural characteristics of Europe change, Davie sees the generational mechanisms for the transmission of religious culture coming under increasing strain, particularly among younger people where these memories are most precarious and where the collective identification with religious institutions is weakest. Given that religious institutions are the primary guardians and cultural transmitters of the Christian perspective, their decline and progressive disengagement from European populations, which Davie does not contest, has important implications for the persistence of the Christian faith in Europe. Put another way, how are individuals to be satisfactorily socialized into the norms of religious belief and practice in a climate where religious institutions are becoming progressively weakened? How are religious memories to be maintained when their institutional guardians are struggling to survive in the face of general indifference? The answer has to be, 'with great difficulty' and despite the apparent persistence of residual religious beliefs, this looks very much like yet another variant of secularization.

While this account of the social and cultural transformation of religion in England and Wales only scratches the surface, nevertheless, it furnishes compelling evidence for the progressive loss of the salience of religion in England and Wales in both its associational and cognitive dimensions. However, care should be taken in assuming that evidence like this, on its own, points to a general, across-the-board, decline in religious belief and practice, let alone the presence of something like secularization. That is where theory comes into play. Certainly, institutional indices of decline in both England and Wales suggest that the reach of religious institutions into the general population has diminished throughout the twentieth century and that this trend has become more pronounced in recent decades.

Nevertheless, there are geographical variations and variations by denomination and institutional type. This decline is not uniformly distributed among the denominations, opening up the possibility of growth in some sectors, although this is less likely to be among those mainstream groupings of liberal persuasion. There is also the problem of the mismatch between indices of religious belief and measures of institutional affiliation. Clearly, religious belief can exist without the benefit of denominational membership or even association with other believers, but what exactly does this mean? Does it represent a radical shift in the practice of religion in modern European societies (Davie, 1994, 2000) or is it merely further evidence of the progressive disengagement of European populations from their religious institutions and the ongoing secularization of European societies (Bruce, 1996, 2001)? It is to these questions and the paradigm in which they are framed, the 'secularization thesis', that I now turn.

THE SECULARIZATION THESIS – AN OVERVIEW

Defining secularization

The original meaning of the term 'secularization' is grounded in the historical processes surrounding the Protestant Reformation (Casanova, 1994). It was, quite simply, a way of describing the transfer, or more properly, the expropriation, of material assets (land, property, monies, etc.) from religious institutions into the secular sphere. A well-known historical example of this would be the dissolution of the monasteries during the reign of Henry VIII. The term then gained increasing currency as a way of describing processes whereby functions or roles that were traditionally the domain of the religious sphere came to be relocated within the secular sphere. For example, European universities and schools are by and large no longer under the control of church authorities. Hospitals and health care, social care and welfare, with some exceptions, are no longer operated by religious orders. Where once these roles were the exclusive province of the church, they are now primarily administered by the state or by private enterprise.

Secularization has also progressively been applied to the realm of ideas and meanings, morality and ethics. For example, one would be hard pressed to find anyone today, other than religious fundamentalists, who would accept in its literal entirety the biblical account of creation, or the full implications of the doctrine of original sin. If we no longer believe that the Earth is the geographical centre of the solar system or that infants who are unfortunate to die unbaptized go to hell, that is largely because there are other, competing non-religious explanations that the majority of us now find perfectly sensible and satisfactory. In the same vein, moral and ethical stances are no longer the exclusive province of religious institutions. In recent years, values such as universal human rights to privacy, toleration, freedom of thought and freedom from discrimination have evolved largely out of the political sphere, but are no less 'moral' or 'ethical' for this (Chambers, 2003b). In contrast, Fevre (2000) suggests that it is primarily the values of the marketplace that are coming to predominate in Western societies, leading to a moral and ethical vacuum, while Davie (2000) appears to suggest that nothing is coming through to replace religious values. Nevertheless, the fact remains that the loss of the social, economic and political power that religious institutions used to wield and which ensured their capacity to enforce their world-view, has opened the way for the public acceptance of ideas and meanings that are no longer exclusively grounded in religion.

More recently, secularization has come to be equated with another term, 'modernization', a process that is also seen as corrosive of religion. Arguably, historical factors associated with modernity, such as industrialization, urbanization, the emergence of mass societies and the growth of individualism and the notion of individual rights, have all undermined the power of religion in modern societies (Bruce, 2002). All this activity and change has led many social theorists to argue that secularization itself is not so much the aggregate of a number of historical changes but is rather an identifiable process in itself, albeit linked to the project of modernity. As such, the notion of secularization has taken on the qualities of a paradigm, usually identified as 'the secularization thesis'.

This thesis presupposes that there is a historical trend involving increasing differentiation of the various aspects of social life into specialized spheres, each with their own specialized institutions and groups: family, polity, economy, church. Historically, even after this process had happened at the structural level, religious ideas retained their hegemony at the intellectual level. The next stage is therefore the loss by religious thought of its intellectual hegemony, followed by the rise of a scientific materialist world-view and its eventual hegemony, modernism, followed by the collapse of that hegemony and its sequel, postmodernism. The cultural corollary of these intellectual changes is the steady reduction of the salience of religious meanings at the cultural level.

Very provisionally, we might say, then, that 'secularization' is the process whereby religion ceases to be a significant part of the common life of members of a society. As such, secularization is a historical process, particular to the Western world (Mehl, 1970: 61) and occurring, *not in religion itself*, but in the process of the historical development of *societies*. As secularization relates to church history, Roger Mehl (1970: 67–8) suggests that it can be viewed in two ways: as a journey from social insignificance (the early church) to social significance (Christendom) and back to social insignificance (privatization and marginalization), a picture that essentially leaves the future closed; or as a constant engagement by the church with changing social forms, resulting in the constant transformation of the church, a picture that leaves the future open.

Secularization – a contested thesis

If secularization has been largely taken for granted within mainstream British sociology, warranting little sustained discussion (Wilson, 1992; Holton, 1996), within the sociology of religion, the secularization thesis has constituted the main framework for a lively post-war debate. At times this debate has appeared almost entirely self-referential, reflecting an increasing tendency among sociologists of religion to discuss the phenomenon in terms of each other's theories rather than in terms of what is happening on the ground (Sharpe, 1983). Writers such as Bryan Wilson (1992) and Steve Bruce (2002) have consistently defended the idea of secularization against their critics. Others have argued for the modification of the thesis (Shiner, 1967; Turner, 1991; Casanova, 1994) or, even, its abandonment (Glasner, 1977; Stark and Bainbridge, 1985). David Martin has both attacked the idea (1969) and then come to accept it (1978), although a certain ambivalence towards the concept remains within his work (1991, 1997). Notwithstanding such a diversity of opinion, in recent years, particularly among those theorists operating at the more empirical level (Gill, 1993; Hornsby-Smith, 1992; Finke, 1992; Davie, 1994), criticism of the secularization thesis has grown apace, further undermining its paradigmatic status.

Academic rivalries apart, one could be forgiven for wondering how so many theorists, and the list is not exhaustive, could come to such a diverse set of conclusions about the same subject, religion. Sharpe suggests that much of this discourse is merely a reflection of continued confusions as to what secularization might be in the first instance, rather than how it might be measured (Sharpe, 1983). Arguably, this confusion in itself reflects confusions over prior definitions of *religion* and resultant attempts to identify secular-ization in the light of these. As a rule of thumb, the more inclusive the defini-tion of religion, the less likely it is that secularization is seen to be actively undermining religious belief and practice (Towler and Chamberlain, 1973; Hamilton, 1995; Kim, 1996). Simply, if religion encompasses almost every-thing in life then religious decline is an impossibility. Conversely, the more religion is seen as a distinct social institution within a unified set of social structures, the easier it is to identify secularization as a process corrosive of religious belief and practice (Currie, Gilbert and Horsley, 1967; Bruce, 1996).

In terms of method, secularization theorists tend to emphasize first the idea of Christendom, that is, the coincidence of church with society, and then chart the gradual separation of the two and the decline of the social significance of religion (Wilson, 1966, 1982; Turner, 1991; Bruce, 1996, 2002). This perspective has been criticized as the product of an over-societalized conception of religion, that downplays or ignores the role of implicit religious belief at the individual level and the implications of the personal nature of religious belief (Luckmann, 1967, 1983, 1996; Sacks, 1991; Kim, 1996). Simply, what these critics are arguing is that, despite the evidence of decreased participation in activities such as churchgoing, there is also plenty of evidence to suggest that religious beliefs still remain salient for many people, albeit in highly privatized and increasingly unorthodox forms. This type of criticism tends to emphasize the universality of religion and religious institutions in all cultures, at all times, although why this is so is not made at all clear. For the theologian, the answers to this may be self-evident, but adopting a more objective position, the sociologist can only point to this as an assumption that needs confirmation. Historical and cultural contingencies, whereby religious institutions come to prominence at various points in the history of societies, should not be mistaken for universal conditions (Casanova, 1994). On the other hand, if religion is a universal condition, then secularization is impossible in the sense of the demise of religion and we can only talk of congruent social and religious transformations.

Both these positions are, of course, an over-simplification of the real picture and this has been reflected in the ways in which various theorists have utilized elements from both perspectives to drive their arguments forward. Peter Berger (1967, 1971, 1973) has emphasized the necessarily enduring role of religion as the best defence against the existential fears that are an integral part of the human condition, notably the problems of meaninglessness and death. At the same time he recognizes the corrosive impact of secularization or secularizing forces on individual religious belief. For others, institutional decline is not necessarily seen as a barrier to the continued salience of religion at the level of the individual. Beckford (1992) sees the freeing up and deregulation of religion as indicative of the transformation of religion from being a social institution to being a freestanding cultural resource or form. Roger Mehl sees the loss of the public social significance of Christianity, which he does not contest, as an indicator of Christianity's continued health. As it takes on a differentiated minority character, as 'the *corpus Christi* ceases to be confused with the *corpus christianum*', then it can 'rediscover its specific nature', a nature that has been obscured with its over-identification with, and legitimization of, social and cultural structures (1970: 65–8).[4] All in all, given that secularization is deemed to have a number of possible outcomes, this suggests that, either, sociologists are legitimately drawing disparate conclusions about the same processes or, more likely, what they *mean* by secularization differs, which, of course, will colour the way they arrive at their conclusions.

Conceptualizing secularization

In this vein, Peter Glasner (1977) contends that any definition of secularization must necessarily reflect a prior definition of religion. He suggests that there are at least three possible ways of defining religion. Each core definition will produce its own particular variations on the secularizing process in a mirror effect. Adopting Cohn's model of the three dimensions of religion – the institutional, normative and cognitive (Cohn, 1970) – Glasner argues that secularization also needs to be defined in these terms.[5] In doing this, he distinguishes a number of possible types of secularization along each dimension: These are, on the institutional dimension, *decline, routinization, differentiation* and *disengagement*; on the normative dimension, *transformation, generalization, desacralization* and *secularism*; and on the cognitive dimension, *industrialization, urbanization* and *modernization*. It follows on from this type of model that the limits of secularization may vary in strength and effect along each dimension. Indeed, one can envisage scenarios where developments along one dimension may run in the opposite direction in other dimensions. More certainly, it allows us to explain the type of discrepancies between measurements of institutional decline and measurements of levels of personal religious belief that have puzzled contemporary commentators. On the other hand, where religion is subject to an all-inclusive definition, then secularization as an analytical concept is unhelpful, given that it is not clear just *what* is subject to secularization and *how* we might define (let alone measure) that secularizing process.

Perhaps Glasner's most striking contention, though, is that the secularization thesis, in whatever forms it takes, functions largely as *a social myth* with no basis in empirical reality, and both Thomas Luckmann (1983) and Robin Gill (1989) have more recently reiterated this proposition. On the basis of these types of assertions, one could be forgiven for thinking that, within a discipline that emphasizes the 'scientific' nature of its enquiries, this is a fairly damning proposition. Epistemological considerations aside, what I believe it points to is the *nature* of the debate and the cultural baggage that it brings in its wake, rather than the substantive content of the arguments.

In part, I would argue, this is a by-product of the feelings aroused by the subject itself, religion.

The study of the sociology of religion, understandably, tends to draw into its orbit many individuals who retain affective links with a living religious tradition. Conversely, it also encompasses atheists who are attracted to the project of a 'scientific' explanation (or explaining away) of religion. This combination tends to make for lively and sometimes polemical debate. While the formal rationale for the objective sociological study of religion is 'methodological atheism' (Berger, 1973: 106, 182; Chandler, 1997: 240), nevertheless, as Hamilton (1995: 2–11, 167) suggests, in reality individual alignments with particular theoretical positions often seem to be influenced by prior intellectual and ideological orientations. For example, Bruce Lawrence raises the possibility of the intrusion of value judgements into research, noting that this seems particularly so in the case of the debate about secularization (Lawrence, 1989: 62). Conversely, Steve Bruce (1992: 1–3) has argued vigorously that this is generally not the case and that supporters of the secularization thesis have no particular axe to grind. Taking the middle ground, Stephen Hunt (2002: 14–15) suggests that, while the concept of secularization should be recognized as having strong ideological overtones and therefore should be treated with caution, it still constitutes the best available theoretical framework for understanding social and religious change in Western societies.

I have described the origins of the term secularization and its subsequent development as an analytical concept for examining and understanding social and religious change. As I have noted, academic acceptance of what has come to be known as the secularization thesis has not been universal and the idea has increasingly been subject to sustained criticism. Moreover, theories of secularization are necessarily tied to theories of what religion is. The more open and inclusive the definition of religion, the harder it is to identify secularizing currents. When allied to a belief that religion is a universal social and cultural imperative, secularization becomes, by definition, impossible. Conversely, the more closely religion is seen in institutional terms, the easier it is to identify secularization as a process tied to other areas of social change and negatively affecting religion. More controversially, these methodological issues can be seen to have ideological overtones that may negatively affect objectivity. With this in mind, I now move to a consideration of the main theoretical currents surrounding social and religious change in Western societies.

THEORIES OF SECULARIZATION AND SOCIAL
AND RELIGIOUS CHANGE

The past three decades have seen a rapidly growing body of literature focusing around the theme of secularization, and its sheer volume poses problems for any writer seeking to condense the main lines of inquiry in this highly contested field. Much of it is also highly abstracted and consequently difficult to read, a reflection of the complexities of secularization and social and religious change in modern societies. For the purposes of manageability and clarity, and with the student and general reader in mind, I propose to focus on a limited number of what seem to me to be exemplary theorists and arguments. These both reflect the main currents of thought relating to secularization and give a flavour of the public controversies and disputes surrounding this ongoing debate. When describing the theoretical positions of these writers, I will include, where appropriate, elements of others' direct critiques, relevant alternative theoretical perspectives and my own commentary.

Secularization: the Wilsonian perspective

The secularizationist *par excellence* is Bryan Wilson and he casts a long shadow, having, along with David Martin, dominated the sociological study of religion in Britain for the past thirty years. Wilson remains the main figure around which much of the secularization thesis and its critiques revolve (Bruce, 1992) and any critical examination of the literature relating to the secularization thesis must inevitably refer extensively to Wilson's theorizing. For Wilson, religion has its roots in and draws its strength from 'the community, the local persisting relationships of the relatively stable group' (1982: 154). It follows that changes in community structures lead to, or are mirrored by, changes within the religious sphere. The key secularizing concept here is pervasive 'societalization' whereby local communities are increasingly integrated into whole societies, and central to Wilson's thesis is the idea that religion is and has always been highly dependent on social control through personal networks. Simply, it is easier to maintain religious institutions in close-knit communities where individuals have daily face-to-face relationships than within impersonal mass societies where anonymity is the norm. However, in developing this idea, there is a tendency to assume that traditional communities must, historically, have also been religious communities. Both Glasner (1977) and Gill (1993) argue that this particular version of the secularization thesis is dependent on a historical viewpoint in which a 'mythical' golden age of religiosity existed.

Historians and theologians are divided on this point. As far as 'elite' religion in the Middle Ages is concerned, the church *was* spontaneously present in the creative centres of culture (Mehl, 1970; Gellner, 1983). Asa Briggs (1983) also argues that, at the popular level, the boundaries between the religious and the secular were often blurred, which implies that religion did extensively touch the lives of ordinary people. Kung (1995) suggests that medieval religion was a vital component of the lives of the peasantry and the towns-people, both because of the prevalence of uncertainty in their lives and because a unitary Christian world-view, where society and church were interwoven and undifferentiated, predominated. Even in the early modern period, 'Christianity still remained the decisive religious, cultural, political and social framework of Europe' (Kung, 1995: 478). Conversely, Keith Thomas (1971), Geraint Jenkins (1978) and Christopher Hill (1991a; 1991b) all suggest that the empirical evidence from the pre-modern period does not point to any such 'golden age' of religion in England or Wales. The truth is that, except at the elite level, we know remarkably little about everyday pre-modern religious belief and practice and what evidence there is can appear contradictory (O. Davies, 1996). For writers such as Glasner (1977), the 'golden age' of religion is merely a 'social myth', and it follows from this type of argument that theories which are seeking to use this golden age to link the decline of stable communities and the decline of religion are demonstrably 'false'. Leaving aside the implications of a faulty reading of history, Wilson's assertion that religion is tied to the idea of community, and by implication that its strength must decline in a mobile society, can also be shown to be somewhat problematic for two further reasons.

First, while the community thesis is attractive, there are marked regional and situational variations. Certainly, within the context of nineteenth-century industrial south Wales, there is a strong link between solidaristic communities and a vibrant religious faith (Lambert, 1988; A. Edwards, 1990; Harris, 1990; Robbins, 1994). In great part this is linked to the distinctive nature of patterns of industrial development in south Wales, where small settlements, villages in all but name, were established nearby to mines and other centres of industrial activity (Harris, 1990). In contrast, the huge explosion of evangelicalism in nineteenth-century England occurred in conditions of *Gesellschaft* rather than *Gemeinschaft*. It was in the impersonal towns and cities of the new industrial age that religion found fertile ground for its revitalization (Yeo, 1973; Brown, 1992; McLeod, 1992; Gill, 1992, 1993; Hempton, 1994), suggesting that Wilson over-generalizes the influence of traditional communities. Simply, in some situational contexts it was important, in others it was not (Brown, 1992).

Secondly, in terms of theory, Talcott Parsons (1967) has accommodated both social and geographical mobility within a model that rejects the idea of religious decline in favour of a functionalist analysis that incorporates notions of both differentiation and specialization. He argues that while religion has progressively lost many of its traditional functions, as it becomes associated with the private sphere, it still retains its importance as a site for the collective maintenance of traditional values in society. Beckford (1989) notes that this is integral to Parsons's general theory of society, where he lays great stress on the normative aspects of social life – the continuing importance of values, beliefs and norms and their effects on social action. Parsons suggests that there remains a strong connection between religion and morality. Even in its privatized form, religion remains an important element in the process of social control, becoming more so in a society slipping the bonds of traditional communities. While it is true that modern societies are characterized by increased differentiation between the religious and secular spheres, Parsons argues that this:

> Is not secularization in the sense that its tendency is to eliminate organized religion from the social scene, but it is rather to give it a redefined place in the social scene . . . connected with a new equilibrium in the relation between the religious and the secular elements in the social system. (1960: 298–9)

Parsons (1967) also draws an analogy with his theory of the nuclear family, arguing that, although religion now has less public functions, it performs its residual functions in the private sphere rather more efficiently. In his later reworking of evolutionary ideas and in his contribution to systems theory (Parsons, 1966, 1971), he concluded rather more emphatically that religious *ideas* are central to the process of socio-cultural evolution and that religion (i.e. religious ideas) constitutes a 'primary evolutionary universal'. As such, religion can be said to be in a state of continuing adaptation, while remaining functionally necessary for the continued maintenance of the cultural aspect of society. Conversely, Robert Merton (1957) suggests that it is self-evident that large sections of society do not subscribe to religious beliefs and practices, therefore it is doubtful whether it is religion *per se* that is responsible for societal equilibrium.

While both Wilson and Parsons see structural differentiation as being implicated in the social transformation of religion, they come to entirely different conclusions. Parsons sees little decline in the social significance of *American* religion, although it is subject to change driven by systemic imperatives. It continues to remain functional for the well-being of societies (1967). For Wilson (1982), the decline of the social significance of *British* religion is associated with the growing process of structural differentiation going on in society. The separation of religion from its erstwhile functions within the apparatus of localized social control is a sign of its decline in social significance at the institutional level. On a wider systemic level, he sees the influence of religion declining on a number of levels, notably within the political sphere and in the promotion of social welfare and education.[6] Venturing into futurology, Wilson argues that, as religion becomes more privatized, what future it has as an institution is to be found within its most privatized institutional form, the sect. Sects operate as strongly bounded communities, offsetting some of the more anomic aspects of modern societies and providing a strong focus for religious and social identity. While this fortress model has a certain plausibility, short of total geographic separation, it is difficult, given the complex nature of modern associational life and identity-formation, to see how this separation with the secular world can be maintained.

For example, David Martin (1967) sees any simple equation between church and community as problematic, not least because privatization increasingly permeates all associational activities. For Martin, the proliferation of associational forms both mirrors increasing structural differentiation and provides the individual with a number of variable roles, a theme which has been taken up and developed by a number of theorists. D. C. Martin (1995) also notes that, within the open systems of group interaction characteristic of contemporary Western societies, individual identity-formation is based on an open-ended synthesis of many overlapping strands of identity. In a similar vein, Stuart Hall (1992) sees personal identity as reconceived in the form of multiple identities, as the 'decentred subject' is increasingly defined in terms of personal narratives deriving from multiple reference points. In terms of equating the likely future of religion with the growth of sectarianism, Wilson's conflating of religion and community can be seen as over-socialized and deterministic. More pertinently, it is not clear how far individuals continue to see personal religion in terms of distinct faith communities, given that one of the outcomes of pervasive privatization is the trend towards social atomization, which in turn reshapes the way that people relate to the idea of community. Furthermore, within the relativistic environment of 'postmodern' culture, sectarianism itself finds its traditional certainties and boundaries under threat. True, one possible response is heightened resistance to modernizing influences (Bruce, 1996, 2002), but in some cases, notably within the charismatic movement and particularly within the phenomenon characterized as 'post-evangelicalism', a new openness and syncretism can be found (Tomlinson, 1995; Howard, 1996; Walker, 1997). This suggests that, rather than the future of religion being located within sectarian formations of the type characterized by Wilson,[7] it may well be in conditions of post-modernity that fairly loose associational groupings may benefit most from changing forms of identity.

Moving away from institutionalized conceptions of religion, at the intellectual level, Wilson argues that there has been an irrevocable shift away from religious accounts of the world, which have been superseded by scientific accounts. However, as Steve Bruce (2002) notes, while it is incontrovertible that the supernatural has been displaced in many areas of Western cognitive life, this cannot be seen as a simple unilinear and general process of scientific thought replacing religious thought. In a cultural climate characterized by many as 'postmodern', there is increasing suspicion of all 'grand narratives'. Anthony Giddens (1991) suggests that, while religious affinity has always been characterized by the twin themes of trust versus risk, in late modern society these themes now pervade *all* areas of life. If religious thought has undergone a process of intellectual deprivilegization, scientific thought is increasingly not immune from the same processes of radical doubt (Beck, 1992; Beck, Giddens and Lash, 1994). While the jury remains out as to whether society can be described as postmodern, it would not be too contentious to describe contemporary society as pervaded by questions of 'ontological security' (Giddens, 1991: 131–3). Social and economic life at both the individual and collective level is also increasingly characterized by uncertainty. Some writers coming from a religious perspective, notably Sacks (1991) and Tomlinson (1995), see the modern condition as an opportunity for religious institutions, in that increased levels of uncertainty may well open the way for a renewed engagement with the apparent certainties of religious belief and practice.

While this latter viewpoint may be over-optimistic, it does point to the fact that religion still constitutes a significant resource (among others) with which individuals and groups can endeavour to make sense of the world around them. However, the crucial question for any analysis of *mainstream churches* within the British context remains whether the nature of organized religion itself, *as practised in Britain*, can survive as a widespread social practice under the conditions of institutional differentiation and late/postmodern culture. As the ties of authority and tradition that formerly bound religious institutions to societies unravel, then clearly the authoritative status of these institutions diminish (Rose, 1996: 308). Moreover, as Harris and Startup (1999) argue, traditional institutions are left with the problem of balancing their customary function as guardians of tradition with the need to adapt to a detraditionalized environment. Mainstream churches find themselves in a postmodern environment while still being in all their essentials 'traditional' institutions. This institutional tension between tradition and change poses a central dilemma for religious institutions; crucially, whether to abandon long-held principles in the name of adaptation to a changing social and cultural environment (Harris and Startup, 1999: 182–6). For Wilson, the implications of the loss of religious authority and the parallel rise in the internal secularization of the churches are clear (1992: 203–7). Religious institutions either isolate and insulate themselves from the secular world or they slide into increasing conformity with that world and, like the grin on the Cheshire cat, eventually fade away into insignificance.

In reviewing Wilson's theorizing it would appear that he finds most aspects of modern society essentially incompatible with religious belief and practice (1982, 1992). I would argue that there are two overriding problems with his thesis. It is couched in highly general terms, reflecting his reliance on highly generalized data. Moreover, there is an essential reductionism going on in Wilson's thinking, reflecting his essentially materialist approach to the understanding of religion. Materialist approaches to religion are often problematic. When Wilson asserts that religious accounts of the natural world have been superseded (a proposition I agree with, in general terms), he equates this entirely with de-supernaturalization, failing to recognize that many people still seek answers to questions of *meaning* that science cannot answer. This existential predicament, it could be argued, is as much an attribute of modern society (perhaps more so, considering the current uncertainties of life and anomic strains in society) as other attributes of modernity that Wilson delineates. Therefore, I am a little sceptical of his contention that the cultural attributes of modern society are inimicable to religious belief and practice. As Sacks (1991) has argued, science is ill equipped to answer questions of ultimate values and, furthermore, these questions still retain social significance. Moreover, in imputing a *general* mindset to society, Wilson fails to recognize the essential nature of late modern society, which is both pluralized *and* individualized (Hall, 1992).

Secularization – universal process or historically contingent pattern?

David Martin is more circumspect than Wilson about the presence of secularizing processes in society, and in his early writings he argued that the *term* secularization should be abandoned altogether (Martin, 1969). For Martin, it is common-sense concepts and usages of religion that are of key importance, both in their social setting and as the starting point for any sociological analysis, even if these common-sense constructs do not always fit well into analytic models of religion. Despite his early doubts, he later came to recognize that the idea of secularization cannot be ignored as, within the social sciences, it constitutes a social reality in itself, not least as a conceptual boundary which allows analytic limitation and delimitation of religious experience. Certainly, despite his earlier objections to terminology, in later writings he does not reject secularization as a social process capable of sociological analysis (1978). Here, he does think it possible to isolate structural elements or 'co-ordinates' and use them as 'general principles' which can indicate the conditions under which 'religious institutions, like churches and sects, become less powerful and how it comes about that religious beliefs are less easily accepted' (1978: 12). However, Martin has also made it abundantly clear that he does not see secularization as either a universal or an inevitable process, but rather as something subject to historical, cultural and structural contingencies and varying by national contexts (1978, 1991). Therefore, in so far as it is possible to identify something that might conform to a general theory of secularization, it can only be based upon the patterns that emerge from a comparative country-by-country enquiry. Implicit in this approach is a recognition that there will be differences as well as similarities and that there are therefore inbuilt limits to any theory of secularization.

Locating his model of secularization within a historical framework and national cases, Martin charts the progressive disengagement of Western religion from those institutional sites that can convey status and power. Religion returns to where it initially came from, re-emerging among ordinary people as 'personal religion' (Martin, 1978: 3). Despite this loss of institutional power, Martin sees a continuing future for religion in limited voluntary associations which in their communitarian aspect can mitigate the worst effects of the fragmented and segmented characteristics of modern society and which might constitute an authentic point for religious renewal. More pertinently for the theoretical arguments that will be developed later in this book, Martin's thesis carries an implicit recognition that local social-environmental and cultural factors in their varied forms will shape and delimit religious life and practice (Martin, 1978: 91–4). (Again, this is something that Jenkins (1999) has more recently reiterated within an anthropological context.) In summary, Martin's approach to secularization is to see it more in terms of a pattern, subject to many historical contingencies, social, cultural and political, and not as a universal or unilinear process.

Relocating religion – secularization and the world of individual meaning

Peter Berger and Thomas Luckmann are two other influential thinkers, not least because their approach to religion centres on the increasingly pluralistic nature of modern societies. Published in 1967, their *The Social Construction of Reality* was part of the backlash against the then domination of Talcott Parsons in the world of social theory. Rejecting the Parsonian emphasis on systems theory and functionalism in favour of an emphasis on both the individual and meaning, their writing laid the groundwork for social constructionist approaches to society and religion and has continued to resonate with theorists of late/postmodernity. In terms of method, religion is seen as essentially a product of alienation, but also as offering a powerful defence against anomie. As such, it allows humanity to order experience and to construct a coherent, plausible world-view that gives meaning to individual lives. This is essentially a trade-off position. Society, the product of human social action, is highly anomic and this condition leads to 'existential terror', with the prospect of death being the ultimate expression of this anxiety. Religion ameliorates this condition very success-fully, but only at the expense of alienating humanity from its essential self in the process. That said, Berger and Luckmann differ individually in their approaches to secularization.

Luckmann (1967, 1983) sees the sociology of religion as obsessed with defining religion purely in institutional terms. It follows that statistics of church decline (merely one indicator of secularization) are wrongly taken as heralding the withering away of religion itself. While employing the term, he questions whether secularization, in the sense of the widespread decline of religious beliefs, can really exist, as religion is an enduring constituent feature of society, coextensive with social life itself. For Luckmann, because religion is rooted in existential experience, it cannot die. Institutional transformations can and do take place, and in this sense we may talk of 'secularization', but religion can never be eliminated. While he himself makes no such claim, this line of thinking has led some writers (Hamilton, 1995; Hunt, 2002) to accuse Luckmann of 'denying' the existence of secularization as, even if its visible institutions whither and appear to die, religion is merely transposed to another sphere, the private world of the individual.[8] For Luckmann, contemporary transformations of religion are framed by the progressive loss of overarching systems of religious values. As the need for societies to claim a purely religious legitimization recedes, pluralism becomes the new norm, religious practice becomes a matter of voluntary choice and increasingly individuals rather than institutions determine the content of personal religious beliefs. In a sense, what Luckmann is describing is the ultimate realization of the Protestant spirit of free enquiry, whereby individuals determine their own path of salvation in the light of their own individualized belief systems and judgements. As such, this variation on the privatization of religion may be deeply corrosive for the future health of religious institutions, but, paradoxically, may ensure the survival of religion among the general population, even if at the same time it becomes increasingly difficult to measure by conventional methods.

The title of Berger's 1967 book, *The Sacred Canopy*, highlights what he sees as the progressive loss of the type of overarching systems of values which have historically been supplied by religious institutions. Whereas religious values once pervaded all aspects of social, cultural and political life, this hegemony has had to capitulate in the face of competing sets of values derived from politics, the marketplace and, above all, technological ration-ality. Unlike Luckmann, Berger proposes a secularization thesis of sorts, with secularization taking place both at the institutional level and at the level of consciousness. Berger is concerned with ideas, and secularization can be said to involve the corrosion of what he terms religious 'plausibility structures' at the ideational level, in the face of competing secular systems of thought. (Perhaps the best example of this is the replacement of creationist accounts of the world with evolutionary accounts.) This process leads to both doctrinal compromises within mainstream denominations, as they seek to accommodate these new ideas and values, and the rise of sects, which *can* offer an integrated set of definitions of reality.[9] Berger parts company with Luckmann, in that he can see this process of corrosion, if left unchecked, resulting in a situation where religious belief, in whatever form it might take, no longer becomes credible *anywhere* within society (1971). While it is true that religion in Western societies can no longer provide an overarching framework of shared meanings, as Sacks (1991) has argued, religion is, and always has been, more than merely an instrument of social cohesion. Furthermore, he suggests that individual confidence in a religious faith is a subtle quality and may not be as amenable to the corrosive forces of secularism and secularization as Berger suggests.

Putting the most positive spin on Berger's thesis, it seems that, at best, religion will be confined to a residual sphere of social life and in this both Berger and Luckmann are agreed that the future of religion is to be found within the privatized realm. This looks very much like Wilson's privatization thesis viewed from an altogether different angle and the two theorists are not without their critics. Glasner (1977) considers that Luckmann's definition of religion is so inclusive that it makes any religious analysis, let alone an analysis of the effects of secularization, highly problematic. Beckford (1989) suggests that Berger's theorizing is too linked to mainstream Christianity in Western societies and cannot cope with the resurgence of religion as a politico-religious force elsewhere in the world. Mellor and Shilling (1997) also view theories in this vein as too Eurocentric. They contrast the American experience with that of Europe, noting that religion in the USA has always existed under conditions of pluralism and competition, making the notion of one monolithic sacred canopy based on one normative understanding of religion redundant (1997: 189).

Secularization – a multidimensional concept?

Karel Dobbelaere (1981), in his synthesis of the main currents of the secularization thesis, argues that secularization can only be approached as a multidimensional concept. He suggests that the sociology of religion has in the past concentrated too much on the study of one aspect of social structure, namely religious communities, rather than the dynamic relationships *between* social structures. Dobbelaere sees secularization as neither a uniform process nor necessarily inevitable. He identifies three variants of secularization: desacralization, differentiation and transposition, that variously operate at three levels, the individual, society and within religion itself (Hamilton, 1995). These secularizing processes are all characterized by Dobbelaere as forms of what he terms 'laicization' and, in so far as it is possible to simplify Dobbelaere's extremely complex thesis, he seems to argue that, as religious institutions progressively lose their monopoly position, increasingly they have to be marketed within a pluralistic environment. This leads to both ideological and functional adaptation and a reorientation towards the localized environment, defined as 'subworlds'. It is within these subworlds that religion now functions best. Laicization is not a 'mechanical evolutionary process' and as such is, in theory, reversible, depending on the surrounding cultural context and the social actors to be found within it (Dobbelaere, 1981: 150). For all its wide-ranging discussion of different theorists, in the final instance, Dobbelaere's thesis appears to be merely a variant of Parsons's theory of systemic differentiation and the subsequent specialization of subsystems.

Eric Sharpe (1983) argues that, historically, religion is always in tension with society. If secularization is seen as irreligion, then history is littered with examples of secularization followed by resacralization. Mary Douglas (1996) makes much the same point that contemporary secularizing tendencies are merely variations on an age-old theme, and not necessarily restricted to complex societies. (Indeed, these tensions constitute the recurring theme of the Jewish and Christian scriptural narratives.) While Sharpe suggests that we cannot ignore secularization, he cautions against a simplistic analysis. He characterizes the current debate as 'unsatisfactory', mainly because it tends to concentrate primarily at the level of intellectual belief, while giving less emphasis to its existential, social and ethical aspects. Sharpe suggests that religion is best seen as 'multi-functional'. Having identified four modes of religion – existential, intellectual, institutional and ethical – he argues that no one aspect is intrinsically more important than the others, although emphases may vary with situational context and within different religious groupings. Any attempt to analyse secularization must be sensitive to the multi-functional nature of religion. Evidence of decline in one mode of religion may not be matched with parallel developments within the other modes, making it difficult to talk about pervasive secularization.

This theme has been more recently developed by Jose Casanova (1994), who identifies three independent modes or types of secularization: structural differentiation, the decline of religious belief and practice, and privatization. Casanova sees differentiation, the progressive emancipation of the secular world from the control of religious institutions, as both the core of the secularization thesis and an incontrovertible aspect of modern societies. It is unlikely that this trend can be reversed. However, differentiation may not necessarily lead to any major decline in religious belief or practice or even to the privatization of religion. Simply, in some modern societies this happens, in others it does not, depending on the national conditions that prevail in those societies. Historical contingency should not be mistaken for secularizing processes, but should be seen for what it is, a set of circumstances unique to every society. As such, the decline of religious belief and practice may be a dominant historical trend associated with European societies, but it is not to be confused with so-called structural trends accompanying modernity. Likewise, the retreat of religion into the private sphere is an historical option, not a structural trend and it follows that 'de-privatization' is as possible as privatization, even in societies which have experienced secularization in the form of structural differentiation.

This then is the nub of the problem with many of the theories surrounding secularization. It would be foolish to deny that secularization exists as an event. Patently it does, albeit in different forms and at different levels, and differing in strength between national societies. However, as we have seen above, the same general data can inform markedly different theoretical perspectives as to the character of secularization, how it works itself out in modern societies, whether it is a process or not and whether it might be reversible. In the light of these questions, we need explanations that are able to take into account both the constantly changing character of modernity and the equally fluid meanings of religion. For example, and as we have seen above, the privatization of religion debate can as easily be couched in terms of *differentiation* as it can be in terms of *secularization*. The idea of secularization, however, often carries with it implicit or explicit connotations of a process of decline. Differentiation, on the other hand, usually emphasizes or recognizes the adaptive capacities of religion, leaving open the possibility of theorizing religious growth as well as decline. As a conceptual abstraction, this latter approach would appear better placed to facilitate a discussion of the social transformation of religion, an idea that can accommodate theoretically both increased differentiation and the possibility of de-differentiation.

RELIGION AND THE POSTMODERN WORLD

Secularization as structural transformation

Richard Fenn (1970, 1972) has addressed just this problem of placing religion within the context of late/postmodern societies. For Fenn, society represents a social system characterized by increasing differentiation at *all* levels of the system. Cultural systems are no longer capable of producing universally significant accounts of ultimate meaning or moral universes. The end result is *not* the diminution of religion, but the deprivileging of *all* cultural resources, secular and religious, as *authoritative* accounts of the world. Simply, religion becomes marginalized but so do all other cultural accounts. Niklas Luhmann (1974, 1987), in a similar system-based analysis, argues that the process of differentiation has reached a level where we can no longer talk of a single coherent social system. We are left only with a set of self-referencing partial or subsystems, none of which can represent the unity of the whole system. Late/postmodernity is characterized by a reorganized social system where we have, 'in place of the representation of unity, the representation of difference . . . the re-organization of the social system . . . into functional differentiation' (Luhmann, 1987: 104). As such, institutional differentiation or separation *has no implications for decline or growth* within the religious sphere or even the loss of the social significance of religion. The outcome of the trend towards institutional differentiation, for religion or any other subsystem, is that it can only be self-legitimating. Religion is legitimated by nothing but itself, it legitimates nothing but itself. It follows that, if legitimation or de-legitimation does not stem from a unified social system, then it becomes a nonsense to talk about a mono societal secularization process. If religion is self-legitimating, that legitimation must consist of religion's capacity to reproduce itself in whatever form proves functionally appropriate to itself as a subsystem.

Of course, this does not rule out the possibility of dysfunctional adaptations or adaptations that can appear unfamiliar when compared to traditional, mono-culturally grounded forms of religion. Stark and Bainbridge (1985) argue that the future of religion in late/postmodernity will be characterized by a proliferation of sects and novel cult formations. Roland Robertson and JoAnn Chirico (1985) note that the globalizing tendencies characteristic of late/postmodernity have been accompanied by a resurgence of religious fundamentalism and the extensive development of new religious movements. Robertson and Chirico contend that 'new religious frames of reference may be both vehicles for and symbols of the transcendence of purely societal-systemic forms of identity formation' (1985: 232). In this vein, Ian Cotton

(1995) suggests that there are now 400 million charismatic Christians world-wide, their numbers having doubled in ten years, and argues that these constitute a massive cross-cultural and self-referential grouping with operative networks that cross continents. Utilizing the new electronic media of the internet and the fax machine, they are beholden to no centralizing authority and legitimated by no one but themselves. Elsewhere, recent world events increasingly suggest that religion also continues to be a vehicle for political expression and change, something unforeseen to those who once expected a progressive secularization to ultimately reach every part of the globe (Lawrence, 1989; Fox, 1990; Arjomand, 1991). Clearly, these global developments (particularly in the context of a post-9/11 world) and the theoretical questions that they raise are important for any discussion of secularization.

Secularization and supply-side models

Stark and Bainbridge (1985) argue that religion is a social rather than an individual phenomenon and that secularization is not a new eventuality, but is ever present within the religious sphere. Their theory of religion (1985, 1987) is heavily economist, drawing extensively from exchange and rational choice theory.[10] The arguments for and against rational choice theory have been extensively rehearsed elsewhere (Elster, 1989; Craib, 1992; Abell, 1996) but the increasing association with exchange theory and network analysis that rational choice theory represents (Abell, 1996) has proved influential in some quarters. Stark and Bainbridge, and fellow travellers such as Iannaconne, do not see pluralism and the marketing of religion under the remit of consumer preference as either a new phenomenon or inimical to religious traditionalism. They may be influenced in this by the historical development of religion in the United States of America, which almost from its inception has operated in conditions of pluralistic competition (Brown, 1992; Noll, 1992) and sectarianism has always been a predominant feature in American religious life (O'Toole, 1996). On the basis of data gathered in a number of European societies, Iannaconne (1992) claims that there is a correlation between high levels of religious pluralism on the one hand and increased religious belief and higher levels of church attendance on the other. This observation is markedly at variance with much of the theorizing on secularization and religious pluralism, not least because the apparent decline of institutionalized religion can actually be seen as being in the long-term interests of the stabilization and growth of churches. While a competitive religious market creates both 'winners' and 'losers' among religious groups, in the long run it is religion that is the winner.

While this supply-side model appears on the face of it to have a certain plausibility, Steve Bruce (1993, 1999, 2002) has consistently critiqued this view that religious diversity strengthens rather than weakens levels of religious commitment. While this may be the case in the USA (and Bruce is even sceptical of this) the evidence from Europe does not fit easily within a supply-side model which suggests that religious monopolies inhibit demand for religion, while a competitive free market with a wide range of choice stimulates demand. Leaving aside the question of whether we can treat religion as just another product for consumption in the same way as we would baked beans or blue jeans, the facts just do not fit the theory. As Bruce points out, the history of religion in Britain is a narrative that begins with one church; powerful, very influential, organized nationally and meeting the religious needs of the entire population. Post-Reformation, the story is of the development of two broad trends, increasing religious diversity accompanied by progressive religious decline. Arguably, Britain now has more diversity and choice within the religious sphere than it has ever had in its history and yet, on every measure, the British population is more irreligious than it has ever been (Bruce, 2002: 60–2). Looking elsewhere in Europe, we see a pattern where countries such as Eire and Greece still have something very like *de facto* religious monopolies and where religion continues to significantly permeate people's everyday lives (Davie, 2002). None of this suggests that the supply-side model, as it used to analyse European religion, is anything other than a theory based on what Bruce succinctly describes as 'sociologically implausible assumptions' (2002: 62).

Bruce's final comment highlights the essentially controversial nature of the discourses surrounding the idea of secularization. While the above discussion is not exhaustive, it nevertheless points towards the richness and complexity of this debate and also the ways in which sociology itself is deeply implicated in the realization of the secularization paradigm. Of late, this paradigm has shifted from a narrow focus on religion and its institutions to a more holistic and societal approach accommodating an analysis of the relations between different elements of the social system. This seems to me to be a more fruitful avenue for the investigation of the impact of secularization on religious institutions.

Synthesizing the most promising theoretical insights discussed above, we might say that late modern society is characterized by increasing systemic complexity and functional differentiation at all levels. This process is not religion-specific but societal and can be seen as a process of increasing institutional differentiation leading to the deprivileging of the authority of *all* institutions or as a process of the disembedding and realignment of institutions. At the cultural level, ascriptive loyalties are replaced by voluntary associations, as increasing complexity and differentiation leads to the fragmentation of knowledge systems and their reconstitution in conditions of pluralism. Secularization is merely the outworking of these societal processes from the standpoint of religion and church growth or decline has to be understood in terms of society and not religion. The demise of churches comes about when they fail to adapt to changing social conditions and in this sense this process is open-ended. As far as the secularization thesis itself is concerned, it appears to be still conceptually tied to sociological analyses of modernity. While I am sceptical as to the presence of 'post-modernity', the challenge for sociological theorists is to come up with new ways of conceptualizing the effects of systemic, social and cultural change on religion.

CONCLUSIONS

The debate outlined thus far has been carried out at quite a high level of abstraction. Nevertheless, it strongly suggests that explanations of religious transformation must include both reference to religion itself and an analysis of change at the level of social systems. As far as any putative secularization is inferred (or not), socio-economic and cultural forces operating outside of the religious sphere *may* be of crucial importance to religion at various times in history, but this is a relationship of *historical contingency* rather than *societal primacy*. It must also be recognized that religion operates in different modes, each subject to different relations of contingency with the social and systemic environment. Indeed, in so far as we can go on to talk about the secularization of *culture*, that is, those trends affecting the discourse in which the social world is constructed and its disparate elements integrated, this does not in itself imply the decline of religion.

As Owen Chadwick (1975) has famously argued, the hallmark of the secularization of the European mind is the process whereby the *conscience collective* becomes both more diffused and increasingly subject to a rationalized world-view, but in so far as this type of secularization thesis is explanatory of something, it cannot be the decline of religion. For some proponents of the secularization thesis there is a tendency to confuse the latter with the former and this error is compounded when there is a failure to recognize that the secularization of culture is a dynamic process. Under the conditions of late modernity, there appears to be not only a loss of faith in religion but also, increasingly, a loss of faith in the new types of rationality underpinning modernity. If modern life is characterized by anything, it is the progressive de-privileging of *all* institutional structures and systems of thought.

However, when we shift to the question of whether institutionalized religion, particularly in the form of the mainline denominations, is at present declining in Britain, then the evidence cannot be denied. In terms of societal influence, religious institutions, by virtue of their historical presence in European societies, continue to contribute, if fairly feebly, to ongoing discourses relating to morality and social justice. However, the churches and denominations are deeply pessimistic about their current position, as resources are stretched ever more thinly and numbers of adherents continue to decline. The crucial question, then, is what does this presage for the future? We may well continue to experience more decline at the institutional level or possibly, as some observers are now predicting, a bottoming out of this process. Those who see the glass half full suggest that this may lead to a subsequent resurgence of religious belief and practice, although at the present time this is merely conjecture. A more modest prediction is that, whatever the future health of institutional religion, it is not likely to disappear altogether from the European scene, although this is conditional on its ability to adapt to what appears to be a highly secularized environment.

In so far as religion retains any social significance, on the available evidence, this is likely to be primarily restricted to the private world, an adjunct of lifestyle choice rather than in any ascriptive form. There will of course always be exceptions to this rule but in an increasingly secularized environment, individuals for whom religion is an important part of their identity will constitute a shrinking minority. This should not be seen as the end of the story. The challenge for sociology now, it seems to me, is not to continue with building increasingly complex theoretical schema relating to the lacunae of secularization, but rather, as Davie (1994, 2000) and Jenkins (1999) have suggested, to seek to identify linkages with religious institutions and their surrounding populations. In other words, to demonstrate empirically how bodies of believers relate to their surrounding populations and vice versa; to understand how socio-environmental factors and the characteristics and organizational models of religious institutions help or inhibit this process; to identify what is the minimum size for an active religious minority to influence those around them and the mechanisms by which that might be achieved; to seek to understand better the nature of differential participation in religious belief and practice and the self-understandings that motivate the actively religious. The project for the rest of this book is to describe and account for sociologically these various factors within the context of a number of localized case studies which reflect various aspects of contemporary Welsh religious life.

3

Social and Religious Change in Swansea

THE CITY AND ITS PEOPLE

Swansea is the second city of Wales, a place with a long history both as a seaport and as a centre of the metallurgical industry. Situated in the south-west of the country, between the mountains and the sea, it dominates the surrounding industrial and rural hinterland, both southwards and westwards, and marks the cultural dividing line between Welsh- and English-speaking Wales. Home to approximately 220,000 persons, in many ways Swansea is typical of the experience of the great provincial centres of Britain but in some ways it is quite unique.

It is typical, in that the last thirty years have seen the city struggling to cope with major economic and structural changes. The metallurgical industries that were the foundation of Swansea's prosperity have mostly disappeared and even the archaeological relics of the great industries have largely been obliterated by land reclamation projects in the Lower Swansea Valley. The once thriving docks which previously imported ores and exported metal, tinplate and anthracite to the rest of the world are now moribund and much of the waterside has been or is being developed as a yachting marina and up-market housing development. In common with much of Wales, unemployment rates are high, but the demise of traditional industries has been somewhat offset by economic and occupational restructuring and diversification. Service-sector employment now accounts for two-thirds of the workforce, while manufacturing industries account for under a quarter of the workforce.

In terms of housing, and in common with much of south Wales, the city has a high rate of owner occupation, 68 per cent, with only 21 per cent of households in local authority housing. However, 35 per cent of dwellings are of the terraced variety, representing largely working-class occupation, and these are concentrated in the eastern and northern areas of the city, areas of traditional settlement. These areas also contain large local authority housing estates which have many of the social and economic problems associated with the inner-city areas of any large urban conurbation. In marked contrast, the western part of the city, what we might term the suburban fringe, is noticeably more prosperous on all indices. Largely a product of the post-war housing boom, the growth of these suburbs was very much a part and parcel of a trend towards growing social and geographical mobility in Welsh society. In their famous 1965 study of Swansea, *The Family and Social Change*, Rosser and Harris noted a westward drift of upwardly mobile families, creating a distinctive split along class lines between the expanding affluent west and the declining industrial east that still holds today. Twenty-five years later, Swansea had the highest concentration of upper income wage-earners in the surrounding county of West Glamorgan (Symonds, 1990: 25) and it would be fair to assume that most of these individuals and their families continue to reside in the prosperous western suburbs of Swansea.

If Swansea's recent past is fairly typical of the social changes experienced elsewhere, in geographical terms it is unusual. Swansea is an untypical city in that topographically it is more a collection of discrete communities which are often separated from neighbouring communities by physical barriers, such as great hills, rugged rock formations, gullies, rivers and marshes, which are integral features of the Swansea landscape. The city is described locally as 'more a collection of villages' and Swansea residents still talk about 'going to Swansea' when they mean taking a ten-minute bus ride to the city centre. Residents tend to define themselves by the locality they live in, rather than overtly identifying themselves with Swansea and they are recognized as such by other Swansea residents. Rosser and Harris comment that:

> History and topography have combined to produce a sort of cellular pattern of distinct and well-recognised communities within the modern administrative area . . . it is a town with a multiple personality (displaying at times considerable psychological confusion because of this) which cannot be summed up in a single phrase. (1965: 42)

Students of Welsh life will not be unfamiliar with such parochialism and, in this respect, Swansea is culturally close to the social experience and local rivalries of the patchwork of communities that typify the industrial valleys and towns of south Wales. This is unsurprising, given that the fortunes of the city were originally forged in the successive waves of immigration that characterized the Industrial Revolution throughout south Wales. This massive population movement saw the emergence of both a distinctive working-class culture and a collective community structure based upon a solidarity of attitudes and values, and in this the Greater Swansea area is no exception (Edwards, 1990: 14).

This culture could still be found relatively intact thirty-five years ago, even if it was already experiencing strain as the accompanying social structures were beginning to break down in the face of a 'mobile society' (Rosser and Harris, 1965). Continuing economic and structural changes since that time have done much to undermine what remained of this consensus and this has created inter-generational tensions within communities that have all but swept away the old notions of community solidarity, even if a strong identification with place remains (Symonds, 1990: 30). People no longer conform to the pattern of working together in the traditional labour-intensive industries, living together in the same warren of streets surrounding the workplace and worshipping together in the local churches and chapels. While they may still reside together, the loss of the shared experience of place as mediated through localized employment appears to have had a corrosive effect on all local community structures. This is most noticeable in the eastern part of the city where older people still cling to those traditional attitudes and values that are typical of solidaristic working-class communities, and which the younger generation appear to be rejecting wholesale.

Perhaps the most untypical characteristic of Swansea, when compared to English cities, is the cultural presence of an indigenous second language, Welsh. At the time of the 1991 census, 10 per cent of the population were Welsh-speakers, in the sense that Welsh was their first language. However, the number of these Welsh-speakers has been steadily dropping for decades and the overwhelming majority are aged 45 years or older. Despite the fact that all schoolchildren in Wales receive some compulsory Welsh-language education, and while Welsh is everywhere visibly present on road and street signs, the Welsh language appears to impinge little on the daily life of the city, where the preferred medium of communication is English.

RELIGION IN SWANSEA

Swansea is home to a diverse array of religious institutions. Some have deep historical links with the area, while others are more recent arrivals. Among those groups with a long-standing presence are Roman Catholics, Anglicans and the traditional Free Church groupings, both Welsh- and English-speaking. Those denominations that operate primarily through the Welsh language are the Presbyterian Church of Wales (Calvinistic Methodists), the Union of Welsh Independents (Congregationalists) and the Baptist Union of Wales; these groupings can be said to constitute the bedrock of historic Welsh Nonconformity. Other mainstream Free Church groups present in the city include the Baptist Union of Great Britain (English Baptists), Methodists, the United Reformed Church, the Salvation Army and the Society of Friends (Quakers).

Away from the mainstream, there is a lively evangelical presence and, in contrast to the mainstream, many of these are more recent arrivals. Inheritors of the spirit and ideology of the 1904 Revival, the Christian Brethren have a ubiquitous presence in the city as do the various pentecostal groupings; the Apostolic Church, the Assemblies of God and the Elim Pentecostal Church. Allied to this sector are a number of independent congregations, about twenty-five in number, who characterize themselves as 'evangelical', and these range from extremely conservative congregations to examples of fairly radical 'housechurches'. On the periphery, there is also a non-Trinitarian presence, predominately Unitarians, Mormons and Jehovah's Witnesses and more recently a non-Christian presence, of which the largest is Islam, with three mosques, but which also includes a Sikh temple and a very small but highly visible community of adherents to Krishna Consciousness.

What all these diverse religious groups have in common, apart from geographical proximity, is that they are operating, to varying degrees of success and failure, in conditions of quite marked secularization. This is 'secularization' in terms of the abandonment by the overwhelming majority of the population of any significant commitment to religion, something common to most parts of Wales. William Price suggests that: 'The twentieth century has witnessed a dramatic collapse in the influence of the Christian churches in Welsh society . . . attendance at worship has become the activity of a small minority' (1989: 42–6). He notes that this trend, while common to all, is most marked within those churches of the Welsh-speaking Nonconformist tradition, reflecting the parallel decline of the daily use of the Welsh language, and in this Swansea is no exception. The effects of secularization will become somewhat clearer in the discussion below where I briefly examine both the recent history of religious institutions in Swansea and some statistical indicators of the health of these church groups.

RELIGION IN THE RECENT PAST

Thirty-five years ago it was still possible to characterize Swansea as a city with a higher than average level of visible religiosity. The churches and chapels, if not full, nevertheless catered for approximately 23 per cent of the general population, an impressive figure given that at the time the comparable English average would have been approximately 13 per cent of the general population (Rosser and Harris, 1965: 128). Today, there are visible architectural reminders of this religious heritage everywhere and one of the most striking features of the city is the number of buildings that were at one time or another, or continue to be, places of worship. Redundant church or chapel buildings tell their own story, whether derelict or given over to other purposes, but the picture of decline and decay is no less apparent in many of those churches and chapels still in use.

The product of the nineteenth-century race to build bigger and more grandiose structures, and in some cases capable of accommodating huge congregations, these places of worship are clearly increasingly surplus to the requirements of Swansea's remaining worshipping population. One such chapel, known locally as 'the cathedral of Welsh Nonconformity' has seating for 1,500 people and an average Sunday attendance of 150 worshippers. That said, this is by far and away one of the better-attended chapels and this discrepancy between potential and actual use is even more marked when we consider the fate of other large religious buildings. It is not unusual for these large chapels, with seating available for anything from 500 to 1,000 persons, to have an attendance of fifty or fewer worshippers. The picture of a congregation of ten or less people in a damp and dilapidated building designed for 800 persons, limping along with no hope of future growth, is an all-too-common portrait of Free Church life in Swansea.

However, it would be wrong to assume that the religious life of Swansea is, or has been, entirely dominated by the Free Churches, although this might have been true elsewhere in Wales. Swansea is untypical of the wider religious map of Wales outside the south in that it has both a strong Roman Catholic presence among the general population and the Anglican churches have a far higher numerical profile than their Nonconformist counterparts. The presence of Roman Catholics stems back to the historic migrations of the nineteenth century, when Irish Catholics constituted a major reserve army of labour in the newly industrialized south Wales. St David's, the mother church, was founded in 1847 and soon after large Irish Catholic populations could be found in the Greenhill and Docks areas of the city. Today, the estimated Roman Catholic population of Swansea, at more than 10,000, constitutes approximately 5 per cent of the general population.

In terms of Anglican adherence, in 1965, Rosser and Harris recorded that, in ascriptive membership, the numerically dominant denomination in Swansea (constituting 51 per cent of the Christian population) was the Church in Wales. At the time this was a situation untypical of most of the rest of Wales where Nonconformity held sway (1965: 127). Twenty-five years later, Harris wrote:

> The authors of the Swansea study . . . were surprised at the strength of Anglican adherence and activity in an area held to be traditionally Nonconformist . . . there had been a significant shift in the fifties away from traditional Welsh Nonconformity and towards allegiance to English speaking denominations, especially to the Church. This shift was associated with two distinct but related phenomena: Anglicisation and secularization. (Harris, 1990: 55)

Harris suggests that, in the prevailing climate of the day, while younger individuals and families were abandoning both the use of the Welsh language and their identification with distinctly Welsh institutions, it was still not socially acceptable to be 'nothing' in terms of religious loyalties (Harris, 1990: 55–6). In this sense, the upturn in Anglican fortunes was achieved by default, but nevertheless, in real terms, it boosted the fortunes of the church at a time when others were suffering a reversal of their lot. Furthermore, those new adherents now make up much of the current constituency of the Anglican community.

THE NUMERICAL HEALTH OF THE CHURCHES

Statistical measures of decline and growth are only one indication of the health of religious institutions and a very broad indicator in that. Taken on their own they can tell us very little about the process of church growth and decline, other than in what church groups these trends are most marked. Moreover, the numbers of congregations belonging to any particular group and their percentage share of the religious market are in some cases more an indication of their past rather than their present health (Bible Society, 1997: 7). Furthermore, in the case of growth, they cannot tell us how this was achieved or where recruits have come from. (For example, recent growth in one group may be the result of transfers from other groups.) Nevertheless, they constitute a useful starting point for the wider discussion that will follow on from these statistical indicators. The figures themselves are generated from the author's own survey of churches in Swansea (Chambers, 1999: 365–8), supplemented by data from the Bible Society and the Christian Research Association that allows for some comparison with national trends.

Anglicans and Roman Catholics

Today, there are fifty-two Anglican congregations operating in Swansea and estimated active membership constitutes approximately 3.6 per cent of the general population. The strength of Anglican adherence can be further illustrated through a comparison of the relative share of the religious marketplace in terms of attendance at worship. A city-wide survey of church attendance, carried out by the author in 1995, revealed that Anglicans accounted for 22 per cent of church attendance in Swansea, a figure not dissimilar to Welsh national trends, where Anglicans constituted 28 per cent of the total Christian worshipping community (Bible Society, 1997).

Locally, the Roman Catholic share of church attendance in 1995 was also 22 per cent, again appearing to mirror national trends in Wales (Bible Society, 1997). In common with the rest of mainland Roman Catholic Britain, there is a distinct gap between the estimated Roman Catholic population and active participation in the life of the church. While the population had grown by 24 per cent in the preceding decade, numbers attending mass had only risen by 2 per cent (Chambers, 1999). Nevertheless, despite the presence of this trend, the Diocese of Menevia (incorporating Swansea) had the highest recorded rate of mass attendance (36 per cent of the estimated Catholic population) in England and Wales (Catholic Media Office, 1996). In terms of the net growth or decline of congregations between 1985 and 1995 (that is, the percentage of growing over declining congregations) the Roman Catholics in Swansea have seen a 22 per cent net growth and the Anglicans 5 per cent. Overall, there has been a 9 per cent net growth in this sector of the Swansea churches and it can, when compared to other sectors, be described as relatively stable in terms of adherence. Against a backdrop of pervasive religious decline in Wales, this experience is somewhat atypical of the rest of the country and the same cannot be said of the Free Churches.

Nonconformity

Among these Nonconformist groups surveyed in 1995, those historic denominations associated with the Welsh-speaking population accounted for approximately 15 per cent of church attendance and their 'English' counterparts approximately 17 per cent. Together, these constitute the established face of Nonconformity in Wales, albeit an 'establishment' divided along linguistic lines. Over and against these denominations, who tend to be theologically liberal (but not universally so), socially conservative and ecumenical in temper, stand those groupings of an evangelical character. This sector accounted for a not inconsiderable 24 per cent of 1995 church attendance. Numerical decline has been and continues to be very marked among those Nonconformist denominations and independent congregations that were established prior to the twentieth century. While this decline is more marked among those groups catering for Welsh-speakers, it also includes a significant proportion of their anglicized counterparts.

Welsh-medium Free Churches

At the end of the nineteenth century and into the early twentieth century when the disestablishment debate was at its strongest, the Calvinistic

Methodists could, on the strength of their then huge membership, make a strong case for recognition as the 'national' Church of Wales. A case for this could no longer be made and its successor, the Presbyterian Church of Wales, saw its national membership halved from 108,064 in 1970 to 53,300 in 1995 and 350 chapels closed their doors during the same period (Brierley and Wraight, 1995). Matters were marginally worse in Swansea, where membership during this period declined by 35 per cent, a significantly higher figure than the 25 per cent national average. Locally, the decline in church attendance during the same period ran at 26 per cent, slightly higher than the national average (Chambers, 1999). Significantly, only one Presbyterian congregation in Swansea did not report any substantial numerical decline and this was due to a policy of the wholesale transfer and merger of congregations, who were bussed in to this congregation from a number of chapels deemed to be no longer viable.

Nationally, the Union of Welsh Independents saw the closure of 166 chapels and the loss of almost half its membership (49 per cent) in the years 1970–95 (Brierley and Wraight, 1995). Locally, in the years 1985–95 membership declined by 27 per cent (against a national decline of 24 per cent) and church attendance by 34 per cent. The Baptist Union of Wales, which caters for both Welsh-speakers and a smaller English-speaking constituency (mainly to be found in south-east Wales and more evangelical in character) saw a 60 per cent decline in membership in the years 1970–95 and closed 163 chapels. Locally, in 1985 95, membership declined by 28 per cent (slightly higher than the national average) and church attendance fell by 35 per cent. Only one local chapel had experienced any growth and this congregation was very untypical for this denomination's profile in Swansea in that it catered for Welsh-speaking evangelicals.

The overall picture, both locally and nationally, for those Nonconformist denominations catering for Welsh-speakers is of marked numerical decline and numerous chapel closures. The fact that two of these denominations, Baptists and Independents, have their national headquarters in Swansea only further emphasizes the apparent inability of denominational leaderships to stem this tide of decline, even when it is, so to speak, on their own doorstep.

English-medium Free Churches

Elsewhere within the mainstream of Nonconformity, local English-speaking churches have fared somewhat better. In terms of congregations, the aggregated picture is mixed, with both declining and growing congregations and an overall rate of net decline running at around half that of their Welsh-speaking counterparts. Furthermore, there was quite a lot of variation between the fortunes of these denominations in Swansea in 1985–95 and UK national trends.

In Swansea, during 1985–95, Baptist Union of Great Britain churches saw a 17 per cent decline in membership and a 19 per cent decline in church attendance, with net decline in the order of 31 per cent. In the same period, for England and Wales as a whole, membership declined by approximately 4 per cent, while church attendance increased by 2 per cent. Conversely, whereas nationally Methodist membership declined by 13 per cent, Methodist churches in Swansea only saw an 8 per cent drop in membership, although church attendance declined at a rate of 15 per cent and net decline was 66 per cent. United Reformed congregations in Swansea also bucked UK national trends in both membership and attendance. Locally, there was a 15 per cent decline in membership (as against a national figure of 21 per cent). However, church attendance appeared to be fairly stable (declining by a mere 0.4 per cent), a figure markedly at variance with URC church attendance in the UK as a whole, which declined at a rate of 19 per cent. (All UK figures are from Brierley and Wraight, 1995.)

In one way or another, this sector of the Swansea churches appeared to exhibit some variance with UK trends, but this is to be expected, given that they are operating in Wales and not in England and also given that 'national' statistics invariably disguise divergent regional trends. More salient is the fact that what might be termed 'traditional' Nonconformity in Wales has not fared well in the past few decades, and in this, Swansea churches and chapels are no exception with regards to patterns of numerical decline. Indeed, the brief pen portrait above hints at how the experiences of mainstream Swansea churches have been shaped in recent years by the twin processes of anglicization and secularization.

The evangelical churches

In contrast to the mainstream, the evangelical sector in Swansea appeared rather more resistant to secularizing currents. While pentecostals, taken together, only constitute 6 per cent of the religious population of Swansea, in the years 1985–95 they saw some growth, both in terms of membership (13 per cent) and in church attendance (7 per cent). Half the congregations reported some numerical growth. Comparable figures for the UK demonstrate a 28 per cent growth in membership, so Swansea can be said to be somewhat at variance with national trends. Independent evangelical congregations, who constitute a significant section of the Swansea religious economy, accounted for 23 per cent of church attendance. While overall membership dropped by 5 per cent, this was accompanied by a 35 per cent growth in church attendance. It would appear from this mismatch that either this sector is fairly fissile or, while these evangelical congregations have no problem in attracting worshippers, they have rather more difficulty in generating long-term commitment. These issues will be explored in more detail below. By way of contrast, Christian Brethren congregations have experienced an overall 4 per cent decline in membership and 6 per cent decline in church attendance. These figures are roughly in line with the rest of the UK, although with local net growth running at 20 per cent the indications are that declining numbers are a particular feature of some congregations while others have been able to buck the trend. Indeed, in this sense, the overall figures are misleading as they suggest a general picture of decline, whereas the picture in Swansea is rather less uniform. Clearly evangelical churches have proved rather more resistant to secularization but this has been at some cultural cost. Evangelical churches are overwhelmingly English-speaking and as such are a good example of the way in which organized religion generally has become more anglicized and, more specifically, the way in which the Welsh language is becoming progressively disembedded from religion in Wales.

Membership and attendance figures for the different denominations hide significant variations within them and the portrait that they paint is certainly not the whole story. However, on the basis of this limited evidence, a number of broad trends are visible. In terms of decline and growth, Anglicans and Roman Catholics are holding up rather better than many of their Nonconformist counterparts, particularly those long-standing Free Church denominations that constitute the bedrock of Nonconformity in Wales. Among the Free Churches, there appears to be some correspondence between linguistic and theological characteristics and patterns of decline and growth. Evangelical groups appear generally to be better placed than theologically liberal groupings and English-medium churches are faring slightly better than their Welsh-speaking counterparts, although overall decline is most marked in the liberal sector. However, these generalised figures disguise variations within these groupings. As we shall see below, while some groupings may be in a state of overall decline, some individual congregations may be growing and declining congregations can be found in groups that have exhibited some growth.

In mapping the numerical health of individual church and chapel congregations in the city, a somewhat clearer picture emerged. In general, congregations in the western suburbs appeared to have fared significantly better in terms of numerical adherence than those in the traditional areas of residence to the east and this pattern cuts across denominational allegiances.

Clearly, there are also social ecological factors at work. The factors behind these geographical disparities in the numerical health of congregations beg a number of questions that statistical data is ill equipped to answer, and it is to these matters that I now turn. In doing this, it seems best to discuss matters in two parts. First, a discussion of the impact of social change on mainstream congregations (where decline is most evident) and then, secondly, to a discussion of a related issue, patterns of growth and decline among evangelical churches (where growth is most pronounced).

SOCIAL, ECONOMIC AND CULTURAL CHANGE AND ITS EFFECTS ON THE MAINSTREAM CHURCHES

A recurrent theme in much theoretical writing about secularization is the way in which social and geographical mobility both undermines traditional localized religious allegiances and transforms religion itself. Historically, in the Welsh experience, events such as population movements have invariably been accompanied by changes within the religious sphere. As Harris (1990: 57) has demonstrated, this also holds true in fairly circumscribed geographical areas. In a comprehensive set of interviews and informal conversations with church leaders and long-term churchgoers in Swansea in 1995 (Chambers, 1999) a number of themes relating to social, cultural and geographical mobility emerged.

This evidence suggested that the westward drift of families that Rosser and Harris had noted in the 1960s had, in time, adversely affected those churches and chapels situated in the eastern part of the city. Traditionally, these congregations had drawn from the more 'respectable' sections of the working class as well as the lower middle class. These were precisely the people that were taking advantage of post-war prosperity, and the opening up of educational opportunities that had previously been denied them, to move up (in social terms) and to move out (in geographical terms). This new emphasis on social and geographical mobility, coupled with the post-war housing boom in the western part of the city, emptied many eastern areas of precisely that section of the population most likely to attend church or chapel.

As Rosser and Harris (1965: 11–17) demonstrated, 'moving away', even if only a mile down the road, could often break the links between the individual and their 'family' chapel. Many young families, now free in their eyes of the ties and constraints that their communities of origin represented (particularly, the figure of the 'Mam') took this opportunity to curtail previous church activity. For others who desired to continue churchgoing, social and geographical mobility was in many cases accompanied by a change of denominational allegiance in keeping with their new-found social status.

Rosser and Harris noted a recognizable progression of people moving out of the Welsh-speaking chapels and into the anglicised sphere of the 'English' Free Churches or the Anglican Church (1965: 136).

Not all migrated to the western suburbs of the city. The opening up of educational opportunities in the late 1950s and early 1960s introduced for the first time the possibility of a university or polytechnic education for the children of working- and lower middle-class families. These possibilities resonated particularly with Nonconformists, who have traditionally put a high premium on education. Many families saw their children go off to higher education institutions and subsequently to well-paid employment, either in Cardiff, in England, or even further afield. At the time, Swansea offered very little in the way of graduate employment and, for many sons and daughters, the road to education was the same road that was to lead them away from Swansea forever. This haemorrhaging of the brightest and best of the younger generation, particularly from those chapels organized along the principles of the gathered congregation, left those chapels largely bereft of potential future lay leadership and ill-equipped to face the future.

If social and geographical mobility had been the main catalyst in the narratives of decline, this type of observation was not restricted to Nonconformity or to the recent past. Both Roman Catholic and Anglican clerics also complained about a similar exodus of young people and their families. In the most extreme cases these demographic changes had left parishes with congregations that largely consisted of elderly people. One Anglican cleric, who saw little real future for her parish church, whose congregation now numbered ten elderly women, commented: 'They're dying off as you heard this morning now. Our oldest member here is gone. I've buried several during the last year, you know, all those crossed off ones. Nobody will be brought in to replace them.' While this church was clearly no longer viable, what distinguished this narrative from similar narratives in the Nonconformist sector was the continued full-time presence of a paid ordained minister (albeit a deacon) and this highlighted crucial differences in congregational experiences. While Anglican and Roman Catholic churches were not immune to the effects of demographic changes, their rate of numerical decline was in most cases slower than that of their Free Church counterparts. This can be seen as a reflection of the fact that they were in some respects better placed to resist and adapt to the effects of change. The crucial difference here was not external but rather appeared to be related to differing forms of church organization.

Within the Free Church sector, gathered congregations, typical of many of the chapels, are responsible for their own government and financial maintenance. Lambert (1988: 98–9) has likened these Welsh chapels to 'self-governing ecclesiastical republics' and this apt description perceptively captures that tension between the formal independence of the congregation and the fact that all financial costs must be met by the congregation with little or no outside help. Like any independent association, in the final instance the books need to be balanced and, for most, employing someone in a full-time pastoral capacity is an insoluble financial burden. From the evidence gathered in Swansea, it would appear that when a Free Church congregation falls below eighty active adult members, and if outside help is not available, then it becomes impossible financially to maintain full-time professional leadership.

Clearly, the residual effects of mobility on congregations located in areas characterized by the out-migration of churchgoers have left many congregations in a weakened state. Lack of resources, financial and human, has led to a progressive crisis in terms of leadership, with congregations having no ordained minister or having to share a minister with others. In this regard, Swansea chapels and churches are not untypical of the experiences of their counterparts elsewhere in Wales. In an interview with the author, the last remaining full-time Welsh Presbyterian minister in West Glamorgan noted that when he arrived in Swansea in 1960 there were thirty-five Presbyterian ministers in the West Glamorgan area. His stipend was now only being met because his own congregation was an amalgam of four previously distinct congregations and, understandably, he was pessimistic about the future of his presbytery. Another minister of the United Reformed Church commented that it was only his half-stipend from a university chaplaincy that allowed his congregation of a hundred members to retain his services. In a number of other cases, part-time hospital chaplaincies fulfilled the same function. Many other Free Church ministers were only able to carry on by accepting multiple oversights of chapels, effectively limiting their activities within each individual congregation to occasional preaching.

More common though were the many cases where the leadership of struggling chapels devolved down to lay personnel, often untrained elderly men and women. Among those congregations that had a long-standing culture of ministerial dependency (and there were many of these), the process of decline invariably picked up in pace once they lost the services of a professional minister. With a few isolated exceptions, lay leadership only appeared to be effective among those congregations that had never had the benefit of a paid minister in the first place. These tended to be small 'mission'-type churches, more evangelical in character and often founded by a family or families in the mid-twentieth century and the calibre of what was essentially an untrained leadership (but often persons whose occupational background was professional) was often high. Conversely, the Anglicans and Roman Catholics, denominations with a territorially based organization, can and do subsidize operating expenses (and in the case of the Anglicans also ministerial stipends) in poorer parishes from central sources. Despite their own recurrent financial problems, they can still provide a level of pastoral oversight that the Free Churches can only dream of and this continued source of local leadership provides both direction and some confidence in the future.

Of those individuals and families who migrated to the western suburbs, some nevertheless chose to continue to return to worship in their churches and chapels of origin, in many cases providing invaluable numerical and financial support, and sometimes lay leadership, to struggling congregations. These continued loyalties often reflected the considerable investment, often over two or three generations, that individual families had put into membership of a particular church or chapel and this attachment to a particular place of worship has been an abiding feature of Welsh Nonconformity up until fairly recent times. By way of contrast, Anglicans and Roman Catholics, with their more universalistic orientation, found it relatively easier to transfer to other congregations as they moved elsewhere in the city.

The sense of attachment to place has often been something of a two-edged sword where the chapels have been concerned. Even where congregations have diminished to below twelve active members, determined efforts are made to 'keep the doors open' rather than transfer to a more viable congregation and risk a loss of identity. Passions can, and do, run high, particularly if closure and merger is forced by the denomination, as has repeatedly been the case with the Presbyterians. Conversely, Independents and Baptists, being technically members of associations rather than denominations, can do as they wish. As self-governing entities they cannot be forced to close their doors and the upshot of this has been that tiny congregations have continued to worship in buildings that are in many cases structurally unsound, attacked by damp, mildew and dry rot and subject to vandalism. One elderly deacon, musing on the condition of surrounding chapels and their people's unwillingness to countenance the idea of merger with another congregation, suggested, rather poignantly, that:

> Naturally, tradition dies very hard you know and there are a lot of people like that. They're in a place where they've been born and bred and they're reluctant to leave, to go. Hopefully it will never come to that [with us], you know that some sort of revival or growth will happen with all the churches, which is possible, but the trend of the times, there's a cycle now . . . and it's bound to come back to where it started.

This optimism that another 1904-type revival might emerge to reverse the process of decline is somewhat sociologically misplaced, if understandable, given that many elderly worshippers are only one generation removed from those events. There are many tiny groups of elderly worshippers in Swansea, struggling to maintain buildings that can seat hundreds, unable to explain the calamity that has hit their chapel and waiting in hope that another great revival will come to rescue them from extinction. In effect, they have given up on human agency to reverse events, such is the perceived tide of indifference to organized religion among the general population. This picture does not tell the whole story though. If the chapels represent one link with a happier past, other heirs of the 1904 Revival are still to be found whose story is in some ways more positive. It is to these groups that I now turn in order to clarify our understanding of the nature of church growth and decline among that sector of the Swansea religious economy that appears most resistant to the currents of secularization.

PATTERNS OF GROWTH AND DECLINE AMONG EVANGELICAL CHURCHES

Swansea has both a relatively strong evangelical sector, whose adherents could quite justifiably be characterized as the true heirs of the 1904 Revival, and a long history of engagement with evangelicalism. In general, evangelical churches have an enviable reputation among their more mainstream Christian counterparts (and also among some sociologists) for being able to buck many of the trends associated with secularization. Evangelical churches and their congregations, we are told, are less likely to be declining in numerical terms and more likely to have experienced some growth. They are more likely to attract younger people and to have congregations which better reflect the general demographic characteristics of their surrounding populations. Most importantly, in a climate of marked indifference towards organized religion, they are seen to be able more effectively to recruit from the religiously unaligned general population (Bible Society, 1997). Viewed in this light, evangelical churches would seem, in many ways, to be the answer to the prayers of those elderly congregations described in the preceding section. The question, then, is how far these evangelical congregations might be a catalyst for a general revival of fortunes of the Christian church in south-west Wales?

The answer is, under current conditions, that this remains something of an open question. While there are growing evangelical congregations in Swansea (and some impressively so), this growth is, by their own report, overwhelmingly generated by recruitment from other (mainly evangelical) church congregations. A number of prominent evangelical ministers and lay leaders saw this reliance on transfer growth as a major cause of concern for a sector that prided itself both in its ability both to evangelize effectively surrounding populations and to generate sacrificial levels of commitment among its existing adherents.

One well-placed evangelical minister described the Swansea evangelical church scene as 'a merry go round'. In seeking to account for both the high levels of transfers generally and the loss of many of his own members, he laid the blame squarely on his fellow Swansea evangelicals who he dismissed as 'seeking novelty in preaching . . . and when it wears off, they move on'. Others used terms like 'spiritual gypsies' and 'wanderers' to describe the way in which a considerable proportion of worshippers circulated through various evangelical churches without settling in one for any great length of time. This was seen by those in the know as something endemic to the area. Even within the fastest growing church in Swansea, the leadership expressed great concern about this trend. One remarked that competition between the churches had led to much 'adding', whereas these churches should be seeking to be 'multiplying', that is, making genuine new converts rather than attracting transfers. Another leader in the same church commented that within this congregation (which he did not think was untypical) there were three times as many floating worshippers as committed members, adding that: 'We see these wanderers as really being incapable of any real commitment, they're just *not* membership material at the moment. Until they show the commitment, we don't press them about membership' (emphasis in the original transcript). Comments such as these do in some measure explain the statistical anomaly whereby membership in independent evangelical churches dropped by 5 per cent over a ten-year period, while attendance rose by 35 per cent. Clearly, figures like these cannot merely represent the circulation of the same numbers of individuals between these churches. The shape of the figures suggests real growth but all the anecdotal evidence suggests this is primarily transfer growth. There are a number of possible explanations for this mismatch.

With a few isolated exceptions, evangelical congregations in the eastern part of the city are declining rapidly. Population movement and the associated demographic factors have taken their toll over the years, as they have with the mainstream churches, but this was somewhat mitigated by the decision of some churchgoing families to continue to support their chapels of origin, despite moving to the suburbs. Anecdotal evidence suggests that many of these individuals are now increasingly 'giving up' on these congregations as they continue remorselessly to decline, and are seeking to relocate themselves in the more buoyant evangelical congregations in the suburbs. That said, and given their individual histories, these individuals are far more likely eventually to transfer their membership, rather than become floating worshippers.

Geographical factors apart, there are also a number of what have been described as 'new' churches (Bible Society, 1997), relatively new arrivals on the Swansea church scene and mainly charismatic in orientation but not exclusively so. They are 'new' in the sense that they marry an evangelical theology with a thoroughly modern approach to matters of culture. As a movement, the 'new' churches can be said both to seek to resist secularizing forces and simultaneously to endorse certain aspects of modern culture (Hunt, Hamilton and Walter, 1997: 3). Church services are culturally in tune with modern trends; dress is casual, music is contemporary (often electrified, with guitars and drums) and the general ethos of worship is informal and as far away from traditional understandings of 'church' as is possible. Understandably, this movement has proved attractive to the younger members of more conservative evangelical fellowships (notably the Christian Brethren) and many individuals and young families have left these to realign themselves with various 'new' churches in the city.

On a broader cultural and historical note, there has always been a long tradition of 'hearers' in Welsh chapels. These are individuals who might identify with and attend a particular place of worship for many years, possibly all their life, without taking on formal membership. Historically, the 'hearer' epitomized the tension between commitment to the idea of a moral community (and a desire for local respectability) and the reality of formal commitment to chapels which could be highly oppressive in their dealings with members, seeking to control every area of their lives (Lambert, 1988: 102–11). The floating attendees to be found in Swansea today are very different in some respects, but there remains a tension between ideological commitment to evangelical religion and a hesitancy to become too closely involved with those aspects of social control (and possibly the economic responsibilities) that accrue with formal membership. Evidence gathered in interviews also suggests that there has undoubtedly been some movement from the mainstream denominations of what we might call 'part-time hearers'. To be found at preaching services, these are individuals who are ideologically dissatisfied with their own mainstream churches or chapels, particularly regarding the content of preaching. Anecdotal evidence suggests that this species of churchgoer emerged in the 1970s at a time when, in the words of one respondent, the mainstream denominations were increasingly becoming 'infected with liberalism'. However, despite their theological leanings, they still retain considerable affective ties of loyalty with their local church or chapel of origin, which they continue to attend on a reasonably regular basis, often making a point of attending the communion service there. These individuals can be found making the rounds of those places of worship which are noted for the quality and 'soundness' of their preaching ministries.

Of course, this Janus-faced approach to churchgoing does not always endear itself to religious professionals of a more liberal theological outlook. Moreover, from the perspective of declining mainstream churches, the evangelical sector represents unwelcome competition in a marketplace characterized by a progressively declining religious constituency. Within both the evangelical and mainstream spheres, transfer growth is understandably seen as something of a problem and this has effectively created strains on the relations between different churches and, in the case of evangelicals, very visible fissures between different groups. The upshot is that the Swansea church scene appears to the outsider to be very fragmented, with little sense that the churches are in any way united in a common purpose. These strained relations must have some impact on potential recruits and may even be inhibiting the general numerical and psychological health of many congregations. It is to these matters that I now turn.

RELATIONS BETWEEN THE CHURCHES

'Is he sound?' or 'Are they sound?' are turns of phrase that are still commonly to be heard among more conservative churchgoers, reflecting the residual effects of a long history of widespread evangelical activity in the city. Documentary and anecdotal evidence suggests that a hundred years ago evangelicalism was a dominant force in church life, both among the Free Churches and within Anglicanism. Indeed, many Anglican churches were heavily subsidized by the Church Pastoral Aid Society, in some cases up to the 1960s, and even a cursory examination of surviving parish magazines from the early twentieth century reveals a very marked evangelical stance. Evangelicalism among Anglican congregations in the city is largely invisible today. What remains is a commitment to conservative, biblically based and theologically orthodox preaching from the pulpit, coupled with a pastoral ministry that takes a fairly liberal stance towards public social issues and questions of private morality.

With the exception of some Baptist congregations, the long-established Free Churches in the area can no longer be described as evangelical, either in terms of theological orientation or proselytizing zeal. The very oldest cohort of church and chapelgoers can remember when evangelicalism was the norm and in many cases their personal attachment to its outward forms – 'sound' preaching, Sankey songbooks and teetotalism – remains intact. However, what we might term the intermediate generation, those individuals in the 40 to 65 age group, for the most part decisively rejected this lifestyle and orientation in the post-war years and are very antipathetic towards any show of religious enthusiasm. (Although there are, as noted earlier, individuals who are dissatisfied with this shift in orientation.)

The same can be said for many Free Church ministers working within the mainstream, particularly those of the same intermediate generation. This generation of ministers, mostly trained in Wales, reflects the liberal theological climate that was current in the theological colleges from which they graduated and which is very evident in their preaching. Their attitudes towards evangelicalism range from outright hostility or suspicion to uneasy coexistence with neighbouring evangelical churches within what often appears to be a framework of both familiarity and mutual incomprehension. These tensions are exemplified in the following extract from an interview with a Free Church minister:

> Theologically, I'm a middle of the road man. What I find difficult to understand is when you speak of evangelical churches or charismatic churches, well, they are on the increase, and I can't understand why they seem to attract people. I was brought up in an evangelical family where my parents were fundamentalists. Well now, though both have died I have a great respect for my parents but I moved away from that position and I think myself that the position I hold is fairer. Looking back over my education and so forth and my reading of theology, I think that I've moved away from that evangelical position but, take for example [the Presbyterian Church of Wales], we have about a hundred and twenty ministers. I would say that of those hundred and twenty that only perhaps ten or fifteen at the most would hold say a fundamentalist position. I mean, some of my friends, we beg to differ you know, but we're still friends, yet they haven't made such a big impact on our denomination. Because I can think of a minister friend whom I would regard as an extreme evangelical but his churches have gone down more than anybody else I believe.

While this statement sums up the uneasy relationship between the mainstream and evangelicals, it also suggests that, in terms of the recent past, the evangelical tradition is not far away in the memories of many churchgoers. Evangelicalism also impinges on the lives of the Swansea churches in other ways. Many of the weaker mainstream chapels are dependent on visiting lay preachers, many of whom are evangelicals, and the three Christian bookshops in the city are firmly evangelical in orientation. Furthermore, the Swansea Council of Churches remains organizationally weak, not least because there are many evangelical congregations who reject the spirit and principles of ecumenicalism. This spirit of factionalism also spills over into the evangelical sphere and it would be a mistake to view evangelicalism in Swansea as a cohesive entity. The reality is that it is riven with factions and disputes. So much so that it would be easy to conclude that, for many evangelical congregations, 'the enemy' is not so much 'the enemy without', secularism or theological liberalism, but 'the enemy within', that is, other evangelical congregations. This factionalism reflects both theological differences of opinion and competition for adherents and is reflected in the high levels of transfer activity noted above.

In interviews, many evangelical ministers kept their harshest words for other evangelical congregations who were perceived as either doctrinally suspect or engaged in 'poaching' or 'sheep stealing'. This siege mentality was most visible among the more conservative evangelical congregations who appeared particularly prone to losses in the younger age groups. Understandably, this was a cause for concern as this was precisely the age cohort (16–40 years) they could ill afford to lose in terms of securing the future of individual congregations. However, for many conservative evangelicals, what was even more galling was the fact that these erstwhile adherents were mainly transferring to what they regarded as theologically suspect groups within the 'charismatic' (that is, neo-pentecostal) and 'housechurch' sphere.

Historically, factionalism has been an abiding feature of Welsh Nonconformity (Harris, 1990: 51). While this is markedly less so now among the mainstream denominations, which appear to be too exhausted to squabble with each other, it remains very evident within the evangelical sphere. In the mid-1990s, the main bone of contention centred on the so-called 'Toronto Blessing' (today it would be the Alpha programme) which had been enthusiastically received by some congregations and decisively rejected by others. In general, conservative evangelicals viewed the growing number and profile of Charismatic churches in the city with some suspicion if not outright hostility. In part this was due to reservations about the theology and practice of neo-Pentecostalism (notably 'speaking in tongues' and being 'slain in the Spirit') and in part to do with the loss of so many of their young people to these groups. While certainly divisive, the battle-lines surrounding this new phenomenon did not necessarily fall along the established fault lines of conservative evangelicals versus Pentecostals. Some of the longer established Pentecostal churches were also wary of this movement, in part because they saw it as inherently superficial compared to classical Pentecostalism, and not least because it was attractive to many of their younger adherents who were voting with their feet in increasing numbers. On the other hand, some Pentecostals saw it as a proven means of revitalization and renewal for their own churches or as a necessary adaptation if they were to retain their younger elements. Again, while some conservative churches were very publicly vocal in their criticisms of this movement (in both pulpit and the local press), others, while steering clear of the phenomenon, remained publicly silent.

A flavour of this disputatious evangelical culture can be gleaned by one evangelical minister's characterization of the state of the evangelical churches in the city:

How would I describe the church scene here? Confusion, confusion. I mean, I've been in this city for ten years and I've seen much of church life, therefore I'm not deceived by what I see. I've seen what goes on. *We've* even lost a lot of people because they want to go elsewhere, because 'more is happening'. But when you analyse what's going on elsewhere, what's happening, well *there's nothing happening*, it's just a crowd attracts a crowd. I mean, we're living in a society and living in a church age where everyone is looking at themselves and therefore we've lost the whole concept of what Christianity is about. (Emphases in the original transcript.)

While typical of one strand of evangelical thinking, what is interesting here is a refusal to accept and adapt to the changing needs of both members and prospective recruits, or indeed, to recognize and engage with the cultural shifts taking place inside *and* outside the churches. In contrast, the rationale behind much of the thinking in the 'new' churches is more sociological in that they are, in many cases, seeking to bridge the gap between 'church culture' and popular culture, thereby displaying some understanding of the problems churches are facing in an increasingly post-Christian society. Their failure in terms of recruitment to attract significant numbers of recruits from the general population is partially offset by their success in attracting recruits from other churches, but these in themselves constitute a finite resource. Furthermore, this growth has served to highlight profound divisions within the evangelical community, divisions which arguably inhibit any concerted approach to the re-evangelization of the unchurched population. In the light of this factor, and given the current social and cultural circumstances in which these churches operate, it is difficult to see how the evangelical sector, in its present condition, might become a catalyst for any significant religious revival in Wales.

Where then does this leave the Welsh churches, in terms of their mission to the general population? Clearly, the mainstream churches are experiencing problems in recruitment, but this might also be said of their evangelical counterparts who are mainly drawing new recruits from elsewhere within the community of Christians. While recruitment of the latter type clearly leads to individual church growth it does nothing to raise the profile of Christianity with the general population. Secularization is as much about the loss of social significance of religious institutions as it is about the declining numbers of churchgoers. Indeed, strictly speaking, numerical decline is not secularization but merely an effect of secularization, whereas the loss of the social significance of religion (differentiation) is clearly an aspect of secularization. Whereas evangelicals tend to have a fairly narrow view of what mission is, the religious mainstream tends to approach mission in a more holistic manner, interpreting it in terms of social significance and of local church–community relations and it is to this aspect of religious life and some attendant problems that I now turn.

CHURCH AND COMMUNITY

The religious mainstream in Swansea provides us with a somewhat different picture from the evangelicals and this is reflected in the very different concerns of the local clergy and ministers. Nevertheless, a sense of shared situation, not least the problem of continued numerical decline, diminishing resources and the pressures these create is never very far away from the thoughts of religious professionals operating in the city.

Despite the very good statistical indicators relating to mass attendance in the Diocese of Menevia (36 per cent of the estimated RC population) individual Roman Catholic priests were in many cases deeply pessimistic about both the immediate and long-term future for Roman Catholicism in Wales. In 1995 a diocesan meeting was convened in Swansea to discuss the implications of the discrepancy between the estimated 24 per cent growth in the Swansea RC population and the much lower 2 per cent growth in mass attendance. In a stormy meeting, the parochial clergy came under sustained criticism by the bishop for what he saw as their failure to capitalize on the growth of the RC population by converting this into significantly increased mass attendance.

In reply, the local clergy were deeply sceptical about the validity of the statistical claims made by the church. They argued in particular that there had been a significant over-estimation of the RC population in the city and that, in the light of this, the picture was not as black as painted. Nevertheless, all were in agreement that there had been a significant drop in mass attendance over the past decade. This was most apparent in the falling numbers of young people attending, although congregations were fairly well represented in the 30 to 40 age brackets, a generation visibly absent from many of their mainstream Protestant counterparts. Likewise, and again in contrast to their mainstream counterparts, male worshippers were fairly well represented and indeed, the demographic profile of the average RC congregation in Swansea compared very favourably with their surrounding populations, and in many respects was nearer to the experience of evangelical congregations. This would suggest that, despite the bishop's disquiet about falling numbers, actually the Roman Catholics were in a far more favourable position than many of their mainstream Protestant counterparts.

Individual priests appeared far more optimistic about the health of their own congregations. Some priests commented that the loss of teenagers was often temporary and that many returned when they married and had children of their own. One priest had even seen a marked increase in teenagers attending mass, both at his own church (on a Saturday night) and in the local RC comprehensive school. (His explanation for this was straightforward in that both were venues where their parents were not likely to be attending and therefore were not likely to 'embarrass' their children by their presence.) Other priests, while commenting that 'conversions' were so rare as to be almost non-existent, nevertheless noted a steady if small number of lapsed Catholics returning to the church in mid-life. Numbers aside, an increase in lay participation in the life of the church was noted and welcomed by almost all the priests interviewed, particularly the presence of lay eucharistic ministers and members of the Society of Vincent de Paul.

Parish priests were well placed to note other changes also. As historical RC patterns of settlement in the city have changed, the Catholic population is now far more dispersed throughout the city and clerical contact on a daily basis is much reduced. Furthermore, in an echo of observations made by evangelical ministers, some priests noted that individuals were increasingly prone to attend mass in a number of churches, attending weekly but varying the location. The role of Catholic social clubs was in marked decline everywhere and this was seen as a very visible sign of the weakening of traditional Catholic social cohesion. One priest commented that, in Swansea, it was only in those churches located in long-standing solidly working-class areas where the type of social cohesion expected of a Catholic parish persisted. However, he qualified this observation by noting that these churches now had the smallest congregations. Matters were very different in his own, middle-class church located in a leafy suburb of Swansea:

> You get people living in the same street, but they come to different masses, so you get a situation where people never meet each other and never know they are fellow Catholics worshipping in the same church. They go to half-past six mass and perhaps [the people] across the road, they come to the same church but they're coming to a different mass.

On balance, he felt that the neighbouring Anglican church, drawing from the same local middle-class constituency, exhibited much greater social cohesion. An interesting observation perhaps, but more for the light that it throws on clergy concerns. Given the relatively strong performance of the Roman Catholic Church in south-west Wales, it is difficult to account for the widespread feeling of pessimism among clergy on the ground and their masters.

Given that the Roman Catholic Church in the UK generally only really began to experience numerical decline from the 1970s on, some may have felt that the church might have been rather more immune to the same secularizing currents that had bitten deep into the Protestant churches. If so, the experience of the last few decades would have done much to dispel that line of thinking. However, the majority of serving priests in Swansea had spent most of their working lives ministering against the backdrop of numerical decline and had few illusions about the difficulties inherent in their position. What really seemed to fuel their pessimism was the progressive breaking down of Catholic social solidarity in the face of embourgeoising trends.

In conversation, priests repeatedly drew unfavourable comparisons between Swansea and the nearby steel-making town of Port Talbot, which has a significant and long-standing Catholic population. Port Talbot, it was suggested, conformed much more to traditional patterns of RC residential settlement and, as a result, levels of social cohesion were high. One priest commented:

> You take the difference now between St Joseph's Port Talbot and here. Terrific social cohesion there, because when the Irish came over, they lived in the streets around St Joseph's and unlike Greenhill [a traditionally Catholic area in Swansea] those streets were not pulled down. In Swansea the local Catholic population went out to places like Blaen Y Maes with the Council but in St Joseph's Margam it's a very strong parish. It also has the advantage that a great number of people in the parish, men primarily, well they work in Margam steelworks so they have something in common. Now, when they meet each other in church, they're meeting each other in the week. Now *here* it would be different because everyone's got [a different job] you know, there's no one place where men of the parish are employed.

What is interesting is that this observation echoes the experience of many of the chapels in that the strength of local congregations, both in terms of numbers and cohesion, was highly dependent on a very clearly defined set of local factors. These would include stability of residence over successive generations and close proximity of kin, a high degree of social, occupational and economic homogeneity and close ties of mutual cooperation between kin and neighbours. Conversely, growing occupational heterogeneity and social and geographic mobility inevitably weakens and undermines the traditional grounds of religious adherence.

In comparison to their RC counterparts, Anglican clergy were rather more sanguine about issues relating to congregational decline. Certainly, given that there has been a long-term decline in the fortunes of the Church in Wales for most of the twentieth century, they have had much longer to get used to the idea. This is not to say that Anglican clergy were complacent about numerical decline, particularly if they were experiencing it first hand in their own congregations. Nevertheless, despite long-term decline nationally, urban congregations in Swansea remained remarkably buoyant compared to the experience of other sectors of the Swansea churches. On the basis of their own experience and that of other clergy, priests frequently suggested that the general trajectory of decline may be 'bottoming out'. In a fairly typical comment, one priest remarked of his own parish: 'As you know our increase is small and I suppose when I talk of the "increase" here, it's more that there has not been any decline at a time when everyone else is declining.' In part, observations like this reflect the fact that Anglicans have continued to benefit somewhat from that recent pattern of social and geographic mobility associated with embourgeoisement and resultant changes in religious allegiance. However, Anglican parishes in the eastern part of the city have certainly not been immune to the general pattern of decline that has overtaken all churches in this area. Parish records demonstrate that, forty or fifty years ago, many of the churches located in these areas of decline were as full as their Free Church counterparts and in these happier days, congregations of two or three hundred were common. That said, given that nationally Anglicans have never been other than a minority grouping in a predominately chapel culture, the fall from grace has not been as hard as that experienced by the Nonconformist denominations. Furthermore, the understandings of Anglican clergy about the nature of their ministry are very different from their counterparts in other mainstream churches.

The nature of Anglican ministry is inclusive and clergy have a duty to minister to the surrounding religiously non-aligned population as well as to their congregation. The levels of personal commitment required of worshippers are not high when compared to, say, the evangelical churches, who require a 'conversion' experience and the adoption of a rigorous and disciplined world-rejecting lifestyle before there is full acceptance into the worshipping community. Clearly, in evangelical congregations, believing comes before belonging. However, most clergy in Swansea would agree with Robin Gill's assertion that

> In matters of faith, belonging is primary. Intellectuals are apt to forget this. We are so concerned with thought that we frequently convince ourselves that *belief* is primary. People believe and then they belong, so it is assumed . . . in that order. In contrast, I am convinced that the order is mostly the other way around – we belong and then we believe. (Gill, 1994: 27–8)

This idea of belonging without any necessary criteria of belief makes it easier for individuals in the local community to slip into attendance, given that the church ethos is inclusive of them and does not seek to impose unrealistic levels of commitment before any real involvement has begun. With one or two exceptions, Anglican clergy in Swansea saw these weak boundaries as a positive strength in their ministries. Furthermore, they also emphasized the importance of maintaining a 'middle of the road' profile rather than veering towards extremes of churchmanship which might be seen as a form of gatekeeping. One commented: 'The more rigid some policies in individual parishes become, the more isolated they have become from the community in which they are set. Your reason for being there is to be there for *everyone*' (emphasis in the original transcript). The importance of an inclusive orientation, where clergy minister to the needs of the whole community and not just the congregation, was a point that was repeatedly emphasized: 'It's not like a congregational church that says they're the only ones that I'm here for, because usually they're the ones that I spend least time with. I give all my time to the community, which is the parish vision of Anglicanism, right?' This inclusivity is also reflected in a relatively higher level of local community use of church facilities such as church halls, and as one priest commented: 'It's not a *huge* step to go from there [the church hall] into church for anything, provided the same warmth is offered to them there . . . the same feeling of identifying with them and making them feel comfortable' (emphasis in the original transcript).

In the same vein, a number of priests who were describing a steady trickle of previously lapsed Anglicans returning to the fold suggested that this could partially be attributed to the fact that channels of communication remained open through the local pastoral ministry to the general community. Certainly, local use of church facilities and the occasional offices of baptisms, weddings and funerals were overwhelmingly seen as a good thing and as something that marked out Anglican ministry from that of other churches. Priests also repeatedly commented on the increasing inability of the Free Churches to attract candidates to the ministry or to find the money for ministerial stipends. This lack of professional ministry on the ground was seen as a significant, indeed even primary, fact in the rapid numerical decline of the local Free Churches. In contrast, priests felt that the main reason why Anglican congregations in the city remained relatively healthy was because they still had incumbent clergy giving direction and focus to their congregations.

In the light of this strong commitment to the Anglican vision of parish ministry, older priests particularly were both concerned about the falling number of clergy vocations in the Church in Wales and the future implications of this trend for the existing parish system. In this vein a local canon and parish priest voiced his disquiet about the potential 'grouping' of parishes to offset the fall in clergy numbers:

We've seen what has happened with the Free Churches, with ministers having oversight of more and more congregations and when there's no resident minister these churches go down very rapidly indeed. I suppose that I could say that I fear that were there to be too many groupings of Anglican parishes for a similar reason [the lack of available clergy] then we would find some staggering falls in congregations because they didn't have a minister, because that's important. I still think it's very important for the vicar of a parish to live in the parish. He must be part of the community. It wouldn't do if he lived in another area and came in.

The down side of this model of ministry was that, with one exception, clergy felt that it was very difficult to involve lay people in the running of parishes. Parishioners expected clergy to be responsible for most, if not all, areas of church life and were reluctant or felt poorly equipped to assume significant responsibilities themselves. However, this was a common strand throughout Swansea, affecting all groupings and not merely Anglicans.

In summary, these two examples of different institutional approaches towards church–community relations give food for thought. Clearly, the experience of Roman Catholic and Anglican parish ministry is not strictly comparable, given the continuing salience of ethnicity in RC membership and the fact that RC priests minister to a circumscribed population. In contrast, Anglican ministry is more truly inclusive of the surrounding population. However, in both cases, the experience of these churches suggests that, given the right mix of social environmental conditions and an organizational structure based on the territorial unit of the parish, it is not impossible for churches to make an impact on their surrounding population. True, this parish-based model of mission appears to work best in precisely those social conditions (long-standing working-class communities) that are fast disappearing. Nevertheless, the presence of an inclusively orientated pastoral ministry, with religious personnel resident on the ground, appears to offer some confirmation of the continued social salience of mainstream religion in local communities. This is, however, only one side of the equation. Churches are both social *and* cultural institutions and as we have seen in the discussion of the high rate of church transfers, the cultural orientations of congregations cannot be excluded from any analysis of the health of church groups. Clearly, contemporary society has been marked by significant cultural shifts across the board and a crucial question is how the internal cultural characteristics of churches might inhibit or promote congregational growth. It is to this question that I now turn.

CHURCH CULTURE AND SOCIAL CHANGE

From my discussion, it should be apparent that the continued reliance on a professional ministry within much of the mainstream is indicative of a certain conservatism within Swansea church life generally. Certainly, the housechurch movement (exemplifying, as it does, 'do it yourself' religion) has not found this part of Wales a particularly fruitful area for expansion. William Price (1989: 40) has characterized Anglicanism in Wales as being very conservative and this observation might be extended to Welsh church life generally and to Swansea as a microcosm of wider national trends. Throughout Swansea, ministers and clerics of all persuasions emphasized the deep conservatism of their congregations and their reluctance to accept change. Even among the few 'new' churches, leaders stressed the need to handle change thoughtfully and sensitively if significant sections of their congregations were not to be alienated. It would, however, be a mistake to assume that this conservatism always takes similar forms, particularly when we are talking of Swansea. There are a number of distinct types of conservatism related to different types of churches.

The conservatism of the 'ecclesia' type churches (Anglican and RC) is essentially to be found in a liturgical conservatism orientated towards a middle way and eschewing extremes of either 'high' or 'low', coupled with what might be termed an 'orthodox' line in teaching and preaching. However, this is often to be found in tandem with a pastoral ministry that adopts a realistic stance towards the exigencies of modern society and culture and is sympathetic to the frailties of human behaviour. For example, marrying couples who are already cohabiting or baptizing the children of unmarried parents is no longer an issue for most clergy in this sector.

The same cannot be said of the more conservative evangelical congregations, where biblical fundamentalism is invariably coupled with an extreme moral conservatism. This combination often makes it difficult for these churches to engage in any meaningful way with their local communities, particularly in working-class areas or on the new housing estates. One minister, based in one of Swansea's older local authority housing estates, told me that a number of young families (where the parents were in long-term common-law relationships) had begun attending his church but had eventually left after being told to choose between the church or each other. Relations with the local unchurched population were also not good, mainly due to this minister's refusal to accept or overlook the lifestyles of local residents. He summed up the dilemma:

> We've had a number of people saved from the community, but they've all gone back and all on the same issue, immorality, and it's very hard. You say this is what the Bible says, we appreciate you're desperate, we just can't condone it. I've had people come to my house and tell me, quite openly, that they are living together and sleeping together, but would I mind if I buried a relative? Thirty years ago no one would have *thought* of walking into a minister's house saying they were living an immoral life. So yes, they've all gone back on that issue. It's

very hard and I think it's an issue the church should not bend on. Otherwise, who calls the shots?

This type of gatekeeping and boundary maintenance is not uncommon and explains in part the failure of evangelical churches to interface with working-class communities and their subsequent decline. Furthermore, this ideological conservatism is often compounded by an overall cultural conservatism in church life and worship generally. However, theological and moral conservatism does not necessarily preclude innovation in the organizational and worshipping life of congregations. This is the case with the 'new' churches operating in the city, who have been prepared to explore ways of making themselves more 'relevant' in a changing social and cultural environment.

By way of contrast, many mainstream congregations, while having no strong theological commitment to conservatism, are nevertheless imbued with a spirit of conservatism in what they do. In many cases this is exemplified by an almost pathological resistance within congregations to any hint of change. In the case of the Welsh-medium churches this is particularly so, although, unlike their anglicized counterparts, this is not so much a refusal to adapt to changing cultural and social conditions as an inability even to comprehend the implications of these changes. The loss of a predominantly Welsh-language cultural milieu, the virtual disappearance of the Welsh-speaking communities that were the backbone of this culture and the failure to attract a new generation of Welsh learners are all received with dismay and incomprehension.

Indeed, this failure to attract young people and families is a theme echoed among all the varied religious groupings in Swansea. Some groupings, notably the 'new' churches and, to a lesser degree, the Roman Catholics, have, as I have noted earlier, proved to be rather more culturally in tune with the needs of young people. At the other end of the spectrum, the Welsh-medium churches appear most affected by the absence of the young, although this is merely a matter of degree. Generally, it is a commonplace of Swansea church life that there is a 'missing generation' and the demographic profiles of most churches reveal a dearth of what might be termed 'key age categories', those individuals capable of child-bearing, and thus the internal reproduction of declining congregations. Swansea is not untypical in this: the findings of the 1995 Welsh Churches Survey and statistics generated elsewhere in the UK reveal very similar demographic patterns. Nevertheless, the marked conservatism of the majority of Swansea churches and chapels reflects a culture that appears almost frozen in time, hardly the most attractive environment for those brought up in a totally different culture.

It is a fairly common observation within the Welsh church scene that there appears to be a cultural lag between the experience of churches in

England and their Welsh counterparts, and that this gap increases with distance from the border. Certainly, the general religious life of Swansea is, in many aspects, more reminiscent of the situation in England twenty or thirty years ago. This cultural distanciation is even more marked within local chapel culture which tends to conform to the general cultural attributes extant in the 1940s and 1950s. This cannot be said of the general cultural life of Swansea, which differs little from that of any other British city. It follows that the cultural gap between the chapels and churches and the general population, especially the young, is particularly marked. Simply, there is little to attract younger people to become active worshippers and, in the case of the chapels, this constitutes what can only be termed an alien cultural environment for the younger generations.

This has serious ramifications for both internal reproduction and outside recruitment. As McGraven and Wagner (1990) have noted, individuals find it hard enough to commit themselves to the religious life, without having the added burden of crossing ethnic, linguistic or class barriers. This principle applies as well to age groups and it follows that potential recruits will find it easier to make this transition within a religious grouping that best reflects their prior cultural experience. In Swansea, the handful of churches that are attracting young people in numbers have both significant numbers of other young people or young families present and offer distinctive forms of worship that are culturally relevant. This is not so at the other end of the continuum. Here are to be found Free Church congregations, primarily composed of elderly women, often worshipping in over-large, damp and crumbling buildings and using forms of worship which have hardly changed in a century. The social and cultural life of these chapels remains firmly rooted in a by-gone culture and the increasingly faint echoes of collectivist community structures which limp on in the activities of the Ladies Guilds and Sisterhoods and the sparsely attended meetings for worship. Simply, there is nothing here to attract the younger generations.

THE CHURCHES: PROSPECT AND CHANGE

Taken together, the picture generated by the Swansea churches is fragmentary, with a plurality of individual group agendas. Some churches are looking forwards but many are looking backwards. Some are seeking to convince individuals of the continuing relevance of religion, others merely affirm their rejection of an irreligious world. Some are seeking to expand the boundaries of inclusiveness, others are seeking to reinforce the boundaries of exclusiveness. All this activity (or inactivity) is largely self-referential, carried out in a climate of growing indifference to organized religion and increasingly divorced from the lives of the majority of the general population.

Like the religious landscape in the UK as a whole, the pattern of success or failure is patchy, both in terms of geography and church type. Comparatively, certain types of religious group are doing rather better than others, both in terms of maintenance and mission. Certain geographical areas appear either more, or less, conducive to churchgoing. Taken together, these two factors appear to have significant effects on the decline, survival or even success of individual congregations in Swansea. In broader terms, any individual church growth is taking place in the context of a general decline of churchgoing and a parallel loss of influence of institutional religion. These trends are particularly marked in Wales and, in this respect, Swansea is no exception to the general Welsh experience. Indeed, the current religious situation in Wales is in many respects now much nearer to the English experience. Certainly, Wales is increasingly differentiated from the rest of the so-called 'Celtic Fringe' where, statistically, churchgoing remains fairly buoyant.

This decline in the social salience of organized religion, while indicative of secularization, nonetheless also incorporates a number of factors that are distinctively Welsh in their provenance. The role of Welsh Nonconformity in shaping both a sense of 'national' identity and a distinctive communitarian culture is central to an understanding of how organized religion has come to lose salience in Welsh society. The rise and fall of Nonconformity exemplifies more generalized trends within the religious sphere. Talking in general terms, and this would apply to any industrial (or more properly post-industrial) region of Wales, the economic and structural changes that south and south-west Wales have experienced in the last thirty years have both significantly undermined the ethos of Welsh Nonconformity and undercut its constituency. The individual Welsh chapel was the concrete expression of communities that lived, worked, worshipped and died in tightly circumscribed locales. The chapel was an expression of solidaristic community life and expressed that life to others. The chapel was the voice that encapsulated the social, political and economic life of the community, but, in a dialectical relationship, also derived its life from the community. Simply, it was the totalizing expression of habitus, both derived from and informing community life.

However, these interconnecting strands, social, economic and political, which appeared so strong, were only so because they were interwoven. The span of the twentieth century saw these strands progressively unravel, rendering increasingly problematic the place of the chapel in local communities. The political strand was the first to be broken as the Liberal Party increasingly lost its constituency to the Labour movement. However, the social and economic strands remained connected while people continued to live and work together and the rope held, even if it was increasingly fragile. While men continued to work in identical or similar occupations, local populations remained socially, economically and culturally homogeneous, with everyone effectively 'in the same boat'. It was the subsequent decline and then collapse of the traditional industries that effectively broke the rope. With the collapse of community all that was really left was a sense of place. This left the chapels, in most cases, high and dry. Their modes of organization, their activities, their modes of expression: the interpretative framework that structured human experience and made sense of the self were all predicated upon a notion of habitus that was no longer relevant to the overwhelming majority of the population. The only remaining function that many chapels had left was as a time-travel capsule into the recent past. Unfortunately, it is in the nature of younger people to look forward, only the old seek to embrace the past.

Two central processes inform this progressive disconnection between religious institutions and the general population: first, changes at the socio-economic level, notably the decline of heavy industry and the related progressive breaking down of homogeneous communities based on a close link between work and residence and the growing trend towards structural differentiation; secondly, the progressive embourgeoisement of sections of the 'respectable' working class and their movement away from traditional areas of residence to the suburbs, in the process shifting the centre of gravity of local religious institutions away from their historic roots in working-class communities and transforming religion in the process. Whereas Welsh religious institutions historically sought to transcend matters of class (and in doing so connected with the widest possible constituency), churchgoing has been transformed into something more closely resembling the experience of the English churches. Certainly, the latter part of the twentieth century has seen a distinctly Welsh religious culture and practice fading away into something that closely approximates English suburban religion.

Clearly, Welsh religious institutions are now forced to operate in social, economic and cultural settings that are a long way from their traditional roots in a relatively undifferentiated society. Clearly, too, the understandings of churchgoers about their place in Welsh society and the future of their respective religious institutions are also undergoing change. It is to these changing understandings and the notion of social action that I now turn. In the four case studies which follow, the ways in which individual and group social action are conditioned by both local social environmental factors and informed by the subjective meanings and interpretations of the social actors involved will be explored in some detail. Beginning with a composite study of congregations which have declined to the point of extinction, I shall then move on to three studies which encompass a working-class Anglican parish, a suburban Baptist congregation and a successful independent evangelical church. Each case study will seek to expand upon and illuminate issues raised in this chapter with a view to building a more complete picture and a more nuanced understanding of the significant changes that have affected and informed Welsh religious life in recent years.

4

The End of the Line

It was a cold Sunday morning in January 1996 when I first visited 'Zion' (not its real name). A Baptist church situated in a rundown working-class district of Swansea, it is a large, imposing building capable of accommodating 650 worshippers that has now fallen on hard times. Indeed, at first sight it appeared to me to be derelict, with broken windows, graffiti-covered doors and all the signs of having been subjected to a sustained and long-running campaign of vandalism. My first impression, despite having been in recent telephone contact with the church secretary, was that I had arrived too late and that the church had finally closed its doors on its worshippers, yet another statistic in the story of Welsh church closures. It was not, however, closed. Inside were six elderly women and one elderly man preparing to commence the weekly service of worship. As they struggled to find me a useable hymnal from a pile of musty and mildewed volumes, it became apparent that the cold, damp and decayed interior of the church was in no better condition than the outside. The content of the service itself was little better as we limped through an act of worship that was as cheerless and uninviting as the building itself. My overwhelming impression was: why on earth would anyone want to step through these doors on a Sunday? Despite the best efforts of the congregation to welcome me, there appeared to be nothing that could possibly attract newcomers and certainly nothing to induce younger people to attend this particular church. The smell of decay was more than just the deterioration of a building, it signalled the death of a worshipping congregation.

It was not always so. Talking to the women in the congregation afterwards, they told me of a very different church. This was a full church where, if worshippers wanted to guarantee themselves a seat, they got there half an hour early. It was a church that was vibrant, with the spiritual and social life of the local community revolving around its services, meetings and activities. It was socially and politically aware, providing a number of local councillors at both borough and county level. Within the denomination it had a high profile and built up many contacts with other churches, even as far away as Holland, Germany and Switzerland. Locally, Zion was a

byword for a successful and thriving Baptist church. This was the church of
their youth and there are many such congregations and stories to be told in
Wales. According to the 1995 Welsh Churches Survey: 'The vast majority of
churches in Wales are very small . . . over half of the total churches in Wales
have a total attendance, including children, of 25 or fewer and the most
frequently reported size is 10' (Bible Society, 1997: 20). Understandably, the
authors of the survey suggest that these congregations are likely to have a
very limited impact (if any) in, and on, their local communities. Lack of
human and financial resources, the loss of professional leadership, old and
dilapidated buildings, and congregations primarily made up of the very
young and the very old, all taken together, hardly augur well for the future
health of the Christian religion in Wales (Bible Society, 1997). Does this
mean, then, that institutionalized religion in Wales is coming to 'the end of
the line'? The short answer is no, but a qualified no. Where faith groups
have the resources and the will to adapt to changing social and cultural transformations, then their future remains at least open. Certainly, there are some
isolated cases of churches that appear to be thriving, even while those around
them continue to decline. However, for the majority of traditional expressions
of faith and practice, those sections of the Christian church that are struggling
to keep their doors open in the face of the widespread apathy of the Welsh
people to organized religion, it seems very much like the end of an epoch.
Swansea, in common with the rest of Wales, has many congregations who fall
into the latter category and it is to these churches that I turn first.

In this chapter I introduce the stories of four churches that are all in various
ways very close to reaching 'the end of the line' and one church that,
through unforeseen circumstances, has been given a new lease of life. While
the following three chapters will be built around single ethnographic case
studies, this chapter proceeds a little differently. In the case of the life of
churches like Zion, there is very little for the ethnographer to investigate.
What remains of corporate church life is little more than one service for
worship on a Sunday morning. Any foci for investigation are in the past,
where individual narratives of growth and decline are situated. There is
very little to engage with in the present, other than the oral histories of those
remaining worshippers. These interviews carried out with elderly church and
chapelgoers offer a fascinating insight into a cultural and social world that is
fast disappearing. Furthermore, despite denominational differences, a very
similar picture emerges, with the same general processes that have proved so
corrosive to churchgoing and very similar (even interchangeable) events in
individual congregations highlighting and marking the progress of decline.

This is therefore something of a composite case study. While focusing on
the story of Zion, which is in many ways an exemplar of the effects of secularization, I shall also draw on ancillary interview and observational material

gathered in four other churches. These are: 'Hope Chapel', an English Baptist church; 'Shiloh', a Welsh-medium Independent church; 'Faith Tabernacle', an evangelically orientated Presbyterian church; and 'St Jude's', an Anglican church (not their real names). All are located in those traditional working-class areas in the east of Swansea and all are in a marked state of decline, with average attendances of twenty persons or less. Hope Chapel differs slightly from the others in that, while it has experienced marked decline since the 1950s, special circumstances have arrested this decline for the time being. These circumstances will be discussed in relation to the future prospects of the other churches featured in this chapter.

THE ENGLISH BAPTIST STORY

'Zion' is situated in 'Eastside', a traditional working-class community that has seen better days. Roughly 7,000 people live in a residential area that is tightly bounded by various topographical features that give the locality something of an island feel. (Indeed, until the 1940s, access to the rest of Swansea was by means of one bridge.) The community has traditionally drawn its living from the docks located nearby, which, until economic restructuring in the 1970s, was the largest local employer. The docks are now a rapidly fading shadow of themselves and very few people gain their employment from this source anymore. The rate of economically inactive adults is twice the Swansea average, although unemployment levels are roughly the same, indicating that this is an elderly population. Industrial pollution has been a problem in the past and is reflected in the fact that many people in the locality have a long-term limiting illness. Those in work are largely in manual occupations and 56 per cent of households fall into social categories IIIm and IV, rising to 76 per cent when categories IIIn and V are included. Ethnicity is overwhelmingly white and the population English-speaking. The inhabitants are slightly less mobile than the Swansea average, but the presence of affordable housing draws young families into the area, although they tend to move on as their financial circumstances improve.

There are still many families in the area with a long history of residence and association with the docks and these constitute a core of long-established, inter-connected and crosscutting social networks, which still underpin relations within the community. However, these 'local' people tend to emphasize the changes that have taken place in the past twenty years and point to the presence of a substantial proportion of newcomers to the area as corrosive of community structures and 'neighbourliness'. The area now has many of the social problems associated with any inner-city location:

drugs, vandalism, theft and a higher than average incidence of lone-parent families. There are ten active church congregations in the area: three Anglican (all grouped in one parish), one Roman Catholic, one Congregational, one Brethren, one Presbyterian, a small evangelical fellowship and Zion Baptist Church. The high proportion of churches in what is quite a small geographical area is more a reflection of the past religious history of the area than an accurate indicator of present religious adherence, and the state of the Nonconformist churches particularly is not good. With the exception of one Anglican church and the Roman Catholics, congregations are predominantly small, female and elderly.

My first point of contact at Zion was 'Albert' (all names have been changed), the church secretary and unpaid leader of the church. Albert told me that he had been associated with Zion for seventy-two years and that it had been his parents' and grandparents' church. In 1981, after a thirty-year pastorate at the church, the last full-time minister retired and Albert and the remaining deacons took over the running of the congregation. By 1985 membership had fallen to thirty-one persons and continued to fall to twenty-one in 1990 and to fourteen members in 1995. Some of these remaining members are very infirm and at the time of this study average attendance was between six and twelve persons. Albert is now the sole remaining church officer, the others having died or moved away, and he is responsible for leading the church. He works in an unpaid capacity and is accredited by the Baptist Union of Great Britain as a lay preacher.

The Baptist cause in the area began with a children's work initiated in 1875 by a local woman and her husband in their home. The district around the docks was in the throes of birth as an urban community, in an area that only twenty years before was still a mainly rural location. This was a period of rapid social and economic change. Swansea and the surrounding hinterland was then experiencing an industrial boom and in 1881 the expansion of existing port facilities and the building of two new docks was accompanied by the construction of many dwellings and an influx of workers and their families into the area. Many of these were Baptists drawn from elsewhere in Glamorgan and further afield and it would appear that one of their priorities was to establish a visible worshipping presence in the area. Up until this point in time the only religious presence in the locality had been a solitary Anglican church which had pre-existed the urban community. Clearly, there was a lack of facilities for Nonconformists moving into what was then a rapidly expanding community and, as a result of the pioneering 1875 work, the Baptist congregation was formally founded in 1881, when a constitution was drawn up and deacons elected. Worship was initially in a tin and wood structure and this was replaced in 1884 with what became known as the 'New Chapel', which accommodated 300 worshippers. From the outset this building was deemed too small. Contemporary church records described it as 'inconveniently crowded' and it was replaced in 1905 with the present structure, the 'New Church', a building designed to accommodate twice the number of worshippers.

At this time, the church could rightly be described as a focal point for community life. A surviving copy of the 1933 *Jubilee Souvenir* records that prior to the Great War, Zion played:

> [A] great part in the religious and social life of the district. It was a scene of great prayer and preaching. Heaven was brought down to earth and its walls are hallowed with memories of those who pleaded with God for the salvation of men. Choir and congregation sang the songs of Zion, and many now sing the song of Moses and the Lamb.

Albert commented that in his father's and grandfather's time, the social, economic and worshipping life of the community were closely inter-connected. Elders and deacons were men of some status and substance, often local shopkeepers or foremen or managers in the numerous local industries or on the docks. In the matter of employment, a friendly report from a church officer to his employer could secure work and it was local common knowledge that employment in certain firms or places was largely conditional on attendance at particular churches or chapels. Families were large and as children became adults and started their own families in turn, they stayed in the locality, often living only a few streets away from their parental home. Males tended to work side by side with their co-religionists, who were often also related. Women inhabited their own social networks based on ties of both family and religion. For the chapelgoers, the pleasures of the theatre and the public house were denied them so they made their own entertainment in the chapels. The life-world of the chapels provided status, some security in a very insecure world and, above all, respectability and a distinctive collective and aspirational identity for working-class families. In a very real sense, the social, economic and religious lives of these Baptists were inseparable.

The Great War marked something of a watershed in this way of life. Men who had served in the armed forces and who had seen something of the wider world (and something of its horrors) returned unsettled and often questioning the role of organized religion. The steady rate of church growth that had characterized the pre-war years began to falter, despite something of resurgence in the early 1930s when membership reached its highest point of 273 persons. (Many 'hearers' and the children of members can be added to this figure.) Despite continued local support for the church, the inter-war years were also a time of growing financial crisis as the congregation increasingly struggled to meet both the debt incurred with the new building and the costs of ministry. Nevertheless, as extant church records showed, a number of able ministers served the church during this period. Another war was again to prove problematic for the health of the church and the years afterwards saw the beginnings of a more permanent decline. The 1981 *Centenary Souvenir* records that in 1946:

> History repeated itself. When hostilities ceased and men and women were discharged from the forces there was no great return to the Churches. [Zion], like other churches, felt the loss particularly of male worshippers. Efforts were made to encourage the people to worship. The Church was faced with serious losses in membership. The weekly collections were at a low ebb, and financial difficulties arose. The minister left in 1949.

This fairly stark assessment of the health of the congregation highlights the precarious financial state of the church at this time and Zion was not alone in this. A perennial problem within the Nonconformist sphere in Wales has been the financial costs of maintaining mortgage payments on church buildings and the costs of ministerial stipends.

In the case of Zion, the roots of this problem went back as far as 1884. The initial growth of Zion in the late nineteenth century was a reflection of, and a response to, the growth of a local community. Given the nature of Welsh society at the time, it is unsurprising that a community in the making should look to the familiar institutional structures of church and chapel upon which to build their own nascent community structures. The story of increase to the church was also a story of increase to the community. However, by the time the 'New Church' was built, the rapid population growth that had characterized the recent history of the area was slowing and the local community was stabilizing in terms of numbers. With hindsight, it is clear that the assumption that the congregation would continue to grow, even though there was no significant new building of dwellings in the locality, was over-optimistic. From its inception the building was a financial liability and the effects of the Great Depression and the high local rates of unemployment which followed the collapse of the south Wales economy exacerbated this in later years. It has remained a liability and it is highly probable that if the decision to rebuild had been held in abeyance until after the Great War a more modest structure would have been seen as appropriate.

Zion has had eight full-time ministers during its history and the records emphasize that the congregation, even at the best of times, had always experienced difficulties in meeting the financial costs of maintaining an incumbent minister. The inter-war years were particularly hard in this respect as many men in the congregation were unemployed and the records note that a discernible drift from the church began to gather momentum in the mid-1930s. In describing this drift, the writer of the *Centenary Souvenir* suggests that personal financial hardship and the falling away were linked phenomena. This falling away was exacerbated by the disruptive effects of the Second World War, not least the billeting of soldiers in the church buildings, which was unpopular locally, and the absence of a resident minister from 1941 until 1946. These years were also characterized as a period of drift and throughout the history of Zion these periodic fallings away appear to coincide with times when the church was without a resident minister. Nevertheless, despite these setbacks, the congregation was still in a relatively strong position in the immediate post-war years and the records reveal the existence of a strong and lively church culture in the 1950s.

The last incumbent minister was called in 1951 and remained pastor for thirty years. Significantly, half the costs of the ministerial stipend were, for the first time, met by an outside body, the Baptist Home Mission Fund. For Zion, this period was something of an Indian summer. Despite growing financial strains, the congregation was still looking forward to the future. There was no sense of impending crisis and this confidence was expressed in an ambitious rolling programme of structural renovation of the church fabric that continued into the 1970s. A new emphasis on purely social activities within the life of the church brought dividends in terms of an increase in numbers, particularly among women. This late flowering of the church was in no small part due to the efforts of an energetic and innovative minister and his partner, who was also active in the life of the church. The previous longest serving minister had spent thirteen years at Zion, somewhat longer than the average incumbency of six years. This was a period of much needed stability in the life of the church, although a policy of 'mission' was becoming increasingly replaced with a strategy of 'maintenance'. In the life of churches this can often lead to complacency, and certainly, as late as 1981, there appeared to be little or no recognition that this was a critical period in the life of the church, even though numbers by then had been steadily dropping for forty-two years.

Another significant and related shift in this post-war period was in the theological and organizational emphasis of the church. The early life of the church was founded on a strongly evangelical theology and the active presence of energetic and extremely capable lay leaders. Elders and deacons were selected for their spiritual and administrative qualities and were directly accountable to members on both counts. From the 1950s on this was less likely to be the case. This was a time when a definite cultural sea change was emerging within the congregation, heralding a shift away from a distinctly evangelical witness and way of doing things. This appeared to be congregationally rather than ministerially driven and women were an important force for change. Despite initial resistance from the minister, innovations such as church bazaars and an amateur dramatic society (both anathema to conservative evangelicals) were introduced and long-standing organizations like the Band of Hope and the Young Men's Institute fell into abeyance. The stated rationale for these new social activities was to generate much-needed income for the church but increasingly their social function predominated. The profile of women's social organizations and activities was raised, indicating that they were now becoming a more powerful force within the congregation as they began to outnumber men significantly. Theologically, the church retained a formal commitment to the evangelical tradition but in practice this was interpreted in an increasingly liberal manner. At the same time, power was becoming progressively concentrated in the hands of the minister rather than with elders and deacons, something which Albert, then a relatively young man, was ambivalent about:

> Thirty-one years. He had a controversial ministry . . . a long time, over a number of years you know. He tended to be autocratic see? He didn't give members that licence to use their talents and gifts, not that I criticized him in any way, but that was the trouble, I felt he stifled people's gifts and talents . . . He was autocratic in that way.

The knock-on effect of this approach to ministry was that those younger individuals who might have moved into a more active membership were discouraged from contributing and putting into practice their own suggestions and ideas. This was compounded by the fact that there were also a number of genuine and successful innovations emanating from this minister and increasingly members became more passive.

Indeed, this was an individual ministry that was both high profile and seen as successful. This minister was a committed ecumenicist and relations with other churches were good. He accrued many offices at both national and local levels: president of the British and Foreign Bible Society, council member of the Free Church Council, chairman of the South Wales Joint Board, and secretary of the Swansea District and West Wales Baptist Association. He personally established links between Zion and Baptist churches in Europe, and also pursued an active political career as a local Labour Party councillor, being made an alderman of the city in 1970. Understandably, these activities were time-consuming and often clashed with church activities, occasionally causing friction within the church. Laudable as these activities were (and there is no doubt that they also raised the profile of Zion), it is hard not to draw the conclusion that all these efforts overstretched this minister and masked a benign neglect of the congregation.

Numbers continued to decline, either through deaths or members moving away, and there seem to have been no moves either to try and recruit new members or even to encourage those who had moved to homes elsewhere in the city to continue attending at Zion.

Even if there had been a concerted campaign by the church to retain members, it is doubtful that this would have brought about much success. In remembering this period of time Albert conceded that: 'I can't recall *anybody* who continued in their membership and worship once they moved away, although they *had* the transport. I don't know why. Because it was a working class district perhaps?' (Emphasis in the original transcript.) The corrosive effects on the life of the church of the growing embourgeoisement of the congregation can be seen in a longer extract from conversations with Albert:

> The main reason [for decline] was that in the so-called affluent years of the sixties and seventies, people had more money and were richer in the financial sense. They upped and went out to more affluent areas like Tycoch and Mumbles and other places you see. Whole families, whole generations, whereas they used to save up and stay. Like my mother and father, when they got married. It was the custom in pre-war years that you rented two rooms and normally lived in the same district in which you were brought up. You grew up in that community and your children and grandchildren followed after. That just collapsed, and there again young people also started to leave. They had the opportunity to go to university and they never came back. My son went into the RAF. He never came back to Swansea. He married a girl in Norwich and he lives up there now. So, if they went into banking or any other business, they had to go away to find a job and for promotion. So that infrastructure of church life collapsed. It was a family gathering in those days you see.

By the 1980s, the effects of this exodus to greener pastures were all too apparent in Zion. The choir had dwindled in numbers and for the first time was entirely female in composition. Uniformed youth organizations like the cubs and scouts had been disbanded in earlier years and eventually even the Sunday school closed. The active social life of the church began to decline, significantly altering the community aspect of the church. As deacons died or moved away, there was no one willing or able to take over their individual responsibilities. In 1989 the last organist died, hastening the eventual demise of the choir. Of the raft of activities which sustained the life of the church, very little now remains:

> We used to hold monthly church meetings. Always the last Monday of the month was the Deacon's Meeting and the Wednesday was the Church Meeting,

and then if there were new members joining the church, on the following Sunday, the first Sunday of the month which was Communion, they were taken into the church. But that's gone by the board now. Most of them come here on a Sunday morning and they won't come out in the nights. They come here on a Sunday morning and they tell you, 'We'll be indoors now to the next Sunday'. So there's that decline (*pause*) I mean, this *was* a hive of activity seven days a week. In the old days we had Band of Hope Monday. You had choir on a Tuesday. You had mid-week prayer service on a Wednesday. You had Sisterhood in the afternoon, Wednesday afternoon. On a Thursday we had Young People's Fellowship and then there was Friday, perhaps a practice for a Passion Play or even a Nativity Play. So, it was only perhaps the Saturday when the church was being neutralized you see. As older members, as families moved away and older members passed on, died, (*pause*) there was nobody willing to come in and take their place see (*pause*) to take over the office (*pause*). The community went down. (Emphases in the original transcript.)

Community use of Zion is now restricted to the occasional wedding or dedication of a child and funerals, all of which Albert is licensed to conduct. Former local ties and past family affiliation to the church are the main reason why couples choose to return to get married in Zion, often for no other reason than because their parents were married there. (Local residents prefer to use the local parish church for weddings, or if they are remarrying, the local Congregational church.) Very occasionally, local people with some past familial connection to Zion choose to have their babies dedicated there and these can be big public occasions with up to fifty family members attending. None of this is translated into churchgoing. Zion has also become a fairly popular venue for funerals, of which there are many. In some cases this is again because of prior associations with the church. However, Zion is also a venue that is looked upon favourably by many funeral directors in the city, not least because Albert is licensed to conduct funerals and because of all the available seating. These funerals provide both a welcome source of revenue and a continuing affirmation of the public presence of the church in the community.

However, none of this in itself is enough to secure the future of the church in anything but the short term, and it is only a matter of time before the doors close for the last time. The building itself is a continuous drain on remaining finances and most of the capital fund, built up in the good years, has now been spent. Albert himself is in remarkably good health for his age and remains active and energetic, although how long he can continue to provide leadership to the congregation remains an open question. Indeed, given the age and infirmity of the remaining congregation, it is unlikely that his services will be required for much longer. Albert himself sees no future for Zion in its present circumstances. He estimates that the yearly cost of supporting a minister would be in the region of £20,000, a sum beyond the means of the present congregation, and they cannot, given their circumstances, call another minister. While the other Free Churches in the district are also in an advanced state of decline, he considers that there is no likelihood that these congregations might merge to give themselves another few years of life: 'We're all in the same boat as far as congregations are concerned but people are loath to leave their own church and to try to get them to do that is the most *difficult* thing in the world' (emphasis in the original transcript). The one positive move that Albert felt might have given the church a new lease of life was to have demolished the existing building and replaced it with sheltered housing and a modestly sized hall for worship. He is in close contact with the congregation of another English Baptist church, 'Hope', that has successfully seen a project like this come to fruition.

'Hope' Baptist Church is situated approximately a mile away from Zion in a more central location within the city. In many ways the history of Hope mirrors that of Zion; a once thriving congregation, founded in 1871, with a small, faithful remnant who have for many years battled in the face of continuing decline to maintain a large building, capable of accommodating a thousand worshippers. In an almost identical narrative to that of Zion, the congregation had dwindled to twenty-five members, when in 1992 they were approached by a major Welsh housing association with a proposal that was to prove a lifeline. The housing association had identified a need for a sheltered housing complex for elderly people in the area and it was proposed to Hope that it relinquish the title to the land on which the chapel stood and the existing building be demolished to make way for housing. In return, the housing association would design and build a new chapel, capable of seating 150 persons and located on the ground floor of the proposed block of flats. The proposal was accepted and the congregation temporarily removed to a nearby church while the demolition and building work was completed. They moved into the new building in 1995 and the congregation, now drawn from the existing members and residents of the flats, has doubled in size. The new chapel is bright and welcoming and has extensive facilities, including a fully equipped kitchen and wheelchair access, which are particularly suited to the needs of an elderly congregation. More importantly, it is now situated at the heart of a community (literally living on top of the church) who by virtue of their age are more culturally attuned to churchgoing and the church has proved successful in recruiting from these residents. While it is unlikely that the demographic profile of the church will change much, it is likely that as older members and residents die or move into care homes, these losses might be offset through recruiting from new residents. The church thus has a realistic chance to reproduce itself, even though the demographic profile is likely to remain at the upper end of the age scale. The renewed sense of forward-looking optimism at Hope has also allowed them to take on the services of an able part-time minister.

In the light of this very positive experience, Zion pursued this option to the point of having architects plans drawn up by the Baptist Housing Association but they were unable to take the project further due to lack of funding from the Welsh Office. It is now 'on hold' and it is likely that events will overtake Zion in the very near future. During the course of my conversations with Albert, another chapel in the immediate district closed its doors for the very last time, the congregation having dwindled to six elderly women. Zion has been able to continue to keep its doors open but remaining capital assets are being rapidly depleted, with no hope of replenishment, and it is only a matter of time before these resources are exhausted or the remaining congregation die. Simply, the church is almost bankrupt in terms of both human and financial capital and there seems no way back from this position.

What the story of Zion affords us is a comprehensive picture of the life of a church from its inception and growth to its decline and imminent demise. Every story such as this contains its unique features but also certain factors which appear common to the narratives of many other churches in the district, and indeed, of the wider Welsh experience. Before proceeding to discuss the experience of other churches in a marked state of decline, it will be worthwhile to isolate and discuss the main factors that contributed to the growth and decline of this church.

Clearly, the first point to be made is that the congregation was established because of need felt among a local population, which was prepared to organize itself in these matters. In common with much of south Wales, the area had recently made the transition from a rural to an urban locality and there was a distinct lack of local amenities. What began as a fairly modest attempt to afford some religious provision for local children was subsequently translated into the establishment of a Baptist congregation and a project to build a place of worship to meet the needs of Baptists moving into or already living in the district. Thus, the growth of the church was informed by the growth of the community. Community growth was economically driven and people were attracted to the district, first and foremost because of new opportunities for employment. In common with the experience of much of newly industrializing Wales, emergent community structures were dense and highly reliant on cross-cutting social networks which linked the social, economic and religious spheres and which had the institution of the family at their heart. In the matter of religious allegiances, this was first and foremost essentially a family allegiance. This nexus of domicile, employment and religious life was a very strong foundation for building community life, but a foundation that would be severely weakened if any element of the nexus was put under strain.

Two world wars and the intervening Great Depression put some strains on this network of relations but in their essentials they remained intact. However, economic restructuring and the social and geographical mobility associated with the post-war years, coupled with the growing privatization of the family, were all factors that proved corrosive to both traditional working-class family life and to solidaristic working-class communities. For a church that took much of its strength and life from these family and community values, the effects were immediate and, ultimately, irreversible. Indeed, through this lens we can begin to see that it is not so much some abstract concept like 'secularization' that has been at the root of Zion's decline, but rather the fact that congregational life is dependent on and extremely sensitive to local social and economic changes. Simply, it is these socio-economic transformations that are the primary motors of cultural change, particularly at the localized level of community and church.

External socio-economic factors aside, there are a number of factors internal to the religious sphere that must also be accounted for. It is now generally recognized that late nineteenth-century Wales saw a competitive race to build more and bigger buildings for worship, leading to the over-provision of churches in urban areas. Certainly, from the start, the 'New Church' was a great financial burden on the congregation and in retrospect the decision to build in this manner can be seen to be misconceived as what had been a growing population was now stabilizing itself. There is also the question of leadership. It is apparent that, after its initial inception, the pattern of growth within the church was not constant and drift and decline was demonstrably linked to those periods when there was no resident minister. Prior to 1941, ministers were charismatic individuals, evangelical in their theology, energetic and able, giving strong leadership and their arrival always coincided with an increase in numbers. However, the post-war years saw a cultural shift within the congregation that de-emphasized the distinctively evangelical characteristics of the church. At this point, with a third generation now in place in the church, routinization in the shape of the transition from charisma to office was clearly taking place. At the same time, the blurring of the distinctiveness of the strict Baptist lifestyle led to the cultural boundaries between the churchgoing and non-churchgoing populations being weakened. Initially, this led to very modest growth, predominantly among local women, but this could not be sustained for very long. In many ways the last ministerial incumbency can be accounted a success in terms of raising the public profile of the church, but it did not lead to any sustained growth. Rather, it can be seen as a period of benign neglect that over the years entrenched the trend towards ministerial dependency.

This combination of a ministerial autocracy, the departure of many of the young people into higher education and the loss of many families to the suburbs, left the church bereft of potential future lay leadership. At the same time there appears to have been little real recognition of the seriousness of Zion's position and no planning for the future by the minister or the deacons. It was 'business as usual' despite the fact that the church was rapidly failing. Given this lack of attention to the future, it is unsurprising that families moving elsewhere in the city did not seek to retain their active links with the church.

I now turn to some other voices from Swansea's constituency of elderly churchgoers and leaders. The stories below, while all having their unique features, nevertheless reflect many of these trends and issues and again exemplify the inexorable shift towards local social and cultural marginalization that religious institutions have experienced in the face of social, economic and cultural change.

OTHER VOICES

The story of 'Shiloh', a Welsh-speaking chapel situated a mile to the north of Zion, in what was once a village setting, has many parallels. A large imposing building capable of seating 800 worshippers, this chapel was once a major centre of Welsh Nonconformity in West Glamorgan but is now reduced to a membership of twenty-eight and an average of ten worshippers on any Sunday. The congregation is affiliated to the Union of Welsh Independents (*Annibynwyr*) a grouping which 'lost' 269 churches in Wales in the years 1982–2000 (Brierley, 1995, 2001) but which continues to represent approximately 6.6 per cent of the active Welsh Christian population (Brierley, 2001). Like Zion, Shiloh is affiliated to an association of gathered congregations rather than a denomination in the strictest use of the word, which gives it a great deal of latitude and independence in the matter of policy decisions, not least as to when the doors close for the final time.

The 'village' is located in what was historically both a rural location and a centre of the mining and copper-working industries. Over the course of the twentieth century it was gradually absorbed into what is now the city of Swansea and was until the 1950s an overwhelmingly Welsh-speaking community with a strong sense of local social solidarity. The post-war years saw the construction of large local authority housing estates in the district and the influx of a large English-speaking population into the surrounding district. At the same time, the Welsh-speaking population was steadily shrinking and by 1995 it had declined to a point where only a few elderly persons still used the language on a daily basis. The traditional industries that were the economic mainstay of the area have largely disappeared, along with any sense of community in the traditional sense, and local unemployment rates are high.

As early as 1648 a dissenting congregation was recorded as meeting in a local farmhouse and out of this grew Shiloh, which was the 'mother church' for dissenters in the district. The present church building, an imposing porticoed structure in the Greek classical style, was erected in the early nineteenth century, replacing a smaller chapel dating from 1672. Locally, Shiloh has an illustrious history and was responsible for planting seven daughter churches throughout Swansea. For much of its history, the stance of the church was firmly evangelical and it was touched deeply by the 1904 Revival. 'William', the current church secretary, now an elderly man in his seventies, recalled that in his youth Shiloh was the vibrant social and cultural heart of the community:

> Oh yes, I remember it full. We used to have special services and they used to take the seating from the vestry and put it in the aisles of the chapel to accommodate the people you know. So many (*pause*) and I remember, one of our late members here, he hasn't long been dead, his father was deacon here and he was telling me [when] the church had gone down then. 'My father's always complaining' he said, *'when the membership had gone to four hundred odd.'* He complained! If he lived today now (*pause*) down to two figures. (Emphasis in the original transcript)

Unlike many chapels and churches, Shiloh did not experience any significant falling away after the Great War and this was largely due to the residual effects of the 1904 Revival which found a greater resonance within the Welsh-language churches. Decline began to set in, initially very slowly, after the Second World War. The area was changing rapidly, and changing in ways that were not conducive to the continued health of Shiloh. William takes up the story:

> Well, the building of the estates, which was all open ground before they came along see? And where I live, on the main road there. That was just one street all the way down and more or less, every house was a Welsh [-speaking] household you know? Families, big families. But since they've built the estates. The people that come in you know, English[-speaking] people you know? So (*pause*) they're predominant now. You know, the old people dying and there's other people coming in, but unfortunately, they're not Welsh people you see? Welsh-speaking people. So, everything has changed, [people] dying and moving to different areas. We've got children brought up here who moved to Cardiff you know? And even further afield. Well, there was

nothing here for them really. All we had here was a few pits and the steel
industry. That was the main thing.

Here, despite linguistic differences, we see a similar pattern to Zion's
experience emerging. We see the breakdown of the community base of the
church, as the effects of social and geographical mobility start to bite, leading
to the loss of the families that were the mainstay of the chapel. A combination
of increasing educational opportunities for young people in the 1950s and
1960s with an employment base that was largely structured around traditional heavy industries and manual work led to a further drifting away of
those young adults necessary for the internal reproduction of the congregation. Later, when even these industries began to collapse, there was very little to prevent young people from moving away. No moves were made by
the chapel to try to accommodate the religious needs of the influx of
English-speakers by changing the linguistic policy of the chapel and this
population remained untapped and largely unchurched.

In part, this lack of missionary zeal was a reflection of internal changes
that had taken place in the post-war years. Culturally, there was a marked
de-emphasis on the formerly evangelical character of Shiloh and a move
towards routinization. Financial difficulties emerged, both in the maintenance
of the building, which was deteriorating rapidly, and in the funding of the
ministerial stipend. The all-age character of the congregation was changing
and the average age of the congregation rising. In the 1970s the Sunday
school (which had at its height once boasted 1,000 scholars accommodated
in two schoolrooms and the vestry) was closed and in 1985 the last minister
left as the congregation was unable to meet his stipend. William was
highly critical of the character and quality of post-war ministerial leadership generally in Wales:

> There's a lot to blame with the ministers as well I feel, over the years you know?
> They seemed to be complacent and you know, 'everything is all right *now*'.
> They never looked ten or twenty years ahead; they never envisaged what
> would happen. What *has* happened anyway. They just, you know, 'I'm com-
> fortable – we're here' and all the rest of it. But they never seemed to *think* you
> know? That something would happen and all that would change completely.
> (Emphases in the original transcript.)

By the late 1980s, the building was to all intents and purposes semi-derelict,
with the remaining congregation now forced to worship in the vestry. A
salvation of sorts presented itself in the 1990s, when two substantial
legacies allowed the rapidly dwindling band of members to engage on
extensive renovation work on the building, a project that the parent

association repeatedly called into question as a waste of resources. William was quite frank about the potential benefits of the work on the chapel. They cannot hope to attract newcomers to the chapel, given that the community base of the church has collapsed. They have made approaches to various choirs and other cultural groups with a view to transferring ownership of the building, but to no avail. Renovation merely ensures that the fabric of the building remains intact so that, in William's words, 'we can keep the doors open until the last one of us dies'. Admirable as this dedication to the chapel and the congregation it serves is, it has not been without its critics. The Union of Welsh Independents, as noted above, was very opposed to the renovation work, seeing no future for the dwindling congregation in its present circumstances. Its preferred option was the closure of the chapel and the merger of the few remaining worshippers with another local congregation, a policy that the Presbyterian Church of Wales has frequently resorted to throughout Wales. However, unlike the Presbyterians, the union can only act in an advisory capacity, as it has no formal powers to impose closure on independent congregations. Despite the views of the denomination and in the light of the forced mergers of a number of local Presbyterian congregations, the closure and merger option was vehemently rejected by the remaining congregation who remain determined to retain their independence to the last.

The vexed question of the 'rationalizing' of congregations is very much a live issue in Swansea and the Presbyterian Church of Wales has been at the forefront of initiating this policy. 'Faith Tabernacle', an English-speaking Presbyterian church, is one such congregation that has come under pressure from the local presbytery to close its doors. It is also an interesting case because, unlike the other congregations under discussion in this chapter, the disposition of this congregation is still firmly evangelical. Again situated close to the docks and a stone's throw from Zion, this congregation was established in the early twentieth century as part of the Forward Movement (a sub-association founded by the Presbyterians in the late nineteenth century to evangelize the influx of English-speaking workers and their families into south Wales). Like Zion and the other local Nonconformist congregations, and notwithstanding its evangelical ethos, this congregation has experienced marked numerical decline in the latter part of the twentieth century. German bombing during the 1939–45 war destroyed the original chapel building and the present structure, capable of accommodating 200 worshippers, was opened in 1956. In this respect the congregation of Faith Tabernacle is in a more advantageous position than others in the area as the present building is both manageable and structurally sound. However, in all other respects, a very similar narrative emerges.

The membership now stands at eight persons and the average age of the congregation is 71 years. A husband and wife team, 'John' and 'Pat', who are respectively the church and pulpit secretaries, have for many years provided leadership to the congregation. Born and raised in the locality, they now live in one of the western suburbs, commuting back to the church on Sundays. John worked on the docks for thirty-eight years and Pat worked in the local post office. Both are now retired and, while they may live elsewhere, they remain very committed to the local community. Both bemoan what they see as the loss of community spirit in the area and cite the influx of newcomers into the area as the primary cause of this. In their younger days, community life and local social respectability was very much wrapped up in the life of the churches and chapels of the area, as John recalled:

> It was the done thing for people to be seen going to church on a Sunday. I remember the street (*pause*) well, if you can picture [Zion] at the top and [the congregational chapel] half way down, and both services started together and they finished together and you couldn't see the street for people (*pause*) just outside, just coming out. I mean, there was no rivalry between the two, but that was the done thing you know, people (*pause*) it was to be *seen* to be going (*pause*) with their bowler hats on and so on. (Emphasis in the original transcript.)

This way of life is now a distant memory and, apart from the small and faithful congregation, there is now no local community use of the chapel for weddings, dedications or funerals. John and Pat are committed evangelicals and the ethos is still strong within the worshipping life of the congregation, although the average age of the membership means that in practice there are not the resources to actively evangelize the local unchurched population.

Despite the widely held assumptions that evangelical churches are somehow more successful at attracting and holding on to adherents, this has not been the case with Faith Tabernacle. Like many other small evangelical congregations in this part of the city, they have been no more immune to the same social, economic and cultural factors that have proved so corrosive to the practice of churchgoing generally. Decline became noticeable in the 1950s and again was largely driven by post-war affluence and the westward drift to the suburbs. Admittedly, this process was slower and even in the late 1950s the Sunday school could still boast a hundred scholars. However, by 1973 church membership was in the forties and in 1980 the last full-time minister had retired and left the church. John commented that, at that time, 'There was a big going away of ministers from the Presbyterian movement . . . and of course they never came back . . . no replacements. It didn't affect north Wales so much but it affected down here a tremendous amount.' By 1984 the Sunday school had closed and a year later the membership had dropped to twelve people, a number that was to stay fairly constant for ten years. Eventually numbers began to drop again, and despite their evangelical convictions this was a development which John and Pat were fairly sanguine about. Given their extensive personal contacts with other local congregations they are aware that the same pattern of decline is affecting nearly all the local churches and that, given the average age of their congregation, they can do nothing to redress this situation. However, one bone of contention was the fact that some local evangelicals chose to attend the big 'preaching' churches in town rather than supporting struggling local congregations. John commented:

> The car makes you independent doesn't it? I've always put forward that what makes people become Baptists, Congregationalists, Presbyterians, you know, when they start off, is because they live near to that particular church. I mean, [Zion] catered for all the people up there, they all became Baptists. My grandparents and my parents went a little further down the street to save climbing the hill and they became Congregationalists. But now people have cars, they can be independent, they can *really* choose now can't they? (Emphasis in the original transcript.)

In this matter of choice, John and Pat see their church as having little appeal for younger people, compared to evangelical churches in the suburbs.

> Well there's no life in the church. I mean, we sing out of a hymnbook, a lot of charismatic churches don't use the hymnbook do they? They've got screens on the wall or they know the choruses off by heart and we don't do that. It's a trend that people like this sort of thing. Here (*pause*) how can I say it? (*pause*) It's hard (*pause*) you go in as if you are in a straitjacket. Whereas, if you go to the Gospel Hall up there and the youngsters are going about in pullovers and jeans and so on, and there's a relaxed atmosphere you see? And youngsters like it because this is the trend isn't it? I mean people don't wear suits today you know, if they can help it. You go to our church (*pause*) I mean, we're only three men and we're all dressed in suits. All the ladies are dressed nice but perhaps somebody coming in from the outside would feel (*pause*) restricted. And I think this is what's happening in the Free Churches, you know? I think we're too old and staid. I mean, you've got to realize that we're seven attending members. We've got one that's housebound, there's one over 80, two over 70, and you say to yourself, 'You only want *something* to happen' and straight away you're down to unmanageable figures you know. (Emphases in the original transcript.)

Pressure from the presbytery over the small size of the congregation was a constant factor in the early 1990s and this crystallized when the name of the church was put forward, as John said, 'out of the blue' on a list of churches recommended for closure. As there was no prior consultation, the congregation was able to mount a defence based on the lack of communication, gaining a reprieve, but only that. John considers that closure is inevitable and is now only a matter of time, whatever the wishes of the congregation. Understandably, this experience has led to some disillusionment with denominational structures. Within the Welsh context there appears to be little recognition by denominational leaders of the continued salience of a sense of place and family connections within working-class Nonconformist culture. John sees the local presbytery as little more than 'a talking shop' and he suggested that there was widespread dissatisfaction among local Christians with denominations that appear remote from and unsympathetic to the needs and desires of local congregations. John and Pat have no desire to continue within the Presbyterian movement once closure happens. They have identified a number of thriving evangelical churches nearer to their home in the suburbs and one of these will be their likely destination.

Church decline in the eastern sector of the city is not restricted to the Free Churches. While the Anglican parish system has partially protected congregations from many of those factors which are implicated in decline, in some cases, closure appears inevitable. One such case is that of an Anglican parish located in a rundown district adjacent to the city centre and comprising two churches, 'St Jude' and 'St James'. Originally set in a rural location, the church of St Jude has seen a community grow up around the church and then depart. While the terraced housing remains, along with many derelict and boarded up churches and chapels, the area is now home to a substantial ethnic minority community of south Asian origin. There is considerable ethnic friction between the few remaining local people and these incomers. St Jude's is virtually the only remaining church presence in the area and along with St James has an aggregated membership of fifty people. Local white residents retain a strong affection for St Jude's, symbolizing as it does some sense of continuity within a local environment that appears to them to have changed out of all recognition. Numbers attending for worship are sometimes very low, often numbering single figures, and worship alternates between both buildings with the two congregations merging every Sunday. However, local community use of the churches for weddings, baptisms and funerals remains high, particularly so in the case of funerals. Many families who have moved out of the area also like to return to the church to mark these life-cycle rituals. There is also a playgroup, based at St Jude's and run by local mothers under the auspices of the church, and this operates in a sectioned-off portion of the worship space. There is no parish hall and the church building is large and dilapidated and clearly unsuited for the needs of either the predominately elderly and female congregation or the playgroup.

The parish is served by 'Avril', a 67-year-old deacon who lives in the district with her partner (and who we met in the previous chapter). Her appointment was unusual in itself, in that at the time she was the only female in the diocese in a full-time stipendiary ministry. The historic vote which permitted women into the priesthood was still some way off in the future and Avril herself saw her appointment as more of a holding exercise in a marginalized parish, rather than a genuine breakthrough in the gender politics of the church. Nevertheless, her presence had been warmly received within the parish, not least by female members of the congregation, and despite her age, she was recognized by all as an energetic and able church leader. Despite the many problems associated with a deprived parish and the general decline of churchgoing in Wales, she sees a continuing role for the church in the locality. Local people still look to the church for the occasional offices, the playgroup is thriving and a junior church still operates, even though numbers are very low. Pastoral work takes up much of her time, as does arranging funerals (of which there are many), and she also visits the local schools regularly. However, there is an economic question mark over the future of the parish. Avril commented:

> Because we're poor churches, they don't quite know what to do with us. The Bishop seems quite happy at the moment to leave me here. The Archdeacon, he's marvellous, very helpful. I find generally that people are very sympathetic to us but they don't quite know what to do with us because of the money. Unless we can get hold of some committed young people, not children now [but] young parents (*pause*) I don't know. I don't know what the fate of the parish is going to be (*pause*) unless the Church authorities see this place as a mission area and are willing to say 'Right, let's look at it together. What can we do?'

Despite all the optimism in the world, realistically, that particular outcome is highly unlikely. The fact that much of Avril's time is increasingly spent on arranging funerals indicates a far more likely outcome. The social and cultural character of the district has changed, with the majority of the local population now identifying themselves with non-Christian faiths. The ratio of persons of white ethnicity continues to shrink and the majority of weddings and funerals are now of people who used to live in the district. The state of the church buildings is a constant source of concern for an impoverished congregation, as is the annual quota that they must pay to the diocese. At the same time, clergy vocations are declining throughout Wales and clergy are spread increasingly thin on the ground, putting strains on the parish system. In the light of these factors and without the continued goodwill of the church authorities, there appears to be little long-term future for this parish, as it is presently constituted.

While Avril remains in post these matters remain in abeyance. However, once she retires, there are no plans to appoint new clergy to the parish.

Whether the diocese will move immediately to close both buildings is an open question, although there are concrete plans in place to merge the parish with its nearest neighbour. The other priests in the deanery, while fully appreciating the seriousness of the economic plight of the parish, see any merger as a retrograde move. One well-respected senior priest with a long history of parish ministry in Wales rehearsed a number of potentially negative outcomes. Any merger into another parish would inevitably result in the loss of a local identity and focus for the church. Furthermore, he considered that the most likely outcome of the loss of an incumbent cleric would be the collapse of local churchgoing, even if the buildings remain open. Given the fact that these congregations are currently barely viable, any further numerical loss would raise serious questions about the continued viability of maintaining a visible presence in the area. Clearly, this parish is not alone in its experience and, despite the different contexts, all these narratives have clear parallels with each other in that each congregation has been severely affected by the impact of social and economic change at the level of local communities. I now turn to a more theoretical discussion of these issues in order to frame the narratives in succeeding chapters.

SECULARIZATION AND SOCIAL AND RELIGIOUS CHANGE

One of the core elements of the secularization model is the concept of societalization: the idea that the social significance of religion declines in proportion to the decline and dissolution of small communities. As modern societies become more complex and impersonal, as face-to-face relations and local social networks are replaced by more attenuated forms of social interaction, organized religious activity, it is suggested, inevitably declines. Compulsion in matters of religion is replaced with voluntarism, the cultural transmission of religious ideas and values is inhibited by competing non-religious world-views, and religion ceases to be an integrative force for social cohesion. The evidence of the case studies outlined above would appear to confirm this thesis, but only up to a point. Contemporary religious decline implies an earlier narrative of religious growth, and it is here within these narratives that we find much that is distinctive about the nature of Welsh religion and much that renders any universal theory of secularization, as it applies to Western Europe, somewhat problematic.

Typically, processes of modernization that lead to deep structural changes, notably industrialization and urbanization, are seen as inevitably leading to the loss of the social significance of religion. These structural changes are related to the idea of social differentiation and the movement from homogeneous communities based on face-to-face relationships and with a high degree of mutuality (*Gemeinschaft*) to more complex forms of social relationship (*Gesellschaft*), where relations are individualistic, impersonal and anomic. This process is generally located in the early nineteenth century and within transitional narratives associated with rural–urban migration and the growth of modern industrialized societies. While this may have been the case with other national societies, industrialization was to have a very different impact within Wales. Within the Welsh context, it was primarily industrialization that provided the impetus for the growth and consolidation of Nonconformity and also the re-emergence of Roman Catholicism as a force in industrial areas. Clearly, the initial phases of industrialization and urbanization (and by implication modernization) can increase as well as diminish the social reach of religion.

The churches and chapels that we have visited in this chapter are very much part of this distinctively Welsh narrative. As we have seen, they grew up side by side with the new communities that provided the labour for the nascent industries of this part of Wales. Significantly, these new communities were generally small in size, socially and economically homogeneous, and underpinned by a culture of mutual cooperation between family and neighbours. Families lived in close proximity in tightly packed streets and this was very much a public and open society where everyone's business was known by everybody else (or so it seemed) and shared community experience loomed large in people's consciousness. Central to this culture of mutuality were the chapels (and later the trade unions) whose internal life was both shaped by, and in turn helped to shape, these new working-class communities. The churches and chapels provided individual and familial status and respectability and a structure for leadership within the community. They offered the vision of a dignified and disciplined lifestyle for families who were economically marginalized by subsistence wages and the uncertainties of broken employment patterns. Through their message of sacrifice and fellowship and an implicit critique of materialism, they validated a common lifestyle that could not hope to aspire to anything approaching material affluence. Furthermore, in an industrial milieu where sudden death, injury and illness were commonplace, they provided the hope of salvation and the promise of a life to come. Life was given both dignity and meaning. At the same time, the churches and chapels sought to generate a sense of civic responsibility, providing hope that the material circumstances of the community might be improved in time. At the individual level they allowed for differentiation within the community (by specific church or chapel membership) while affirming (through the shared commonality of belonging to the Christian faith) the essential solidarity of the community and its undifferentiated nature.

In all this, they were a class-based expression of religious belief and practice. Local religious institutions were the concrete and visible expression of those social, economic and cultural bonds that shaped and held working-class communities together. As such, they were as much the product of the systemic changes that industrialization had wrought and were therefore highly vulnerable to further social and economic change. Key global events (notably two world wars and a world-wide economic depression) intruded into the lives of communities, initiating strains in the relationship between local religious institutions and their surrounding populations. More tellingly, growing post-war affluence, and the opportunities this opened up for personal improvement and individual self-realization, undermined the communitarian ethical and value bases on which the church and chapels were grounded. Changing employment patterns exacerbated this shift. Heterogeneity in employment increasingly became the norm as the traditional industries contracted and new employment opportunities opened up. Improved access to educational opportunities both expanded people's horizons and increasingly took people away from their birth communities. By the 1960s increasing social and geographic mobility was undermining both traditional family structures and localized familial religious allegiances. Geographic mobility took many people out of the immediate orbit of their local church and chapel while upward social mobility undermined the historic Welsh identification with a distinctive form of working-class Christianity. That this new-found mobility hit Nonconformity most forcefully is unsurprising, given the traditional emphases within the chapels on individual self-reliance and self-improvement, probity and frugality. For many of the younger working-class adherents of the chapels, these values served them well as they took advantage of expanding opportunities. Unfortunately, this drive towards self-improvement also emptied many chapels of future generations of worshippers.

Factors internal to the churches and chapels also contributed to this demise. Long-standing internal problems associated with the maintenance of buildings and the provision of ministerial stipends became more pressing as congregational numbers dwindled. A growing culture of ministerial dependency and ministerial myopia in the face of a rapidly changing and radically different social world left congregations ill prepared to face the future. Cultural shifts within the chapels and a growing worldliness contributed to a blurring of boundaries and the erosion of a distinctive evangelical lifestyle at the same time as many new leisure opportunities were emerging. Respectability was no longer synonymous with church or chapel membership and a specifically Christian upbringing for children and young people was decreasingly seen as an essential grounding for later life and civic responsibility. The relatively rapid decline of Sunday schools, so graphically described in some of the accounts above, has in the longer term led to a crisis of cultural transmission. Among the Welsh-speaking churches, the progressive erosion of the language base upon which they were founded was another key factor in decline. Indeed, given the fact that this sector of the religious economy was experiencing a dual crisis of cultural transmission, religious and linguistic, it is unsurprising that they have declined so rapidly in those parts of Wales where Welsh has all but ceased to be the language of the home. Evangelical churches in working-class districts have been no less susceptible to the processes outlined above and, despite their greater emphasis on the religious socialization of children in the home, in many cases decline has been as marked as in the 'broad' churches.

Perhaps the greatest irony is that the expansion of Welsh religion, and Nonconformity in particular, was primarily the product of an increasingly mobile society. These structural changes, first, internal migration, and then, increasingly, migration from England and elsewhere, allowed religious institutions to develop a set of social functions that were crucial in ameliorating some of the more anomic and dehumanizing facets associated with newly industrializing societies. Within the Welsh context it is clear that, for a time at least, because of the close identification of many Welsh people with Nonconformity, indigenous religious traditions were in a position to adapt with some success to the processes of societalization. This was not to last, although the churches and chapels fought a rearguard action up until the 1960s. From that period on, it is clear that this same mobile society (albeit in a late twentieth-century guise) was effectively undermining the community roots of the churches and chapels. As churchgoing populations moved out of traditional areas of residence, denominations and congregations were left with the burden of an over-abundance of places of worship that were too large for the current needs of their adherents and a constant financial drain. At the same time the number of religious professionals was shrinking, leading to an under provision of ministers, who became increasingly overstretched in terms of pastoral oversight. Crucially, this also happened at a time when the primary cultural transmission of religious values was proving increasingly difficult in the face of growing societal indifference to the claims of religious institutions. For many churches this became an unequal struggle, as congregational numbers dropped and ageing congregations struggled to maintain the corporate religious life with diminishing financial and human resources. Perhaps the most significant (and poignant) element of the narratives outlined above has been the sense of congregations struggling to cope with and make sense of wider forces that appear to them to be out of their control. In this sense, what we have seen appears very much like 'secularization'.

However, not all churches in Wales have failed to adapt to social change and even within the context of the traditional working-class districts discussed above there are isolated instances of churches and congregations who appear to have achieved some limited growth in difficult local circumstances. These churches are important for our discussion because, given that they are operating in the same type of conditions that have proved so corrosive of religious institutions generally, they offer a further layer of insight into the scope and nature of secularization as it is experienced in working-class communities. The following chapter will examine, in rather more depth than the above studies, one such example: an Anglican parish that has in the past experienced both marked numerical decline and, more recently, significant numerical growth.

5

Turning the Clock Back

I first visited the parish church of 'St John' (not the real name) on a crisp Sunday morning in November 1995. Situated in the same dockside community that I briefly explored in the preceding chapter, the tall spire of St John's dominates the local skyline. It creates both a visible marker of the church's presence in the district and, from further afield in the city, it signifies the presence of this long-established working-class community. Other than its impact on the skyline, it is not an imposing building and the interior is a typical product of nineteenth-century Anglican aesthetics. The only features of noteworthiness are an unusual gold and mosaic reredos and a window in the lady chapel that reflects the district's maritime heritage. More noteworthy was the congregation on that day. Numbering about forty people, mostly adults, two-thirds of them women, many elderly but not exclusively so and very visibly working-class. The service itself was unremarkable: liturgically middle of the road and with a traditional Prayer Book ethos, although the whole proceedings were suffused with an air of informality. One small child spent most of the service running around, sitting with various people, all who were welcoming to him. Everyone appeared comfortable in what they were doing and people seemed to know why they were there and what they were about. Afterwards the people were very warm and friendly and there was no sense of elitism, that sense of the middle class on show, as can be the case in so many Anglican congregations. As people drifted away, it became apparent that most people were on foot, suggesting that this was a localized congregation, and (as I discovered later) reflecting the very low incidence of car ownership in this district.

My only previous acquaintance with this church had been through telephone conversations with the vicar who had participated in a survey of churches that I had recently conducted. The limited amount of information that I had gleaned by these means intrigued me. In a district where the practice of churchgoing had radically declined in the preceding three decades, this church had recently doubled its congregational size within the space of three years. While this was remarkable in itself, given the unremitting picture of decline among the local Free Churches, what was even more interesting was the fact that these were mainly, but not exclusively, returning members. This narrative of departure and return was intriguing and, as I later found out, was underpinned by a very complex mosaic of social relations and a troubled parish history, where the question of identity loomed large.

The parish comprises three churches: the parish church of St John, and the smaller churches of 'St James' and 'All Souls'. The first two are located within the warren of streets that make up this dockside community, while All Souls looks down on the community from a large hill which overshadows the district. The overwhelming majority of worshippers at St John and St James are working-class, while the congregation of All Souls might be better described as 'of working-class origin', their move up the hill having been in social as well as geographic terms. Ninety-three per cent of church members live locally. Many are related to each other and, in some cases, they also have family links with the local Free Churches. Two clergy, the vicar and his curate, serve the parish and both are relatively recent arrivals to the district, the former having been inducted in 1994 with a remit to try to restore the fortunes of the parish after two decades of marked numerical decline. The clergy, who are both resident in the area, are assisted in their work by three churchwardens, two subwardens, three parochial treasurers and a Parochial Church Council (PCC). The three congregations are responsible for finding the necessary monies to meet the diocesan quota (currently £10,000) and in turn the diocese pays the stipends for the two priests and maintains the fabric of the vicarage. In terms of organizational structures, the parish is part of the rural deanery of Swansea, which contains nine parishes, overseen by the rural dean. The vicar is in sole charge of the parish, but is responsible to the bishop through his local representative, the archdeacon of Gower. There is a fair deal of autonomy at the local parish level, where authority resides in the vicar, although in theory the PCC can block his decisions by majority vote, and in this eventuality the matter would be referred to the rural dean. In practice this rarely happens and the PCC invariably follows the line suggested (or laid down) by the clerical incumbent. Clergy meet with other Anglican clergy on a regular basis in deanery chapter meetings and in this way they can offer mutual support to each other. Diocesan structures also offer another level of support.

The parish of St John is therefore unremarkable in that it conforms to the general administrative characteristics of the Church in Wales. In terms of size and population density, it is also fairly typical of a city parish (Harris and Startup, 1999: 31). However, as Harris and Startup (1999: 28) suggest, there is no such thing as an 'average' parish in Wales. Each parish can only be understood in terms of the unique human characteristics of its social actors, the ways in which they make sense of their local worlds and the surrounding social, economic and cultural characteristics that impact on local populations.

This particular parish has many of the hallmarks of a settled working-class community where identity is firmly predicated on a pattern of continuous familial residence and where the idea of the family is strong locally. Family ties provide much of the focus for those local values that order social life and these in turn are buttressed by a complex set of relations with other local families, friends and acquaintances that inform the character of the locality. What follows is an attempt to convey some of these characteristics and the local knowledge and events that inform them. Beginning with a description of the origins of this parish and moving on to a discussion of that 'troubled' parish history alluded to above, I will then proceed to unpack those various human elements and activities which define this parish and its resilience in the face of a difficult situation.

ORIGINS

The origins of all three congregations lie in the nineteenth century, a period of rapid industrialization and growing religious confidence and enthusiasm in Wales. All Souls was built in 1842, a project largely funded by the wealthy Grenfell and Freeman families who had extensive commercial interests in the metallurgical industries. Established to meet the religious needs of local copperworkers living in its immediate locality, it was from its inception a thriving church. Within forty years, a new parish had been carved out, incorporating both this community and another community of copper-workers to the west, and with All Souls at its heart. The new-found status of All Souls as a flourishing parish church seemed secure and it was enlarged accordingly, but the closure of the local copperworks in 1892 and the subsequent demolition of the copperworkers' houses left the church relatively isolated and without a significant role. The existing parish was dissolved and from this time onwards All Souls existed as an outlying satellite, served by the parish clergy of St John's. Left without any local population to speak of, it is likely that the building would have eventually closed, but salvation of a sort presented itself in the 1930s when a small private housing estate, 'Seaview Prospect', was built adjacent to the church. However, despite the presence of this lower middle-class enclave in the district, the fortunes of All Souls have never really recovered and it has remained peripheral, both to the local community and to the fortunes of the parish, although it remains an enduringly popular venue for weddings.

The original foundation of St John's is something of a mystery. Local records suggest that there was a medieval church of St John, but that this disappeared into the sea as a result of coastal erosion. Another building was erected at a later date, but again, not much is known. Local records do not say when this was built, but it is certain that it preceded the establishment of the docks and the surrounding community. It is recorded as being situated in the middle of fields and was still serving the religious needs of the district in the 1870s. The present church of St John, which dates from 1888, was erected nearby to this building which was swiftly demolished and the land given over to housing. The year 1888 also saw the incorporation of the parish as it is today. This was a period when the local community was expanding and the parish was served by a vicar and three curates, a deployment of clergy that would be unthinkable under the financial constraints of today.

In common with the other churches in the district, in their early years these churches were well attended and contributed fully to the religious and social life of the community. Both All Souls and St John were enlarged to meet this demand and in 1920 St James was built to further accommodate the local population. After the closure of the copperworks, the main source of local employment became the docks and this was mainly casual work. As in much of industrial Wales, life was uncertain and hard and poverty was grinding. In this environment the churches nurtured a spirit of working-class Anglicanism that was to pay dividends in terms of a fierce local loyalty to the Anglican Church that persists among those long-standing Anglican families still living in the district. Parish records note that the inter-war years were a time of particularly pronounced economic hardship for local Anglican families and the parish finances suffered accordingly. Nevertheless, Anglicanism persisted, and during the 1950s and 1960s the local churches fared rather better than their Nonconformist counterparts, with Easter communicant figures for 1966 recorded as a relatively healthy 242 persons.

While the Anglican churches in the district have not been immune from the social, economic and cultural changes outlined in the previous chapter, their experience has been somewhat different. For example, the migration of a significant proportion of the churchgoing population out to the western suburbs was a trend that affected the Free Churches much more deeply. In contrast, when Anglican families did move out of the area in the 1960s, while some ended up in new council housing developments in the west, it was mainly to a recently built local authority estate located a mile to the north of this dockside community. This migration was not primarily fuelled by aspirations to upward social mobility but rather by a desire to escape the high levels of air pollution created by the loading of coal in the docks and the often poor quality of local privately rented housing.

Many families found life on the nearby estate particularly unsettling, not least because of the absence of the close community structures that they had left behind and to which they were accustomed. The introduction of tighter environmental controls and the running down of the docks improved the air quality in the district and changes in the laws relating to rented housing, notably the 1965 Housing Act, saw many local landlords seeking to sell their properties in the area. These changes contributed to something of a return of local families, a process made easier by the numerous family links that they still retained in the district. What is significant is that this is a somewhat different narrative from that of the migrating Free Church families. Anglican families, when they initially moved out of the district, were by and large exchanging one form of rented accommodation for another. In both geographical and social terms the distance travelled was not far. Conversely, Free Church families were seeking to move out to move upwards on the social scale, marking this by moving into modest forms of home ownership in the suburbs or further afield. Nonconformists, once they had left the area, tended to break those ties that had held them to the district, travelling back only occasionally to visit older relatives. For working-class Anglicans living on the new estate to the north, conditions deteriorated quickly as anomie and relatively high levels of vandalism and crime progressively took hold. These factors, coupled with changing circumstances within the community they had left, acted as both 'push' and 'pull' factors, drawing many local families back to their place of origin. Nevertheless, by 1980, although the Anglicans were significantly out-performing their Free Church counterparts in the district, the number of Easter communicants had fallen to 117, half the number recorded in 1966. It was at this point that the diocese intervened to try to reverse this pattern of decline. What followed was an experiment with evangelicalism that was to split the congregation and drive many long-standing worshippers away, alienate the church from its surrounding local population and severely test the foundations of congregational identity.

AN EVANGELICAL SEA CHANGE

Despite the fact that this parish had no recent evangelical tradition, and with little meaningful local consultation, in 1981 an evangelical was appointed as vicar, serving the parish for eight years. Another evangelical incumbent, who served the parish from 1989 to 1993, followed him. Again, there was little consultation with local people. It is clear from the then bishop's words to the congregation in 1989, 'This man will fill your church, you will have congregations of four hundred or more.', that much was expected, although as two parishioners dryly commented to me, 'this didn't exactly happen'. A cursory examination of figures of Easter communicants would appear to confirm this fact. Easter 1981 saw 128 communicants but by 1993 the figure was 61, a rate of decline of 52 per cent. Conversely, after this failed experiment, returning members and new recruits accounted for a 77 per cent rise and communicants numbered 108 persons in 1996. Clearly, something had gone amiss in the drive to turn this parish around during the years of the evangelical ascendancy.

While the 1981–8 incumbency was less problematic for the congregation than the 1989–93 incumbency, it nevertheless damaged the standing of the church in the community. This incumbent was a known quantity to local people as he had served part of his curacy in the parish in the 1960s. Then, he was known as a very approachable and down-to-earth cleric, well liked by all in the parish, churchgoers and non-churchgoers alike. In the intervening years away he had at some point become 'born again' and, from the local people's standpoint, had changed out of all recognition. On returning to the parish as a committed evangelical, he no longer appeared to have the same facility to communicate with and relate to the people in the area (although his evangelicalism did resonate with some of the older members and local people who remembered when this ethos was the norm and not the exception in local churches). As the change in his personality and religious outlook became increasingly apparent to local people, he squandered much of the local goodwill he had built up in his previous time in the district. He stood aloof from the surrounding population and swiftly alienated sections of the congregation, so there was an immediate sharp drop in attendance, with forty people 'missing' by the time of his first Easter communion. Privately remembered by some as a good pastor, nevertheless most of his incumbency was marked by a concerted effort among many stalwarts in the congregation to undermine his ministry in order to, as one parishioner put it, 'drive him out'. Eventually, he gave up this unequal struggle and left.

His successor was, in some ways, made of sterner fibre. Not only an evangelical but also a charismatic, his appointment to the parish in 1989 was immediately picked up on the city's evangelical grapevine. Brought in by the bishop to fill the pews, on occasions he did this very successfully. Sporadic special evening services would attract charismatic evangelicals from far and wide and St John's could be packed to capacity. Known in these circles as a place where 'things were happening', this vicar was seen as the man making them happen. Unfortunately for him (and one assumes the bishop who made such great predictions for his ministry) most came only to visit and not to stay. Parishioners were increasingly conspicuous by their absence in these services, where the presence of so many outsiders only managed to alienate local people even more. Given the numbers attending these services, the return in terms of recruitment was extremely modest, with a dozen evangelicals eventually settling into membership. Local people continued to vote with their feet and notwithstanding this small influx of newcomers, figures of Easter communicants continued to drop steadily. Locally, it was felt that the character of the church had changed, not only liturgically, but also in terms of the progressive abandonment of the traditional inclusive Anglican ethos. In the words of his successor, 'as a parish ministry it was a disaster'.

While not everyone I talked to in the course of my time in this parish would have been quite so blunt, a number of common themes relating to this period emerged in these conversations. Buildings belonging to the parish were seriously neglected as a 'people first' policy was pursued, although ironically this policy appeared to totally ignore the needs and wishes of local people. The parish hall attached to the church of St John reached a point where it became so dilapidated that it became a danger to users and was eventually closed on health and safety grounds. Closure meant that local community groups who had used these facilities for years and who had always had good relations with St John's were forced to look elsewhere for premises. Church members were very unhappy about this turn of events, seeing this as a deliberate ploy to create distance between the congregation and the local population. While it is highly unlikely that this was the motivation behind this policy, there certainly appeared to be a failure to realize the central place that the parish hall had in local life and the attachment that local people had to this building and others. By neglecting these buildings, local feeling was that the clergy were both neglecting people in the community and undermining the inclusive relationship that the congregation had always had with the local people. For the small but deeply committed congregation of St James who had vigorously resisted the recent changes, neglect of their place of worship began to be seen as a metaphor for their neglect as people. Pastoral activities, particularly visiting the sick and housebound, were scaled down as energies were directed elsewhere towards parish renewal strategies. For these disaffected parishioners, there was general agreement that, despite the rhetoric of 'people first', clergy had little or no insight into the local working-class culture and the importance of family and friendship networks in and out of the church.

Disquiet about liturgical change was widespread in all three congregations. Many members were deeply unhappy about the often *ad hoc* nature of worship and deviations from established Anglican liturgical practices, the most contentious being the use of unlicensed preachers. The introduction of healing services and the sight of individuals 'slain in the Spirit' and 'speaking in tongues' were also profoundly disquieting to long-term members (even those with some sympathy towards evangelicalism). However, members could, and did, choose to stay away from these special services, whereas Sunday services could not be so easily avoided. Local women complained that these were increasingly overlong, with no fixed time for ending. One long-term member, echoing the sentiments of many others, remarked 'You would be sitting there thinking about the joint in the oven burning, and just *praying* for him to finish. He didn't *care*, he used to laugh about it when we said!' This apparently trivial observation serves to emphasize the then growing cultural divide between clergy and the local community. Sunday lunch is seen locally as an important time when all the family get together and it is an institution of long standing in the district. Married children bring their families to see 'Mam' and 'Dad' and the occasion is seen as more than a shared meal. In the climate of increasing mistrust of the clergy, a minor culinary problem was interpreted by local women as a veiled assault on the family values that underpin the social life of the area. Again, to be fair to this incumbent, this was probably furthest from his mind. Indeed, from his perspective, local 'family values' might as easily have been translated as 'tribalism'. Semantics aside, what is clear is that there was little meeting of minds between clergy and congregation.

This climate of misunderstanding and mistrust was further exacerbated by the small influx into the congregation of middle-class evangelicals from outside the district. It is clear that the then incumbent saw these as useful allies and these individuals were quickly given key roles within the administration of the parish. Suddenly, local members and church officers (and even the organist), who had faithfully served the parish for years, found themselves summarily replaced by evangelical 'outsiders'. While we can only speculate about the motivations behind this move, it is worth considering the situation of the preceding incumbent, whose ministry had been effectively curtailed by the machinations of various members of the congregation. Clearly, a thorough clearout of existing church officers would render this potential scenario far more unlikely in the future. However, a more likely explanation is that there was just too much of a cultural divide between the vicar and the local people. Simply, there was no meeting of minds, and, therefore, it is understandable that the vicar would wish to surround himself with like-minded individuals who would support his vision for parish renewal. Whatever the motivations, the outcome was further erosion of any sense of local ownership of the churches and a further raising of internal tensions. People progressively voted with their feet, choosing to stay away and eventually only the most committed members remained. This was a very difficult time for the congregation and the memories remain fresh among those who endured it. One member said of this time, 'You just had to tough it out sometimes. The important thing was to remain faithful in your attendance.' Another couple commented that, whatever the changes that might be foisted on them, they 'had seen vicars come and go', the important thing being that the congregation 'remain constant' in their faith and practice. This strong sense of congregational identity, forged over the generations in an unbroken hundred years of parish life, was, if anything, reinforced by this period of uncertainty.

Eventually, while the main parish church would be packed with visiting evangelicals for a regular series of innovatory 'renewal days', local people stayed away. While novelties like this might have put the parish on the map with other evangelicals, they were looking increasingly threadbare as a strategy for both parish renewal and local evangelism. By now, the frustrations felt by the vicar with the majority of his congregation, notably the lack of support for him and his church officers and their endeavours, were spilling over in a number of ways. The vicar progressively isolated himself from the congregation, lambasting his critics in the congregation by means of letters, rather than confronting them face to face. (These letters did not go down well within a community where it a point of honour that disputes are settled privately in face-to-face conversations.) Editorials in the parish magazine became increasingly critical of the congregation. Rightly or wrongly, the blame for the failure to recruit new worshippers and the ongoing numerical decline was laid squarely with the remaining members. Towards the end there was a near total breakdown of communication, with the vicar and his family increasingly isolated from the life of the parish. Inevitably, there was a parting of the ways. The vicar took up a new post in England, in pastures more conducive to his brand of evangelical Anglicanism. Many members returned, most of the evangelical outsiders departed, and the diocese drew a line under this particular experiment. In 1994, a new incumbent was appointed, although again, there was little consultation with members. Happily, for members and local people, this person was far more attuned to the local particularities of this working-class parish.

GIVING CONFIDENCE BACK TO THE PEOPLE

Most long-term members, while ambivalent about evangelicalism, laid far more stress on the failure of the previous two incumbents to understand and work with rather than against aspects of local culture. The same could not be said of their new vicar. Born and raised on a Swansea council estate and married with two children, he made a favourable impression with parishioners and members from the start. Gifted with a laconic sense of humour and having a keen insight into the tribalism of families in the district, he is able to observe his parishioners with a certain wry detachment and is not blind to their foibles or, indeed, to his own. Naturally antipathetic to things evangelical, understandably he was not exactly effusive about his predecessors or what they had achieved in the parish. Commenting on his success in doubling the numbers in the congregation, he wryly commented, 'Well, I didn't have a hard act to follow'. A priest with a strong sense of vocation but with few pretensions about his status, and arriving with a deep commitment to turning this parish around, he is clear about where his energies should be directed. In the first of many conversations he laid out his vision for the parish:

> I see my main job here as giving confidence back to the people . . . It's not about getting people into church. It's about myself now, and our curate, developing relationships within the community so that people see us as sound people. People they can relate to, and through the occasional offices, building up relationships with the community and showing the community that we care about them. Giving the community back the facilities that were taken from them. Giving people confidence to see things happening. It's about, in the best sense of the word, turning the clock back. Picking up the best of the past and linking that in with a vision for the future.

His first challenge on arriving in the parish was to address the decline in attendance. During the previous interregnum there was some evidence of ex-attendees spontaneously drifting back and he successfully consolidated this trend by taking the liturgy back to the 'middle of the road'. In practice, this meant the return of Prayer Book worship, and in this he had the wholehearted support of the majority of the congregation. Most of those evangelical incomers (including the organist) who had attached themselves to the previous incumbent did not see matters in quite the same light and quickly disappeared from the scene. Nevertheless, one married couple who had previously been involved in parish administration chose to stay on, initially, 'just for a year to see how things worked out'. To begin with they were apprehensive about the new vicar, but despite his personal ambivalence towards the evangelical ethos, he has chosen to work with these remaining evangelicals and they have stayed. While the few evangelical sympathizers were initially cautious about the prospect of more changes, they managed to find some common ground in the content of sermons. They were helped in this by the new vicar's absolute commitment to theological orthodoxy (as it is understood in the Church in Wales) and the challenging nature of his sermons, both characteristics of evangelical preaching. The vicar also decided that it would be politic to retain two small house groups that had been established during the years of the evangelical ascendancy. Established for the purposes of Bible study and led by the same married couple mentioned above, these groups had proved popular with a small section of the very oldest members. Building on this work and recognizing this particular couple's leadership qualities, the vicar has offered further encouragement of these activities by allowing them to organize a 'prayer chain' which has again proved popular with older members.

Interestingly, despite the troubled recent history of the parish, there has been little or no residual rancour towards those remaining evangelicals in the congregation. In the case of 'outsiders', most had left anyway, but those who chose to stay have now been accepted on the congregation's own terms. The decision to stay is seen by long-term members as an affirmation of the worth of the church and its members. This is particularly important for those individuals and families who, for many years, felt labelled by both clergy and their supporters as 'second-class' Christians who were supposedly devoid of any 'real' spirituality. Now that the balance of power has altered and ownership has been returned to local people, the current contributions to the life of the congregation of those with evangelical sympathies can be better appreciated by all members. This has resulted in a growing mutual respect between the various parties, although as we shall see below when group activities are discussed, clearly demarcated boundaries remain.

The second challenge to the vicar was to address the poor state of the parish buildings. While this is a perennial problem in parishes throughout Wales, as noted above, this had been exacerbated by a policy of deliberate neglect:

> When I came, the situation I inherited, because of the extreme evangelical thing which was all about, you know, spiritual things and all that, 'the buildings weren't important', and so I suppose for about twenty odd years no work has been done on any buildings. The church hall across the road was more or less derelict, unusable, very dangerous. There was no church hall at St James. That was pulled down. So in the first six months I was here, we've created a church hall in the church there, which immediately brought their confidence up. They thought the church was going to close, they'd been fighting that. Former vicars didn't give much time to St James so they were given an immediate boost. Then we looked at All Souls. Again there was no hall there and again we created a small hall in what had been the vestry. We floodlit it, again giving confidence back to the people. Now we've done this to the church hall here and again the church hall is usable now. The church hall was built in the 1950s and was really the centre of all social activities in the community. It hadn't been used for five or six years and now its being used again.

This comprehensive project to reinstate the parish building stock is even more remarkable in that this is not a rich parish. The necessary monies were raised by a concerted campaign of letter writing by the vicar that resulted in finance being made available from sources as diverse as the Welsh Office and the National Lottery. The vicar had no compunction about approaching the latter source, not least because local people were enthusiastic players of the lottery. As the vicar noted, at least they were indirectly reaping some tangible benefits from their expenditure in terms of improved community facilities. While this was an important gain for the community, the thinking behind this project extended beyond the materiality of bricks and mortar. As the vicar repeatedly noted, both the people of the church and the surrounding community had suffered during recent recessions. The district looked rundown and there was a distinct lack of confidence in the future throughout the community. Industry had deserted the district. The local shopping area was shabby and semi-derelict. Even the chapels were closing and being left to the tender ministrations of the local vandals. Within this overall context, this rolling building and renovation project was designed to reassure local people that the church was there to stay, a visible marker that someone cared enough about the community to make a substantial investment in the future of the district.

The vicar sees his third challenge, bringing out the talents and abilities of church members, as perhaps the hardest of all and one that has serious ramifications for the future. As a working-class congregation, he feels that they sometimes lack confidence in their own abilities and potential. In the recent history of the parish this was exacerbated by the influx of middle-class individuals who took over much of the administrative duties, leaving local people disempowered and disenfranchised in their own church. Understandably, this has been very much a learning curve for both the vicar and the congregation:

> I'm a great believer in delegation. That's the way of the future really. Again, I'm struggling a bit with that, the people just haven't got the confidence. I can't just give them a job and say 'can you do that?' because I know that they will come back to me with some problem and it's so easy to say. 'I may as well do that myself'. It's much harder to actually delegate initially and that's the situation we are in now. The hard work if you like is that they have got the abilities, they can do the same as I can, but at the moment there are very few people, very few people that I can really rely on to get on with the job.

While this is a recurring problem for many clergy wherever they are found, it has particular local significance, given the negative effects on congregations of ministerial dependency outlined in the previous chapter. It is also not merely a matter of lightening clergy workloads, as it is becoming increasingly clear within the Church in Wales that the present parochial structure has a limited future (Harris and Startup, 1999). Declining clergy vocations, financial restraints and a parochial system that is increasingly under strain all point to something of a crisis in resourcing the Church. One solution has been the increasing 'grouping' together of parishes in order to maximize clerical and financial resources. However, as Harris and Startup note, this policy is rather narrowly conceived in that it ignores another potential resource, the laity (1999: 66). Within the context of this parish and given the factors out-lined above, the vicar considers that it is highly likely that at some point in the future it may not be possible for the church to maintain a full-time paid incumbent in the district. In this eventuality, the best that the parish can look forward to is some type of team ministry where the laity have a greater role than has traditionally been the case. Looking to the future and learning from the experience of the local Free Churches, it is imperative to encourage lay participation in the parish now if the same fate that has befallen other local congregations is to be avoided.

For example, in the light of the experience of ageing congregations else-where in the district, there is a pressing need to encourage more young peo-ple into the orbit of the church. In keeping with the inclusive orientation of Anglicanism, this is not narrowly conceived in terms of recruitment (although that would be welcome) but more in terms of an open-ended engagement that aims to establish meaningful relationships between the church and the community. The vicar commented on previous failures to do this:

> Our big problem is working with young people. I see that as one of the biggest shortfalls that we have, our work with young people. It really bothers me. We are looking at working with young people in a serious professional way. Not playing at it. Not, you know, a table tennis table and a snooker table and a can of coke in the church hall. . . . Before, we were just playing at it. People would commit themselves to the work, lots of good intentions, big schemes, and then after a few months, well they couldn't always be bothered to go, you know. Maybe it was raining or there was something good on television, so it was too many kids running around with too little supervision. Very disorganized. All we were doing really was keeping them off the streets.

These sentiments are echoed by many in the congregation who feel strongly that the church should and could be doing more for the young people of the area. To this end there is now a small group of mothers, supported by the vicar and his partner, who are seeking to re-establish the church's youth work on a sounder footing than previously. The vicar has stressed to this group that the emphasis this time around should be on realizable aims and a manageable well-planned work, rather than the unrealizable objectives of past endeavours. This is all part of a 'can do' approach that recognizes the crucial importance of 'concentrating on realistic projects that can be done'. Past experience suggests that unrealizable plans soon lead to demoralization and eventually inertia, neither of which is likely to resolve the long-standing crisis of confidence among the laity.

As the involvement of the vicar's partner in the setting up of the youth work suggests, she is an active (if unpaid) co-worker in the parish. A local woman, she is proud of these roots and has an astute understanding of local life, its tribalism, and indeed human nature in general. Well regarded locally, she was described to me by one group of women as both 'one of us' and as 'the first *real* vicar's wife we've ever had. She got stuck in from day one.' She is one of the new breed of 'clergy wives' who, while not prepared to conform to the traditional understandings of a vicar's partner, remains committed to assisting her partner in his work as much as she is able. A nurse by occupation, she finds this work both personally fulfilling and something that gives her an independent life and identity outside the parish. She nevertheless manages to combine paid employment with most of the duties expected of 'a vicar's wife'. Despite her busy life, she has been responsible for a number of initiatives in the parish. One of these was the revamping of the Mothers Union from being a purely social gathering into an active team involved in pastoral visiting and ministry. Another has been the setting up of a loose group called 'the Young Ones' which caters for young women in the parish and she has also reactivated the Sunday school at All Souls.

The curate, who arrived in the parish not long after the vicar and his partner, provides something of a complementary ministry. Formerly a master at one of Wales's leading private schools and a single man, his social situation and cultural background is a long way from that of the local community and the vicar and his partner. Life in a working-class urban parish is about as far as he can get from his previous life experience and he is frank about the fact that he was initially reluctant to take up this post:

> I was hoping for a country parish. When I drove down from Cardiff and passed all those gasholders at Baglan I felt quite depressed and wondered what an earth I was getting into. But as soon as I stepped out of the car and saw this marvellous view of the docks and met the people, I felt immediately at home here.

This feeling has been reciprocated and he is well liked among all three congregations. Importantly, given the previous history of the parish, he is perceived as a deeply spiritual man and a scholarly preacher who lives a very simple lifestyle. The remaining evangelicals and their sympathizers particularly rate him very highly on the strength of these attributes. Generally, he is seen as friendly and approachable and as a person with time for people. Among the small congregation of All Souls, who consider themselves as somewhat socially superior to the other two congregations, his class and cultural background is seen as more appropriate for an Anglican cleric. Significantly, the remaining evangelicals have adopted him as 'one of their own' despite the fact that he makes a point of not being seen to subscribe to any particular party line within the church. In terms of his public persona, he sees it as his duty to adopt a central and orthodox line in his teaching and preaching.

This dovetails well with the vicar's own approach to sermons, which is to present a simple and direct, biblically based message, often related to local conditions, but with an added emphasis on the Anglican liturgical calendar. In its constituents this theological and liturgical conservatism reflects the wider ethos of the Church in Wales which eschews theological extremes, whether high or low. Moreover, it accords with local understandings of the Anglican tradition. Under the previous incumbent, members had to be prepared for any eventuality in church services, the only constant factor being an evangelical emphasis in liturgy and preaching. There was little or no attempt to relate sermons either to the Church calendar or to the cycle of Bible readings. This has changed. There is now in place what we might term a more holistic approach that accords with Anglican tradition. All the elements of worship and teaching, hymns, readings and sermon, are closely related together and mediated through the Church's yearly cycle. Originally reflecting the patterns of rural life, even in an urban setting this engenders both a sense of continuity and a sense of motion. Worship is not static or discontinuous and the liturgical cycle of the Church fits naturally into the changing seasons. As it is repeated each year, this cycle nurtures a strong sense of Christian and Anglican identity and this was particularly apparent in my conversations with older members of the congregation.

While this return to tradition has been welcomed, in other matters practice can diverge quite considerably from other parishes in the city. In a departure from practice elsewhere, and understanding their working-class congregation, both clergy make a point of facilitating congregational interaction after services by not standing in the church porch. They prefer to stand in the back of the church, creating a focal point for informal conversation among the congregation. Consequently, people do not leave immediately but stay and chat for quite a long time. Family news and local gossip is shared, and among the older women news is conveyed about those members absent through sickness. People are updated as to their medical progress and informal arrangements made among the women to visit those who are sick at home or in hospital. Members also use this time to inform the vicar or the curate of local people who may need to be visited by the clergy.

The parish magazine *Outlook* serves as an extension of these informal means of communication. Thoroughly revamped, and edited by the vicar, it is a computer-generated, professionally presented A4 sized periodical, which is on sale in local shops. It seeks to bring together items of local news (including obituaries), reports from the three churches and the groups operating within them, and upcoming events in the parish. It also contains many contributions from church members in a wide sphere of interests and selected human interest stories and news about the wider Christian church that are gathered from various sources. A perennially popular feature is the inclusion of old photographs and articles that recall bygone life and people in the district. An impressive publication, given the limited resources in the parish, it not only serves to advertise the various church activities, but also engenders a sense of solidarity between the congregations and the surrounding community.

This sense of solidarity, or more properly, a sense of shared situation, is also to be found in relations with the local Free Churches. Many members have almost daily contact with members of the other churches and chapels in the district and the clergy are fully committed to the principle of local ecumenicalism. However, despite this fairly high level of informal congregational interaction, formal overtures by the clergy to the other churches have been largely rebuffed:

> There are so many aspects to this work here. Another thing the curate and I would like to look at is offering our hand of friendship to the chapels and say, 'Why struggle about this? Why are you fighting to maintain all these buildings? Come and use our buildings and hopefully over a period of time develop beyond just using our building and to be actually able to worship together. Why do we have to compete all the time?' But it's very much, well, that's seen in a negative way. 'We must keep going.' You can see it going on until they have to close down, and then they'll just stop worshipping.

Parishioners, many of whom are related, or who grew up side by side by their co-religionists, share this concern for the other local congregations. However, they also recognize that any practical ecumenical links of this sort are unlikely to get off the ground because of the long-standing attachments that local people have to particular chapels.

If formal ecumenical initiatives in the district are something of a non-starter, nevertheless the informal social networks and shared understandings that underpin the life of the parish constitute a property common to the locality. This common property is both the product of shared space and the sense of mutually recognized social obligation that flows from generations of living cheek by jowl in constrained circumstances. 'Community' and, by extension, 'identity' are two much misunderstood words, but words that continue to resonate in the social memory of many Welsh people. It is to this aspect of social life – community experience and shared interests and the expectations and moral orderings that flow from these aspects of social relationships – that I now turn.

RELIGION, COMMUNITY AND IDENTITY

If religion is no longer a major resource for the construction and expression of personal and collective identity for the majority of the Welsh population, nevertheless, at the level of local social units, one can still find much evidence of links between religion and social identities. These links are complex, in that they are also informed by other factors – class, gender, ethnicity, age and the raft of local social relations and networks that go to make up the life of micro-communities. In the case of the Anglican parish, and rather like a Russian doll, there are a number of potential identities overlapping and overlying each other. These can best be thought of in terms of 'distances' (although in the sense that it is used here this is essentially an abstraction used to convey a state of mind). First, and most distant, is membership of the world-wide Anglican Communion, then, with decreasing distance, membership at the provincial level (in this case the Church in Wales), then at the diocesan, parish and congregational levels, and finally at the level of subgroups within congregations. Clearly, these multiple variations on religious identity follow a trajectory from the universal to the (very) particular, but in practice these different forms of identity resource have uncertain boundaries and are subject to both the daily requirements of social experience and a certain amount of overlap and bricolage. What follows in this section is an account of the ways in which identity is reproduced and mediated through both the idea of community and the reality of social networks and vice versa. Beginning with brief characterizations of the three congregations that make up this parish and their relations with each other, I shall then proceed to explore the various subgroups within the parish and the nature of their relations with each other and the surrounding community.

Overall, the average number of people in the parish who attend a service for worship on any Sunday is somewhere in the order of 160 persons. The bulk of these worshippers are to be found in St John's, the main parish church. Here there are an average of 100 worshippers, usually divided between eighty adults (predominately but not exclusively female) and twenty children. While the average congregation of St James is far smaller (and older), with only forty-five worshippers, the proportion of children to adults is higher, with thirty adults and fifteen children regularly attending Sunday worship. (These children are predominantly the grandchildren of adult worshippers.) All Souls has the smallest congregation, with fifteen regular adult worshippers and a small Sunday school, recently reconstituted, with no more than five scholars (all drawn from unchurched families on the nearby housing estate) on any Sunday. As these figures suggest, the condition of each congregation is markedly different, although one shared characteristic is that the typical worshipper will be female and in middle age or older. Realistically,

the congregation of St John's has the best long-term future, both because it has the largest congregation and some recent new recruits. The future prospects of the other two congregations are rather more problematic and it is to these that I will turn first.

As noted in my earlier discussion of the religious history of the district, since the destruction of the housing surrounding All Souls in the nineteenth century it has struggled to find a continuing role in the community. It is an architecturally striking building whose stunning interior is one of the best kept secrets in West Glamorgan. Through the years it has remained an enduringly popular venue for marriages but as a parish church it is socially peripheral, neither here nor there in terms of the life of the district. While the creation of the adjacent housing estate re-established something of a role for All Souls, this is largely in terms of the occasional offices, weddings, baptisms and funerals, none of which appear to have stimulated any long-term growth among the congregation. The membership now stands at thirty-two persons, roughly half of whom are now unable to attend the church at all due to infirmity, and the congregational profile is typically elderly, predominantly female and mainly drawn from the immediately sur-rounding community. The last ten years have seen a 16 per cent decline in membership (all through deaths) and a 25 per cent decline in attendance, trends that show no sign of abating. Despite the fact that most of the inhab-itants of the local housing estate are young families, the average age of the congregation is 71 years, and members can be characterized as insular and very resistant to change.

This resistance is primarily a reflection of the age of the congregation, although the factors that have led to their insularity are more complex. Historically, All Souls and a sister church (now fully incorporated in a neighbouring parish) constituted a parish in themselves. After the break-up of this parish, All Souls was not directly incorporated into the parish of St John, although since that time it has been served by their clergy. This arrangement has not led to any strong sense of shared situation with either of the other two congregations and recent formal moves to incorporate the three churches into a single parish (since completed) were met with spirited resistance from the congregation of All Souls.

Geographically, All Souls gazes down on the dockside community and socially the congregation looks down on the working-class inhabitants of the surrounding district. Seaview Prospect represents something of a lower middle-class enclave that is untypical of the surrounding district, which is solidly working-class. Many members of All Souls (although by no means all) feel this contrast strongly and have a keen consciousness of class that is expressed in a certain ambivalence towards their co-religionists below. Certainly, the congregation perceives itself as more middle-class in tone even though most members have fairly recent working-class origins. One churchwarden interviewed wanted little or nothing to do with either of the other congregations who she dismissed as 'the people down there'. This feeling is reciprocated by those local Anglicans who have been so dismissively characterized. They see the congregation of All Souls as 'stand offish' and find their pretensions to social superiority mildly amusing, given that many of the All Souls people had their family origins in the community below. It is a truism that among the established local population everyone knows everyone else's family histories, and in this light these pretensions to social superiority are given short shrift by the people who grew up side by side with them.

Relations between the All Souls congregation and the vicar are also somewhat strained, despite the much-needed improvements that he has initiated to their building. Formerly, robing and the signing of wedding registers were carried out in a small dank vestry packed with the accumulated detritus of fifty years. This vestry has been cleared of rubbish and converted into a compact but bright hall for use by the reconstituted Sunday school, with another vestry constructed in the main body of the church building. Despite the vicar's best intentions (and the very real gains), this project was seen by leading lights in the congregation as 'interference' in their affairs and the much-needed improvements as 'unnecessary'. This culture of resistance to any and all change permeates all aspects of congregational life in All Souls. While this was a useful foil during the years of the evangelical ascendancy in the parish, affirming and preserving a distinctive congregational identity in the face of the threat of change, ultimately this strong identity has proved counterproductive, creating a barrier between the congregation and the surrounding population. While there is some recognition among the congregation that the future survival of All Souls is conditional on connecting with and recruiting from the young families living in the immediate district, in practice this is unlikely. There is neither the will to do this nor the human resources within the congregation to engage in any type of mission strategy. Services for worship are, in their present format, very traditional, with little of the ethos of 'family worship' and there is no desire among the congregation to accommodate the surrounding population on anything but their own very narrow terms of reference. While members of the congregation see each other on a fairly regular basis, their social life appears to exclusively revolve around the church and church activities, particularly the Mothers Union. Efforts by the vicar's partner to revamp the Mothers Union in order to bring it into more contact with the surrounding population were resoundingly rejected and the presence of the Sunday school is peripheral to the internal life of the congregation. Furthermore, members are not engaged in the type of complex kin and social networks that still exist further down the hill and subsequently have little or no contact with the surrounding unchurched population. Despite the best efforts of the clergy to connect with these people, and these have included both re-establishing the Sunday school and an annual barbecue on church grounds which attracted many local young families, the congregation appears largely intractable in its isolationist tendencies. In this light, it is difficult to see All Souls as anything but the personal fiefdom of the congregation and most of their energies appear directed towards maintaining this state of affairs. Understandably, the clergy now appear to be moving towards a strategy of maintenance rather than mission with All Souls, while seeking to attract local families to the nearby congregation of St John. The future closure of the church or, as is more likely, its transition to occasional use, appears inevitable as the congregation ages and becomes more infirm.

While All Souls is not typical of the congregational life of the parish, it is part of a wider picture in Wales, where the agendas for many congregations are increasingly being set by the over seventies. The end result in many cases is the increasing isolation of congregations from their surrounding populations, who themselves are now demonstrating all the hallmarks of indifference to organized religion. Given that 89 per cent of congregations in Wales are now mainly comprised of older worshippers (Bible Society, 1997: 16), this is not a problem that is likely to disappear in the near future. As the authors of the last national church survey note;

> To have only 3 per cent of churches . . . appealing to the younger age band and only 8 per cent with broad based appeal are extraordinarily small proportions. It reinforces the impression that by and large church culture reflects the culture of 45-plus-year-olds and that there is a serious lack of provision for younger age groups. (Bible Society, 1997: 17)

However, to focus purely on age is to ignore the often-complex nature of the relationship between church congregations and their surrounding populations. Ageing congregations are not necessarily feeble bodies and a strong congregational identity does not necessarily indicate insularity or an inability to reach out into the community, particularly where there are strong local social networks in place.

St James is an ageing congregation that, in many of its circumstances, appears to fit this latter category rather more. The church was opened in 1920 to meet the needs of residents living in the east of the district and architecturally it is an unimposing red brick building. The interior of the church has recently been totally refurbished and now presents a bright and airy appearance. Unlike the congregation of All Souls, members here see these renovations as both a much-needed vote of confidence by the clergy in them as people and also some indication that St James might continue to have a future as a local place of worship. The adult congregation is predominantly working-class and female, with an average age of 64 years, but there is also a lively children's work in place which skews the overall age profile to 46 years. Average attendance for Sunday morning worship is forty-five persons, although children make up a third of the congregation and there are only six worshippers between the ages of 26 and 44 years of age. This is a fairly standard U-shaped profile that is typical of the overwhelming majority of churches in Wales (Bible Society, 1997: 16). All the members of the congregation live locally and have lived in the district all of their lives. Adult members have a strong sense of local tradition and a staunch loyalty to their church and each other. Most members would consider themselves to be conservative in both their social outlook and their religious observance.

There is a strong Ladies Guild in operation (once common to many churches and chapels in Wales) and this meets on Wednesday evenings. It incorporates all of the older women in the church and can be said to constitute the centre of gravity of the congregation. While this is a fairly strongly bounded group with a clear-cut corporate identity, it is nevertheless inclusive in orientation, incorporating a small number of elderly women from the local Free Churches. Life for these women has not always been easy and all are either widows or spinsters, who, I was told, have 'shared each other's grief and sorrows over the years'. The guild meeting is for many the social highlight of their week, although the format of the meeting is firmly religiously orientated, with the singing of favourite hymns and prayer. Members of the guild formed the central core of resistance in St James during the evangelical ascendancy and these years are remembered with some bitterness (and some pride). In many ways, this very religious constituency of women might have been seen as natural allies to the clergy during that period. This was not to be, as they considered that the then clergy were only really interested in closing their church and incorporating them into the congregation of the main parish church, an eventuality that they were determined to resist to the best of their powers. The power of a congregation as a site of resistance, even in the face of clerical intransigence, should not be underestimated. It is a point of pride among this formidable group of women that in the years 1985–95 membership and attendance at St James remained stable and that subsequently there has even been a slight expansion of the Sunday school. Their current relationship with the clergy is good and they are supportive of the changes that the vicar has made. Furthermore, the fact that the curate (who is regarded with great affection) lives near to their church and is seen very much by them as their own pastor has helped to cement good relations with the clergy.

It should not be construed that a strong congregational identity is a mark of insularity. Members were keen to stress that they were not 'stand-offish' and that there was a high degree of interaction between them and the congregation of St John's. Kin and social networks cut across and intersect both congregations and as people have moved around the district over the years they have often chosen (as is the traditional Anglican way) to attend their nearest church. In this way, many people now resident in one congregation have an intimate knowledge of the other congregations in the parish. Many of the more mobile St James women also attend evensong and the mid-week eucharist at St John's and there are a core group of twelve women who are very involved in one of the two housegroups in the parish. Relations with and attitudes towards the local Free Churches are open and cordial, reflecting the long-standing culture of the area and embedded local notions of status and respectability (the historical salience being generic churchgoing which denotes respectability, denominational allegiances being secondary). However, for these Anglican women Free Church ministry is not seen as being of the same order as that of the Anglican priesthood, which to them carries more legitimacy. (The vicar commented that 'a dog collar is everything with these people. I never go anywhere without it because they see it as a mark of *real* authority'.) In matters of church order and specifically liturgical traditions it is important, as members stressed, that 'things are done properly', particularly with regard to the consecration of the elements in the eucharist, and this requires the presence of a priest. Conversely, among the local Free Churches, where there are no full-time ministers resident, these churches and chapels are very much seen as operating a 'DIY' ministry and therefore lacking in authority. Notwithstanding this high view of the priesthood, local lay leaders in the Free Churches are seen as doing a good job in the face of very difficult circumstances and there was very genuine regret expressed about the decline of the chapels in the district. This decline constitutes the pervasive backdrop to all religious life within the district and the members of St James are realistic about their future. As members continue to age, and despite the presence of the Sunday school, a future merger of the congregations of St James and St John appears inevitable. Members are now reconciled to this, not least because, as they said, the clergy 'have given it their best shot' and, if the church must close, it will not have been from clerical neglect.

It would appear from the situation of both the satellite congregations that the long-term future for the Anglican cause in the district lies with the parish church of St John. This church constitutes the primary centre of gravity within the parish, including as it does the vicarage and parish hall, and offers the full spectrum of services and activities that would be expected in a thriving parish church. Sixty-three persons are recorded on the electoral roll and on average there are a hundred attenders (including twenty children in Sunday school) on any given Sunday. Adult males are far better represented than in the other two congregations but the ratio of females to males is still very high at 9:1. The average age of adult worshippers is 62 years and, with the exception of nine adults (seven of these with strong local connections), everyone lives within the district. The congregation see themselves as a friendly and welcoming church and this is certainly the impression that comes over to the visitor. The social characteristics of the congregation accurately reflect the class base of the surrounding community and most long-term members would be described as 'respectable working-class', socially conservative and at the upper end of the local social scale. Relative newcomers to the congregation are less likely to fit this type. They still tend to be working-class females, but younger, less conservative and often (by their own admission) do not fit the local stereotypes of churchgoers. The congregation is further divided into a number of recognizably distinct subgroups, some formally constituted around shared activities and some merely informal groupings of people who share similar characteristics. Most members, whether long-termers or newcomers, are strongly integrated into the general life of the surrounding community.

Local connections drive this church and, with very few exceptions, worshippers are also members of various social networks based on kin, friends and neighbours. These networks intersect and crosscut each other and middle-aged and older members appear to know the family histories and current circumstances of all the long-established residents of the district. Whilst the character of the community is changing, with many newcomers not part of these long-established networks, they remain important for those individuals whose local connections go back more than one generation. Most mothers in the congregation still see their married children on a daily basis, not least because they often provide pre- or after-school care for their grandchildren. Grandmothers also try to ensure that their grandchildren (and often the children of neighbours also) attend Sunday school on a regular basis. Conversely, adult children, even when they live nearby, are unlikely to attend St John's on anything but a very occasional basis. Typically, it is daughters rather than sons that make the effort and while they are unlikely to appear on the electoral roll, nevertheless, they still regard themselves as attached to the church.

The district has a lower than average incidence of car ownership and much of the life of the community still takes place on the streets and in the neighbourhood shops. There is much visiting of friends' and neighbours' houses, with people stopping to 'meet and greet' on the street, and this constant round of daily interaction is one of the main ways in which church and chapel members maintain regular contact with each other. However, formal ecumenical contact between the different worshipping communities is seen locally as more problematic. Over the years attempts by the St John's people to extend the hand of friendship to the local chapels and churches have not been fully reciprocated and there have been no similar initiatives emanating from these sources. In contrast, there is quite a high degree of formal contact with Anglican congregations elsewhere in the diocese, primarily through the activities of the Mothers Union. There is much community use of St John's for the occasional offices of baptisms, weddings and funerals, which are always big affairs locally, drawing many people into the church. Even where the individuals concerned are ostensibly 'unchurched', there is invariably a family connection at these events, with members of St John's also attending in their capacity as friends or family members. Educational and recreational activities also bring members of the congregation and local people together, more so again since the church hall has been refurbished. Dance classes, art classes, flower arranging and aerobics classes (all based in the church hall) are all popular activities with female members and local women alike, and there is also a mother and toddler group based in the church hall. Members (particularly female members) see contacts such as these as very important, arguing that it gives the local community the opportunity to see church people as, in their own words, 'people like them' and not as 'a holy huddle'. Activities such as these, while not overtly 'religious' (however that might be defined) are an important part of the complex relationship that the church has with its surrounding population. Their importance, over and above their intrinsic worth to members of the local community, lies in lessening the distance and blurring the boundaries between congregation and local people. Furthermore, it conforms to local understandings, as typified by the post-1945 religious history of the district, of the social functions that mainstream churches and chapels should ideally perform.

One striking absence in this set of relations, given the long history of chapel and church engagement in local political life, is the distinct lack of formal political involvement of the congregation. None of the congregation are members of a political party and none are currently local councillors, although there is congregational concern about local issues such as crime and the lack of facilities for young people. Local community initiatives, such as the re-establishment of the local carnival and the 'Eastside Initiative' (a project to improve local educational and recreational facilities), have been actively supported, but this is the sum total of congregational involvement in local politics. A partial explanation for this lack of political engagement lies with the high proportion of women in the congregation, as traditionally local party-political activity has been a male preserve. There are also other local factors, not least being the virtual demise of the docks as a place of local employment and the subsequent eclipse of trade union activity in the district.

Notwithstanding this lack of outside political activity, it is clear that the church is one of the few voluntary associations in the area seeking to work to improve, even in a modest way, the quality of life in the district. From the perspective of those in the congregation, the years of evangelical ascendancy were a period when the church appeared to those outside the congregation to be distancing itself from the local community. While this trend has now been reversed, nevertheless it highlights the ever-present tension within religious institutions between being *in* the world and being *of* the world. Clearly, previous incumbents and their supporters (in common with many evangelicals) subscribed to a type of world-rejecting Christianity that effectively places itself in opposition to the wider society. Just as clearly, the majority of the people of St John's subscribe to a world-affirming Christianity that seeks to chart a path of being fairly closely integrated with their surrounding social and cultural environment. Moreover, and regardless of theological dispositions, local church members, by virtue of their local provenance and membership of local social networks, are both objectively and subjectively integrated into the wider life of the local community.

In the Durkheimian sense these are 'the categories of understanding' (Durkheim, 1995: 8) with which the social actor interprets the world (in this case the very circumscribed world of the micro-community) both spatially and in terms of affective identifications. Elements of the above description of the parish's recent history might suggest the setting up of an opposition between world-affirming and world-rejecting religious dispositions. Nevertheless, as Durkheim suggests, the relationship between the religious and the social is very close indeed. Part of the troubled recent history of the parish revolved around the perceptions of some actors who saw the congregation as 'too worldly', too caught up in the purely social activities of the church. Others could not conceive of a local church that was not, at least partially, predicated on these things. However, caution should be exercised when making too clear-cut a dichotomy between the religious and the secular and the activities that flow from these characterizations. With this in mind I now turn to a description and discussion of the internal life of the church, its subgroups and people.

There are a number of recognizably distinct groupings based around voluntary activities within the congregation. These might be loosely divided into 'social' and 'religious' activities, although, as a closer examination of these activities will reveal, this distinction is very loose. Unsurprisingly, given the numerical dominance of females in the congregation, there are a number of formally constituted women's organizations: the Mothers Union, the Wives Group and the Young Ones. Traditionally, these have been seen as fulfilling a social function, although, as has been noted above, the traditional role of the Mothers Union has changed, with the emphasis now on visiting the sick and housebound. In the case of the latter two groups, the Wives Group and the Young Ones (described in more detail below), these social activities are contrasted with the housegroups, which were established for the purposes of Bible study during the previous incumbency and which can be described as having an overt religious function. Within the congregation, there is an unspoken recognition that these groups differentiate those individuals with evangelical sympathies from those without them. The PCC, the choir and cleaning and maintenance groups whose activities underpin the general organizational life of the church mediate the different groups and serve to integrate the various members of the congregation.

The Wives Group is the most prominent organization within the congregation and meets once a week in the church hall. Originally established as a Young Wives Group in the 1970s, the change of name reflects the fact that the original personnel (most of whom are still active members) are now middle-aged grandmothers. Current membership numbers are in the mid-thirties and its personnel are among the most active members of the congregation. There is a significant degree of overlap between this group and other groups such as the PCC, the choir and the Mothers Union and most of the women take part in the church-cleaning rota. Members are also enthusiastic users of the various community educational and recreational activities based in the church hall, with dance classes being a particularly popular pursuit.

The format of meetings of the Wives Group is quite formal and usually includes a guest speaker followed by a prolonged period of socializing over tea and biscuits. The women are very involved with fundraising as well as organizing social activities, such as trips to places of interest, and they describe themselves as 'the powerhouse of the church'. This self-characterization is echoed by many in the church, not least the current vicar who considers that it was these women who were solely responsible for holding the church together during the last interregnum. More generally, as a long-established group they have provided a much-needed sense of continuity through the many changes affecting the church. In the course of many conversations with these women, it became clear that they are a caring, mutually supportive group, with a strong degree of collective solidarity, and over the years many individuals have been helped by their fellow members through what were often deep personal crises. However, in some quarters of the congregation, this group solidarity and the evident enjoyment that these women gain from their shared activities has come under some criticism. More seriously minded members described it as 'a social club' and as 'contributing nothing to the spiritual life of the church', an assessment that many in the Wives Group took exception to.

For the sociologist, characterizing motivations for activities as purely 'social' or purely 'religious' is somewhat problematic, given that all group activities are inherently social. In the case of the Wives Group it was not at all clear where one ended and another began. Many members of this group were also deeply involved in the practical and organizational life of the church as well as being faithful in their attendance for worship. They themselves were keen to stress the practical Christian nature of their charitable activities, described by them as 'faith in action' and the mutually supportive nature of the group, which was seen by them as visibly fulfilling Christian criteria of fellowship and pastoral care. In the same vein, participation in outside activities such as the dance class was described (rather optimistically, it has to be said) in terms of 'outreach' into the community. In practice, this appeared to be viewed as a species of 'friendship' evangelism, that is, establishing friendships with those outside the congregation in the hope that they might be attracted to the church.

Members perceive themselves as a friendly and welcoming group and are keen to attract new recruits, particularly younger women, to the Wives Group, whether from outside or inside the congregation. However, they are also acutely aware of their failure in this department, despite the presence of a number of female newcomers to the congregation and their desire to incorporate their married daughters into the group. Interestingly, it is the two factors that contribute most to the overall cohesion of the group, and which do much to explain the group's longevity, that also inhibit other women joining the group. First, the very fact that they are such a tightly cohesive group with a marked sense of collective solidarity means that they are a strongly bounded group. While members themselves do not perceive this symbolic boundary as significant in any way, others see this as their main group characteristic and find the high degree of group solidarity offputting. Simply put, other women expressed the opinion that they would experience problems in becoming fully accepted within this group. Secondly, the rather formal programming of weekly activities, which are culturally attuned to an older generation, does not appeal to the younger women within the congregation. This is particularly so in the case of daughters, whose attendance at church is often irregular, reflecting a generational preference for looser more informal ties and a privatized lifestyle. In contrast, the formation of the Wives Group three decades ago reflected the group values of a generation that still liked to engage in regular communal activities that necessitated a fair amount of personal commitment. Both the vicar and his partner recognize this cultural divide and their response has been to organize activities that are more culturally attuned to the needs of younger women.

This group, the 'Young Ones', is coordinated by the vicar's partner and meets on an occasional basis off the church premises and has an ostensibly social function. Activities might include a visit to the leisure centre or a cinema but usually the venue is a wine bar in the city centre and the format is instantly recognizable locally as that of a 'girls night out'. These activities are very popular with that cohort of women who are infrequent worshippers but who retain strong family ties within the congregation, and this group offers a practical means for these women to continue to affirm their identification with the church, albeit in an attenuated form. In these terms this group is a success, although it is difficult to see how this might be translated at a future date into the type of collective solidarity (exemplified by the Wives Group or Ladies Guild) capable of holding the church together in times of crisis.

If the Wives Group can be described as a socially orientated group with a latent religious function, the housegroup attached to St John's might be described as a religiously orientated group with a latent social function. In common with the housegroup based in St James it meets one afternoon a week in a private house for prayer and Bible study and is led by one of the remaining evangelicals. Housegroup members are all very active long-term members of the church, predominantly female, but not exclusively so, and elderly. While this group ostensibly meets for religious purposes, it is clear to anyone attending these meetings that members take pleasure in socializing with each other. Numerically this group is small, never numbering more than a dozen people, but constitutes an important focus within the congregation for those individuals who are recognized as taking a 'serious' approach to faith. In the case of this housegroup, this is firmly equated with evangelicalism, although the same could not be said of the St James housegroup, which is better characterized as 'conservative Anglican'. It is important to note here that this identification with evangelicalism is not a product of the recent history of the church but is something with much deeper roots. The religious environment of Swansea in the early twentieth century was still dominated by evangelicalism and for those older members this is the type of religious belief and practice with which they were familiar in their youth. Typically, housegroup members also have strong past family connections to evangelically orientated chapels and a conservative social and religious outlook that fits well with the evangelical ethos.

Understandably, members are ambivalent about the recent history of the parish. While the more exotic manifestations of charismatic practice were seen as rather disturbing there was some support within this group for the previous two incumbents. The general consensus was that the lack of success of these last two incumbencies was more to do with a failure of communication rather than with any deficiencies in the message itself. Simply, members believed that previous incumbents failed to tailor their message to the particularities of local culture. In the light of this there is also a certain ambivalence towards the new vicar, not least because he is seen as unsympathetic towards evangelicalism, but this is tempered with respect for what he has done to turn the fortunes of the church around. He is seen as someone who does understand the local working-class culture and who takes a theologically orthodox line in the pulpit, so in this there are points of agreement. However, he is not seen as 'deep' spiritually and housegroup members see the role of their group as compensatory to his ministry, contributing directly to the spiritual life of the church by raising the level of spirituality within the congregation. In this vein, and with the support of the vicar, the establishment of a parish 'prayer chain' (meeting monthly and incorporating both housegroups and the Mothers Union) is seen as another link in this work. Like the Wives Group, they would welcome newcomers and are concerned that they have not been able to do this. They too are a strongly bounded group (the boundary here being a certain theological orientation coupled with a strong group identity) which some in the congregation view as offputting. Members of the housegroup are aware of this and worry that others are not aware of what they do or misunderstand the nature of their group. While housegroup members were not above criticizing the activities of other groups, they were keen to stress that they were not a 'church within a church' and that there was room for all.

The members of those groups on the receiving end of these criticisms also expressed this sentiment and, remarkably, given the recent parish history, there is no evident hostility or residual rancour within the congregation. A major factor in these mutually enlightened attitudes is the fact that the memberships of these disparate groups are an integral part of a number of intersecting networks that serve to unite rather than divide. These networks include those general to the district, including kin, friends and neighbours, shared educational experience in local schools and shared occupational histories. These shared social origins and biographies combine in different ways to foster a distinctive localized sense of identity based on place that tends to mediate between group and theological differences. There are also those networks specific to the life of the church. These draw from the more active members of the congregation who provide the personnel for a number of groups and activities, churchwardens and administrative officers, the PCC and choir, the Mothers Union, youth workers, sidespersons and those responsible for church cleaning and maintenance. The need to cooperate actively in these activities tends to draw people together rather than pulling them apart and in practice individuals, regardless of their theological or other differences, work closely together to promote the social solidarity and collective identity of the church as a whole. There is also the factor of Anglican identity and the Anglican theological tradition, underpinning and running like a thread through the life of the church. This acts as something of a safety valve, allowing individuals and groups to identify with and tap into wider Anglican networks in the city and to affirm a broader abstract identity based on the inclusive principles of Anglicanism. While this can be said to apply in theory to any congregation of the Anglican tradition, this is made rather easier by the fact that the majority of the religious views of the congregation are broadly aligned with that of the current vicar, something that cannot be said of his immediate predecessors. However, it should be emphasized that this portrait of group cooperation and stability is dependent on the mediating and organizing role of the clergy. On occasions, the vicar has had to intervene in disputes between individuals and groups and lay down a firm line, particularly in terms of the direction the church should be going in collectively.

Broadly, this direction is a continuation of the re-establishment of the central Anglican principle of providing spiritual care to the surrounding population (parishioners) rather than just to accredited members. Under conditions of secularization, this is no easy task, particularly in the light of the fact that it is now clear that the majority of the Welsh population no longer automatically subscribe to the tenets of the Christian faith. Certainly, for an Anglican church operating in an increasingly secular world, the assumption that local inhabitants who are not connected to any other religious institution are therefore by default defined as potentially within the Anglican penumbra is a definition in need of some confirmation. Nevertheless, in terms of residual Anglican affiliation, three categories of adherents might be identified: active communicants, occasional communicants and nominal adherents (Harris and Startup, 1999: 61). In terms of the ecology of this parish, these might be further categorized as those individuals active in the whole life of the congregation, those who attend fairly regularly but hold back from that level of group involvement and those who either attend very infrequently or avail themselves occasionally of pastoral services. The challenge now facing the clergy and members of St John's is how to move to incorporate these latter two categories, which might be termed the periphery and fringe, more fully into the orbit and life of the local church.

PERIPHERY AND FRINGE

Those worshippers who attend services fairly regularly but who are not active in the organizational or social life of the church make up a significant body of the congregation. This informal but close-knit grouping mainly comprises older women who attend either the main Sunday morning service or the mid-week eucharist. While faithful in their observance, they do not appear to desire any closer involvement over and above this. This group mainly represents those who left the church in protest during the years of the evangelical ascendancy and who have subsequently returned. 'Staying away' was essentially a passive protest and this passivity is reflected in their relatively low levels of commitment, which are source of frustration to the clergy who would like to see them shoulder more of the practical responsibilities of congregational life. Nevertheless, these women are an important link with the wider community. They engage in a fair amount of interaction outside the church, visiting each other's homes and often shopping together, and many share kinship as well as friendship networks. These, in turn, overlap and connect with those local people who still retain some sense of identification with the church, however nominal. In some cases these would be the adult children of members, but in most cases they are the older inhabitants of the district. The district has a high proportion of older people with long-term limiting illnesses and both clergy and (to a lesser degree) laity expend considerable time engaged in sick visiting. If those in need of a visit are not regular worshippers, initial contacts are usually made by members of the congregation, facilitated through their intersecting social networks, and then passed on to the clergy. Clergy also tend to hear first about bereavements through members of the congregation who will indicate whether a visit is appropriate (that is, whether that person is not counted as belonging to any other religious group). Conversely, couples wishing to be married or to have their children baptized would normally initiate contact themselves through the parish surgery, held weekly in the vicarage. This surgery is again an important point of contact with the surrounding population who come for advice and counselling on issues ranging from debt to drug use within families. Local schools have also occasionally called upon the clergy to offer support to families experiencing problems with their children. While this work on the fringe is an invaluable point of contact with the surrounding population it is not seen by either the clergy or congregation as an overt means to recruitment and adopting a means/ends strategy would be seen as highly inappropriate within the context of a parish ministry. Locally, this would be seen as a betrayal of trust. Nevertheless, there have been new recruits and it is to these that I turn.

These individuals, while they have recently become fairly frequent worshippers, still remain on the periphery of the congregation and constitute a small informal grouping that nevertheless has distinctive characteristics. They number no more than a dozen people, are predominantly female, but not exclusively so, and are slightly younger than the congregational average. Some of this group have transferred from failing local Free Churches and these have tended to be drawn in along existing social networks of friends and neighbours. A typical biography here would include an intermittent pattern of very occasional attendance for a number of years, usually at the invitation of existing church members and sometimes within the context of ecumenical activities, culminating in a decision to transfer. Others appear to have no pre-existing links with the church and have drifted in piecemeal. In these cases, initial contact with the congregation was tentative, typically following a pattern of many months of attendance at evensong before shifting to attendance at the main morning service. Whatever the pattern of engagement, almost all these new recruits (male and female) are married but have been unable to interest their partners in attending the church.

None of these newcomers cited a sudden conversion experience as being instrumental in their decision to begin attending church. While some had been exposed to varieties of evangelicalism in the past, this experience tended to be viewed negatively. Rather, their typical spiritual biography tended to be described as a process of 'seeking', often long and drawn out over months and even years, resulting in a sense of the presence of God in their lives or the sense that their lives were being transformed in some way. All felt that a major element in their persisting with initial church attendance has been the lack of 'pressure' on them from clergy and other members of the congregation to conform to a particular set of standards. St John's is seen as both warm and welcoming but also, importantly, as a place where they can remain relatively anonymous and retain an element of personal privacy. Mention was also made of the high level of pastoral care given by the clergy. Newcomers were befriended and visited in their own homes on a regular basis by clergy and this made a deep impression, further consolidating their attachment to the church.

Most, however, remain on the periphery of the social life of the church and this is given concrete expression in a number of ways. During services the few male newcomers tend to sit on their own, creating a distinct space between them and the congregation. Female newcomers tend to see themselves as a distinct group and sit together at the back of the church. They are not so likely to remain after the service to chat with other members of the congregation, although they do get together regularly outside the church to socialize and visit each other's homes. Their main point of reference is the vicar and his partner, who have actively sought to integrate them into the life of the church in ways with which they would feel comfortable. At the vicar's behest, almost all have become actively involved in those practical tasks that underpin church life. Some are involved in the new youth work, others in cleaning and maintenance and one newcomer has become the church hall bookings secretary. As a strategy for integration, the vicar's policy can be said to be fairly successful in that it has engendered a sense of belonging and has brought this group into sustained contact with other active members of the congregation. Nevertheless, the women in this group have tended to shy away from any active involvement in formally constituted groups and activities within the congregation, not least because they do not yet feel fully accepted by long-term members.

This question of acceptance reflects not so much the internal characteristics of the congregation (although these are germane factors to which I shall return) as those of the surrounding community, not least the strong sense of identity that stems from patterns of continuous residence in the district. Acceptance, therefore, is conditional on being seen to 'belong' and belonging is tied up in membership of the social networks that can be said to characterize the parish's local particularities. Reputation is based likewise on local knowledge, primarily through knowledge of families and knowledge gained through the past dealings and the daily interactions that take place within the overlapping networks that constitute the social life of the district. Acceptance therefore inevitably takes time. Furthermore, the gatekeepers of this local knowledge tend to be the elderly who are its living embodiment. Elderly people are, by and large, both conservative in their values and concerned with continuity. This is exactly the same demographic group that dominates the personnel of the local churches and in this light it is easy to see why relative newcomers within the congregation might feel some frustrations in the matter of acceptance.

TURNING THE CLOCK BACK

It is clear from both this chapter (and elements of the last) that the local religious life of the district is characterized by a concern with continuity and resistance to change. In this, the parish of St John is fairly typical of many of those districts in Wales where small or medium-sized settled communities of long standing might be found. These communities are defined both by shared geographical space and local knowledge, both of which carry a temporal aspect, and in many of these communities it is this temporal aspect, the shared sense of the way things were, that keeps the memory of the religious heritage of Wales alive. True, in many places this collective memory appears to be faltering and fading, and this is reflected in a landscape dotted with redundant chapels and small predominately elderly congregations struggling to keep the doors of their particular place of worship open. Moreover, as the results of the 1995 Welsh Churches Survey (Bible Society, 1997) demonstrate, it is among elderly people that organized religion continues to have widespread salience. In this sense, while we are witnessing the secularization of Welsh society, this is not necessarily the same thing as the evacuation of religion from Welsh society. As Timothy Jenkins (1999: 131) in his study of a similar settled working-class community notes, it is tempting to assume, but is not necessarily the case, that when the elderly start to die, their values and identifications die with them. For Jenkins, the cultural transmission of religious (or any other) values in working-class locales is more stable than it appears. He suggests that this is made possible by the generational cycle whereby individuals in their late fifties and early sixties naturally take on and internalize the attributes and status appropriate to their age. In doing this, they become both authoritative guardians of local knowledge thus saving it from extinction, and by extension, potential recruits to fill the thinning ranks of the local churches and chapels. Of course, the question of recruitment is conditional on a number of factors, not least the continued presence of religious institutions in the local community. The closure of places of worship, fairly obviously, closes down that particular avenue of action, although it does not preclude individuals transferring their religious allegiance to churches or congregations that remain viable. As we have also seen, the migration of families out of their traditional areas of residence has negative effects on local churches. Religious values may still be culturally transmitted and individual and family identification may still lie with a particular place of worship, but in most cases this is unlikely to produce benefits for struggling local churches. This suggests, then, that there are a number of conditions that need to be fulfilled, if Jenkins's assertions are to be confirmed.

The first condition would appear to be the presence of a stable settled community with long-standing overlapping social networks that link congregations to their surrounding populations and vice versa. Those intersecting social networks that characterize the social ecology of this parish and the low rates of social and geographical mobility among Anglicans have certainly facilitated both retention and recruitment at St John's. Secondly, the presence of viable places of worship with a professional leadership and a visible presence in the community provides a strong sense of continuity in a district that has seen considerable economic and social change. In comparing the situation of the Free Churches of the district with that of the parish church, it is again clear that the particular Anglican form of territorial organization, its reach and (despite disestablishment in 1920) its established character, has given this denomination an advantage over other religious groups. Moreover, as C. C. Harris (1990: 58–9) has argued, traditional religion in Wales continues to resonate among communities experiencing economic, social and cultural change. In this light, 'turning the clock back' in this particular parish has been greeted by both churchgoers and the local population as a welcome return to organized religion as they understand it.

However, it should also be recognized that this looks more like a strategy of maintenance than mission. Recent church growth has largely been a matter of pronounced short-term increase by returning members and is unlikely to be repeated on that scale. Furthermore, the character of the congregation is strongly derived from the long-standing family and friendship networks that characterize the district and these structures are being eroded, as is the habit of local churchgoing among younger people. These factors raise hard questions for this parish and in this the future remains open, as it does for many congregations throughout Wales. Whether there is, as Jenkins (1999: 131) appears to suggest, a generational cycle, whereby younger individuals on the periphery of the church might move into a more active engagement with the church as they grow older, remains a hypothesis in need of some confirmation and it is this question that I shall proceed to investigate in more depth in the next chapter.

6

Invisibility

One of the most significant transformations within the Welsh religious sphere in the past century has been the progressive move away from a distinctive working-class religious culture into something that is more firmly middle-class in its provenance. The reach of religious institutions into the Welsh working classes was far more extensive than in late nineteenth-century England and this is reflected in the case studies in the two previous chapters. In theory, if not always in practice, churches and chapels were places where the emerging class differences in Welsh society could be subordinated under the umbrella of organized religion. Within God's house, all were fundamentally equal and the social and economic distinctions that marked the world outside were something to be left at the church or chapel door (Pope, 1998: 4). This was not to last. The advent of socialist ideologies and forms of public organization in the early twentieth century did much to undermine this idea of a classless idyll, as did economic restructuring and the emergence of a 'mobile society' in the mid-twentieth century (Brennan, 1954; Jones, 1969). Since then, the cultural characteristics of organized religion and congregational life have become progressively middle-class in tenor. Swansea is no exception and this is highlighted by the patterns of geographical mobility which have weakened churches in working-class localities while at the same time emphasizing the cultural movement towards a more generalized, anglicized and middle-class church culture (Harris, 1990: 56–7). This transformation is perhaps most visible in those western suburbs of the city where a relatively thriving religious economy might be found.

'Maestref' (not its real name) is one such suburb. An affluent locality, it is largely a product of the post-war housing boom, although there are some housing estates dating from the 1920s and 1930s and some leafy streets of Edwardian villas. The majority of housing is privately owned, the exception being one lone estate of local authority housing built in the 1960s. There are also a number of residential care establishments catering for the needs of the elderly. According to the 1991 census, the local population is in the order of 13,000 persons and there are a total of 5,506 households. This is a solidly middle-class area and the majority of the workforce (59 per cent) is in white-collar employment, primarily in management (44 per cent). The cost of housing is high and this is reflected in the lower than average number of young families residing in the district. There is also a high level of geographical mobility among those still active in the workforce. Many newcomers come to Swansea because of the demands of their occupation and leave again for the same reasons. The district also has a higher than average population of retired persons, reflecting the popularity of this district as a retirement destination.

Primarily a residential area, there is a shortage of public amenities such as shops and public houses, although there are many green spaces. The dominant local culture is that of the privatized household and long-term residents described a locality that has always lacked sociability and community spirit. As one elderly resident commented:

People in [Maestref] go about their own business. It's always been like that. You never had calling in to see people. I've lived here since I was two and I can never say my mother popped in to see anyone. It wasn't like elsewhere in Swansea, you never had Auntie something living next door, it wasn't like that then. There's never been much of a community spirit here, people tend to keep themselves to themselves.

This combination of a relatively mobile population and a highly privatized lifestyle accounts for much of the atomized character of the district and is reflected in the almost total absence of the type of long-established intersecting social networks that we saw in the previous chapter. Nevertheless, there is a relatively thriving churchgoing culture. Indeed, as a prosperous predominately middle-class locality with a significantly higher than average cohort of middle-aged and elderly people, this is precisely the type of area where one would expect to find a thriving religious economy (D. Martin, 1967: 106).

There are many churches and chapels, most with sizeable congregations, in stark contrast to the experience in those areas I have explored elsewhere in the city, and indeed, in many other parts of Wales. All types of churchgoing are represented in the district. There are three Anglican and one Roman Catholic churches, two Welsh-medium and two English-medium Free Churches (all theologically in the mainstream), three evangelical congregations and a small Seventh Day Adventist church. Most churches in the district are either numerically stable or have experienced some growth, the exceptions being one Anglican congregation, the Seventh Day Adventists and the subject of this case study. It is to this congregation that we now turn our gaze in order to further our understanding of the pressures and dilemmas that face so many congregations in Wales today.

MAESTREF BAPTIST CHURCH

Our focus is on 'Maestref Baptist Church' (not its real name) a member church of the Baptist Union of Great Britain, a denomination that represents 5.2 per cent of the active churchgoing population of Wales (Bible Society, 1997: 12). It takes its name from its suburban setting, a place where, at 11 per cent of the population, the rate of churchgoing is significantly higher than the county average of 7.5 per cent (Bible Society, 1997: 10). The twelve churches in the immediate locality reflect a broad spectrum of Welsh religious adherence and (with one exception, the Seventh Day Adventists) they all have substantial congregations. However, Maestref Church stands out from the rest because it is a congregation that has experienced significant numerical decline within a local environment where churchgoing remains a relatively popular activity. During the period 1985–95 membership fell by 34 per cent and now stands at 123 persons, some of whom are permanently housebound. Average attendance for worship on any Sunday is in the order of 91 adults and 24 children and the overwhelming majority of adult worshippers (62 persons) are over the age of 65. While the congregation still remains in a position to maintain a full-time paid minister, it is apparent that the age profile of this congregation is firmly at the upper end and this rate of decline is likely to increase dramatically in the near future.

The congregation is formally organized along the lines of the Baptist formula of the 'gathered church': a type of congregationalism whereby the church is seen in terms of a local body of believers gathered together by the Holy Spirit and operating on the principle of separation from the world. Church government is based on the principle of the autonomy and independence of the local congregation and it is essentially a democratic system. Power is vested in the diaconate and the twelve deacons that make up this body are selected from lay members of the congregation by means of annual elections. Technically, the office of deacon is a ministerial function, with implications for lay preaching and pastoral oversight, but in practice it has increasingly been interpreted in many congregations in terms of an administrative function. In theory, there should be a regular turnover of deacons but in practice individuals might serve in the office for many years and in the process can accumulate much power, particularly if they are translated to the office of 'life deacon'.

The minister is 'called' (appointed) by a meeting of members and is effectively the employee of the congregation and directly accountable to the diaconate. While the minister is responsible for the spiritual welfare of the congregation, the day-to-day running of the church (particularly financial matters) is usually the province of the diaconate. In theory, the minister has only the same measure of power as a deacon and while he might advise a course of action, it is then subject to a free vote of deacons. What he/she cannot do under the terms of church polity is to impose his/her will on the congregation. However, in practice, diaconates tend to defer to a minister's opinion. Many ministers, through a mixture of cajoling and judicious politicking among individual members of the diaconate, can get motions in their favour passed. So although formal power rests in the diaconate, ministerial status acts as a form of countervailing power and in practice local Baptist church polity operates in a state of some tension between formal and informal power structures. In terms of the minister's pastoral duties, these are confined to the oversight of members, attenders and their families and technically do not extend out into the community. However, this does not preclude ministers from becoming involved in an official capacity with local community structures such as school governing boards.

Although Maestref Church is a member church of the Baptist Union of Great Britain, this union is not a denomination in the strict sense. The BUGB is essentially an umbrella organization facilitating the loose association of a number of independent congregations and its role is essentially advisory. While it has superintendents whose functions are very similar to those of a bishop, they lack many of a bishop's powers. They can advise but not enforce decisions and the only real sanction is expulsion of a congregation from the Baptist Union. Such a move would in practice affect an individual congregation very little, as its status would merely become that of an independent Baptist church. Consequently, disciplinary sanctions are hardly ever enforced. In the same spirit, individual congregations can also choose to disaffiliate themselves from the union.

Attitudes within Maestref Baptist Church towards the union are mixed. On the one hand, BUGB membership is seen to confer a certain mainstream cachet on the congregation. In terms of identity, many members of the congregation are very keen to disassociate themselves from the Baptist Union of Wales, which is seen as 'too Welsh' (and by implication too proletarian) and from independent Baptist churches (and some fellow BUGB churches) which are deemed to be too evangelical. On the other hand, deacons often complain bitterly about the BUGB, which is seen as overly bureaucratic, inefficient, a drain on financial resources and distant from the local experience of the congregation. In the final instance, these tensions have been resolved in favour of the benefits of denominational respectability, although as we shall see below there are many other internal tensions surrounding the question of congregational identity.

ORIGINS AND RECENT HISTORY

The congregation was founded in 1911 by a number of families concerned about the lack of a Baptist witness in the district. In 1913 a schoolroom (which became the church) with provision for 200 worshippers was erected, preparatory to the proposed building of a much larger church building on adjacent land. Financial problems brought on by the Great Depression and the fact that the congregation never grew to a point that warranted a much larger building put paid to those plans and a church hall capable of accommodating 150 persons was built instead. These buildings, which are architecturally unremarkable, are set some way back from the road, which is a very quiet street acting as a one-way feeder on to the main road. A neighbouring primary school tends to obscure the physical presence of the church even further and both the location and the set-back aspect of the buildings have contributed to a relatively low level of visibility in the community.

Always an affluent congregation, it has been in the financial position to employ a succession of ministers during its history and the current minister has served the church since 1994. In terms of identity, the very oldest members characterized the pre-1945 congregation as 'moderately evangelical' but the church now sees itself as being in the mainstream with an open communion table. Prior to 1958 the church had a succession of six ministers and it was unusual to see a pastorate that extended over ten years. This was to change in 1958 when an incoming minister began a ministry that was to last for thirty years. This minister was a North Wallian by birth and had trained for the ministry in Bangor, a university town in north Wales. Liberal in his theological outlook and with a marked antipathy towards evangelicalism, he was a fairly typical product of the ministerial training regimes of the mid-twentieth century. Coming south to answer the post-war call for ministers, he had served two pastorates of five and seven years in the Gwent Valleys before answering the call from Maestref Baptist Church.

It could be said that his pastorate, while long, was largely uneventful. Remembered as a good pastoral visitor, who liked nothing more than to visit his flock and take tea with them, he tended to leave the organizational side of church life in the hands of the deacons, so preaching and pastoral visiting increasingly became his sole province. These developments effectively undermined the traditional role of deacons as ancillary lay ministers and marked their transition to what was essentially a body of administrators. Whereas the traditional criteria for appointment to the diaconate had been based on the spiritual standing of individuals and their ability to preach and lead worship, increasingly appointments were linked to relevant occupational skills in the administrative and financial fields. The legacy of these changes remains with the church today and, as we shall see below, it is very much a live issue with the current minister and some members and deacons. The current climate in the church is one of marked ministerial dependency in spiritual matters and there is a lack of deacons capable of leading worship services or fulfilling pastoral duties in the absence of the minister. Nevertheless, during a period when church finances were stable and when membership was approximately 300 with an all-age congregation, this minister was, in his own words, 'a steady hand on the tiller'.

By the 1980s the church was beginning to lose members and there was a noticeable lack of younger worshippers in the congregation. Some unsuccessful attempts were made to recruit new members over the years, mostly by dint of sporadic campaigns of door-to-door evangelism on the new housing estates, but without much success, and in the face of changing attitudes towards religion and a growing indifference to Christianity. The minister canvassed the new council estate in the 1960s, and local people, if not prepared to attend church themselves, were at least still defining themselves as Christians and were in a few cases prepared to send their children to the Sunday school. By the 1970s, when a new private estate was built nearby, attitudes had hardened, with a distinct lack of interest in and in some cases active hostility towards Christianity. By the 1980s what little recruitment there was appeared to be entirely through newcomers to the area transferring from other churches. On retirement in 1988 he chose to remain a member of the congregation, albeit, in his own words, 'in the background'.

Opinions within the congregation about the legacy of his pastorate are mixed. Generally, he is remembered fondly as a good pastor who served the church faithfully for thirty years. However, there were some critical voices raised about aspects of his ministry, and these critics suggested that the religious life of the congregation stagnated during his pastorate, contributing towards a culture of congregational complacency which is still apparent today. This viewpoint, while plausible, is somewhat simplistic given that there is no evidence of active ministerial neglect on his part. A rather more relevant factor appears to be a post-war sea change in the cultural characteristics of the congregation.

The first generation that founded the church was serious about its religion and memories of this evangelical culture are still present among the very oldest members. However, the generation that followed viewed their church affiliation from a much more routinized perspective. Either brought up as Baptists in the family church or marrying into church families, their Baptist identity tended to be ascriptive, based upon cultural heritage or marriage rather than a conscious religious orientation. The energies that the first generation had directed in establishing a Baptist presence in the district were now largely spent and the energies of the second generation were increasingly directed towards maintaining the church as a socially cohesive unit, primarily through the increased provision of social activities.

In a sense this can be seen as something akin to the internal secularization of the congregation, as purely religious activities became increasingly marginal to the general life of the church. It became in the words of one member, 'a happy place to be', an environment in which secular middle-class values might be accommodated within the framework of a communitarian Baptist identity. In practice, this meant the virtual abandonment of many of the original religious and evangelistic aims of the church founders and an increasing focus on secular associational activities such as concert parties, amateur theatricals and lecture groups. In the light of these changes, the post-war years can be characterized as a move towards the creation of a community and a sense of identity primarily centred around shared leisure interests. Sociologically, these changes might be seen as a functional adaptation to the impersonality of suburban life through the reorientation of congregational goals. As far as any ministerial complicity in these changes is concerned, it might only be said that this minister appeared to be accommodating to this cultural transformation and certainly did not challenge it.

By way of contrast, the pastorate of his immediate successor was of much shorter duration, was highly eventful and ended under very inauspicious circumstances. In every respect, it could not have been further from the congregation's previous ministerial experience. Previously an associate pastor in a Baptist church in England, he was appointed almost immediately after his predecessor's initial announcement of retirement. The extreme haste with which he was called, a failure of the diaconate to research adequately his background in his previous church and the decision not to consider any other candidates, all point to a flawed selection process. Critics within the congregation suggested that the paramount concern of the diaconate at the time was to avoid at all costs a prolonged interregnum, which might have exposed their collective inability to take on the oversight of the spiritual life of the church. Be that as it may, from the outset he appears to have been an inappropriate choice for this conservative suburban congregation.

Young and innovative but also long-haired, frequently dishevelled in appearance, a smoker and a regular frequenter of public houses, he did not exactly conform to most members' previous experience of Baptist ministers. Certainly, none of these qualities endeared him to the more conservative members of the congregation and typical comments from this quarter included 'an unfortunate chapter in the life of the church' and 'a disaster for the church'. However, not all members were as harsh in their assessment of his pastorate, pointing to a number of positive outcomes and lasting legacies, including the creation of a Bible study group and a prayer fellowship. He also made moves in the direction of outreach into the local community, setting up a coffee morning and attempted to introduce a modern worship format into Sunday services. This was the last straw for some traditionalists who, unhappy with his ministerial style, voted with their feet. Unfortunately, this new ministerial style also extended to a hands-on approach to all aspects of church life, including, controversially, the church finances. A saga of financial mismanagement steadily unfolded, with mounting unpaid church debts and the utilization (and eventually the serious depletion) of the church's capital assets for the day-to-day running of the church. In 1993 it was discovered by some deacons that he also had a number of serious personal debts, some from his previous pastorate, and when the extent of the financial mismanagement and capital losses became known to members, he was relieved of his ministerial position by the diaconate.

The outcome of this unhappy saga was an interregnum, where the previous minister returned as moderator taking over pastoral and some preaching duties. Due to the reluctance (or inability) of deacons to lead services, lay preachers from local churches also helped out during this period of change. His successor, the present minister, called in 1994, was chosen with rather more care. Understandably, the main criteria for his selection appear to have been personal respectability and probity and theological moderation. The former was assured in the minds of the congregation by his family lineage, which is one of the most prominent in the Baptist movement. The latter by his training at the Baptist College in Bristol, an establishment not noted for theological extremes.

In his early thirties and in his own words 'a moderate evangelical', he is married with one child and this is his first pastorate. On taking up this position, he did not, in his own words, find the spiritual life of the congregation 'particularly healthy' and his ministry has since focused on trying to introduce a cautious programme of change to redress this situation. There have been some successes in tackling the problem of numerical decline. A few previously disaffected members have returned and there has been a very small influx of transfers and new recruits, most of whom cited the presence of this new minister as their main reason for joining. While this influx has slowed decline, deaths in the congregation and young people moving away to higher education have contributed to a net loss of worshippers. Despite these continuing losses, in terms of the potential to recruit new worshippers, the arrival of this small group of newcomers offers some hope for the future, and all things being equal, the future of the church appears to remain open. However, as we shall see below, all things in this congregation are not equal.

The limited sketch drawn so far appears to be that of a conservative congregation unhappy with the idea of innovation. While this is true of many in the congregation, it is not true of all, particularly a very small minority of members who welcome the prospect of change. Understandably, this has led to a certain amount of factionalism, dissent and a lively internal politics, played out both within the diaconate and among the congregation. In many ways, this desire for a new direction in the life of the church and resistance to this project mirrors issues that confront the wider community of Welsh churches. For some members of this church, the crucial issue is creating a church that can face the realities of operating in a post-Christian society. For others, the paramount question is how far they can continue to maintain a familiar church culture in the face of widespread and deep changes within Welsh society. The authors of the 1995 Welsh Churches Survey suggest that one of the central questions facing all churches in Wales is this question of cultural relevance and the need for cultural change:

> The central issue is one of cultural relevance and the cost is our church subculture rather than our theology. Church culture, like any other culture, is invisible, in that we participate in it rather than observe it. We enjoy it without being aware of it. Only when it is removed or threatened is our dependence and fondness for it revealed. But our culture is only a vehicle for our spirituality, not its origin. Church cultures come and go, none are prescriptive, none are normative and none are sacrosanct. All give way after they have had their time. The only question is when. (Bible Society, 1997: 48)

While what follows below does not produce any clear answers or prescriptions to these pressing questions at the macro-level, it does illustrate many of the dilemmas and problems associated with attempting to initiate changes, or even the recognition that change is necessary, at the level of the congregation.

THE CONGREGATION

The members of the congregation are overwhelmingly local, most living no more than ten minutes walk away from the church and are exclusively drawn from the middle classes. As noted earlier the average age of the congregation is approximately 64 and there are many female members over the age of 70, the oldest being 96. Males are under-represented within the congregation (the ratio of females to males being 8:3) and the typical male worshipper is in his late sixties or early seventies. There is a Sunday school with twenty-five pupils (mostly girls of primary school age), but a visible lack of worshippers in the 18–44 years age group. Increasingly, many of the very oldest members cannot attend services with any regularity because of ill health and infirmity and the average congregation on any Sunday is heavily weighted with those in the 55–75 years age group.

Many long-term members have strong family connections with the church and typically describe themselves either as having been in the church all their lives or having married someone with these prior family connections. In many cases their parents or grandparents were founder members of the congregation and had held church office at some time. The present congregation, with a few exceptions, has little or no experience of, and little apparent interest in, church life outside of their congregation, other than gossip from the city's Baptist churches. Many members are very conservative in their general social attitudes and have proved resistant to change within their own church life. Indeed, as we shall see below, having no real point of comparison with other churches, many in the congregation are reluctant to recognize the need for change. However, while the majority might conform to this picture, there is also a small but growing minority grouping of individuals who have drifted into the church over the years who do not conform to this profile. More mobile than the average member and all having experience of other churches, most are more interested in religious matters than the typical members and all are open to the idea of change.

In contrast, in an area of higher than average geographic mobility where people move in and out with some frequency, the majority of the congregation are highly sedentary. Most have never left the area to live elsewhere and have no desire to live anywhere else. Indeed, the locality conforms in many ways to the suburban idyll. Members described it variously as 'a quiet area' where 'people keep themselves to themselves', with a low crime rate and 'decent neighbours', and they are proud of the fact that they are long-established residents with a distinct identity. Individuals tend to define themselves in opposition to their more mobile neighbours (described by one member as 'here today, gone tomorrow people') but there is little sense of a general community spirit. Any affinity with other long-term residents appears to be largely restricted to kin, immediate neighbours or those who attend the local churches and even here, with the exception of kin, social relations are highly attenuated. Close friends are most likely to be found within the congregation and members cannot be described as being embedded in the local community in the ways that we saw in the previous chapter.

The lack of meaningful contact with the surrounding local population and the modest nature of the church architecture is reflected in the fact that there is little community use of the church for weddings and funerals, with residents preferring to use the local Anglican church for these events. The neighbouring primary school (of which the present minister is a governor) holds its carol service in the church and this brings in the parents of the children once a year. While there is also a Young People's Fellowship, this is small, numbering seven individuals, and caters exclusively for the children of members. Occasional concert productions and the annual Christmas Fayre are popular with those older residents who attend local churches. In contrast, the annual Summer Fayre attracts only members of the congregation. Again, the weekly coffee morning is mainly the province of members, although a small group of local childminders is sometimes present. An annual 'holiday club' (recently established at the instigation of the minister) has had some success with local families, despite an almost total lack of advertisement on the part of the church. Conversely, the Sunday school mainly (but not exclusively) caters for children with family connections to the church. These activities and the presence of a Brownie pack appear to be the extent of local community involvement in the life of the church. While other local churches have mother and toddler groups and playgroups (and despite the success of the holiday club), these are absent in this church.

Social life within the church is seen as very important and this highlights the lack of strong intersecting social networks outside the church, even among long-term established residents. In a sense this is a double bind because church members primarily identify long-term membership of the community with long-term membership of the church. Literally, for most members long-standing friendships and relations began in Sunday school, and the church and these friendships have become synonymous with each other. If the local community is considered at all it is seen in terms of 'the other'. The majority of the congregation has little or nothing to do with the surrounding mobile population because they are mobile and little or nothing to do with other long-term residents because they are not church members. Effectively, the congregation exists as a community both in itself and for itself and over the years it has successfully managed to both isolate itself from the local community, consigning itself to something that looks very much like social invisibility.

A CHALLENGE TO CHANGE?

At a meeting of the Baptist Area Association of Ministers held in Swansea in June 1996, the president of the Bible Society in Wales remarked that 'the agenda for congregational policy is being set by the over 65s'. He was commenting on the initial findings of the 1995 Welsh Churches Survey and a related observation from that report suggests that:

> The simplest explanation of the current picture is that we see the church growing older with the people it gained several decades ago. It is a common observation that many churches simply continue to do what they have always done. Admirable as such faithfulness may be, it is not a recipe for growth into the next

generation. The only alternatives for growth into new generations appear to be either continual change within existing congregations or the continual planting of new congregations. For many denominations in Wales neither process has operated to any extent for some period of time. (Bible Society, 1997: 17)

In many ways and despite its origins, the congregation of Maestref Baptist Church can be said to reflect this picture. As one church officer observed: 'They don't want to be challenged, that's what they're used to you see . . . it's safe, it's cosy, they haven't got to think about it. They're just drifting along, drifting along the stream.' This sense of drift and the congregational attachment to traditional activities and ways of doing things is hardly a recipe for meaningful outreach into the local community or even the internal retention and reproduction of the next generation within the church. Nevertheless, as the above comment implicitly suggests, there are some within the congregation who are aware of the need to change in order to survive. These differing orientations are exemplified in the internal dynamics of the church and are mirrored in the various formal activities and informal groupings which, as we shall see below, are in some tension with each other.

There are three distinct informal groups within the congregation and these can be distinguished both by the length of time that they have been in the church and by their interests and the activities they engage in. Long-term members dominate numerically and while they share many of the common congregational characteristics outlined above (notably a strong identification with the church and its history) attitudes towards religiosity differ by generation. The very elderly constitute a distinct social network within the church and have a strong religious sensibility, something that distinguishes them from the post-war generation of long-term members. In contrast, that post-war generation tends to emphasize the social function of the church and are highly ambivalent towards any public demonstration of religious enthusiasm, which they characterize as 'show'. Conversely, over the years there has also been a trickle of newcomers into the church, most of whom also have a strong religious sensibility, something that has not always been looked on favourably by other members.

This lack of a culture of overt religiosity is interesting, not least because it is untypical of the Baptist movement generally and particularly so in Wales. Most Baptist churches in Swansea are to varying degrees evangelical in character and many long-term members regard these congregations with some suspicion. In contrast, these same members spoke warmly of the two Baptist congregations in the city that most approximated their own church culture in terms of class composition, mainstream identity and general antipathy towards evangelicalism. This antipathy appeared to be less a matter of theology (a study of which many long-term members appear largely ignorant) and more a matter of perceptions of class. Many members were genuinely perplexed by the success of a neighbouring evangelical church that is both very middle-class in composition and very lively in its worship. The fact that respectable middle-class people might be attracted in significant numbers to join this type of church was a mystery to many members. On the other hand, they had very clear ideas about the appropriate model for their church.

For the majority, decorum and sobriety are the characteristics that they look for in both their minister and in the public life of the church. Above all, worship services should be low key and dignified with an emphasis on continuity of practice. That is the ideal but, despite the best efforts of the present minister, the reality is somewhat different. Congregational singing, unusually for a Welsh church, is perfunctory and poor and the fidgeting of many members during the sermon suggests that they see it as something to be endured rather than enjoyed. The congregation appears most animated immediately before and after the service, while the actual act of worship appears to be almost an afterthought for many. In effect, Sunday services have become a ritual of habit, something their parents did and which they carry on to the best of their abilities. Validated as it is by past practice rather than present enthusiasm, it has become of vital importance to many in the congregation that the format of the worship service remains unchanged.

How far they have moved from the evangelical ideals and practices of the founding generation (and Baptist norms elsewhere) is best exemplified by the almost complete absence of scriptural knowledge and the lack of even a basic understanding of Christian doctrine among many members. Only a handful of elderly women and a few new members appear to have any understanding of the basic elements of the Christian faith, while the remaining members (and some deacons) are not only quite open about their lack of knowledge but quite unconcerned about it too. It would appear that, while the external forms of Baptist organization remain in place, the core of belief and practice has become progressively devalued and puerilized as belonging has superseded believing.

This is best exemplified by the ways in which many members chose to describe their church in purely social terms. Members talked of a 'warm and welcoming church', with 'a warm and friendly congregation', and these appear to be the prime validations for congregational life in the minds of many. However, some members (mostly newcomers but not exclusively so) questioned the nature of this warmth and whether it really did extend to visiting strangers. Many commented that the church appeared to be little more than a social club for the benefit of its members. While this is something of an over-simplification, the church does have a lively internal social life centred on two organizations, the Men's Contact Club and the Ladies

Guild, that would appear to confirm this observation. Certainly, in the course of many conversations with members they only appeared truly animated when discussing these social activities.

The Men's Contact Club (MCC) was founded in the 1950s after a male member came across a similar group operating in a Bristol Baptist church. Purely secular in orientation, it is basically a lecture group reliant on guest speakers, although in recent years these have become harder to find and members of the MCC have increasingly had to deputize instead. The subject matter for these lectures is wide-ranging, the only constant being that there is never any discussion of religion. It is a rapidly ageing group of thirty, none under the age of 65 and the oldest member is 90. It draws its membership from both active church members and those on the periphery of the congregation, mainly husbands of members and men with long-standing family links to the church.

Actual numbers attending meetings are usually no more than fifteen persons, reflecting the increasing age and infirmity of members, and the format of meetings is that of a short talk followed by tea and biscuits and much energetic socializing. This weekly opportunity to get together is clearly the highlight of the week for many of these men and the group has great social importance for them. It also acts as a focus for resistance to change, reflecting the innate social conservatism (and age) of many of its members. Deacons who are also MCC officers unashamedly use their position on the diaconate to protect the position and privileges of the MCC and any attempt at interference in their activities is sharply dealt with. This has at times created friction within the congregation and many female members are critical of the group and what they see as its excessive control over the life of the church. Despite the fact that the MCC is to all intents and purposes an ancillary group on the periphery of the church, its power base within the diaconate means that it can at times exert a power on the life of the church out of all proportion to its numbers. The situation is further compounded by the fact that the church's fabric committee (responsible for maintenance of the buildings and grounds) is exclusively drawn from those members of the MCC who are also deacons. This gives them a great deal of say in setting the agenda for building use and, thus, in protecting their interests and (when it suits them) the interests of the Ladies Guild. Understandably, for those members outside of these groups, it appears that the agendas of these social clubs within the church have become the prime agendas of the church itself, something that they see as producing an unhealthy conflict of loyalties within the diaconate.

The Ladies Guild (LG) is in effect the mirror image of the MCC. Numbering fifty plus members, it is the most prominent grouping within the church and it continues to grow numerically, reflecting the popularity of its activities among the female members of the congregation. (Unusually, for groups in this church, it has managed to attract a few local women who are not church members or attenders.) The group meets weekly and meetings vary between a format with a guest speaker followed by tea and cakes, musical evenings or the occasional trip to a place of interest. Speakers are limited to approximately once a month, with the minister occasionally speaking on a religious theme. The bulk of the group's activities revolves around singing and they mount three or four secular musical productions a year, with the financial proceeds going to church funds or charities. Members were keen to stress that these concerts were the one church activity that actually raised the visibility of the church in the district. (Although it must be said that the audiences for these productions were drawn almost exclusively from within the congregation and a handful of women from the local churches.) This concert schedule means that the group is effectively in rehearsal for most of the year, and the opportunity to adopt a theatrical persona appears to be something that allows the participants to momentarily escape from the humdrum routine of local suburban living. All the participants stressed how important this group was to them in social terms and indeed, for many, this appeared to be almost the sum of their social life.

Despite the popularity of this group and its activities, it has signally failed to attract into its membership the few younger female members in the congregation. The reasons for this are twofold. First, this is primarily a cultural matter, in that the activities of this group are exclusively centred on activities designed to appeal to older women. Simply, the very few younger members view these activities as culturally irrelevant to anyone of their generation. Secondly, younger women, with a few isolated exceptions (all newcomers), inhabit the periphery of church life. Despite their long-standing family connections, they are infrequent worshippers. Often married to partners who have no pre-existing links with any religious organization and often in full-time employment themselves with little free time, their relationship to the church is at best attenuated. Nevertheless, they continue in identification with the church and it may be that, as they grow older, the activities of the LG may prove a more attractive proposition. However, despite the presence of these women on the periphery, they are very few in number. Many members of the LG told me that their adult children now had nothing whatsoever to do with the church, even when they remained resident in the locality, and there was a general recognition that this raised uncomfortable questions about the future health of this group.

Internal criticism of the LG is far more muted compared to that directed at the MCC. While the minister wishes that the amount of energy that the women put into their musical activities could be directed towards more overtly 'religious' goals, he recognized that 'it was probably the Ladies

Guild that held this church together during its difficulties'. While some newcomers to the congregation have also questioned what they see as this misdirection of energies, this has not stopped many of them from joining this group. While they tended to rationalize their membership in 'religious' terms, emphasizing the charitable nature of much of the group's activities, it was also clear that they saw the social side as a very attractive feature of church life. Indeed, the strong sense of social solidarity engendered in this group and the recognition that this was an important area of church life that had not been colonized by men was universally recognized by female members of the congregation. In contrast, attitudes towards the dominant position of men were largely negative but also highly ambivalent. On the one hand, men were seen as getting far too much of their own way in terms of church policies, particularly so where the activities of the MCC were concerned. On the other hand, it was clearly perceived that if there was any loss of the MCC's privileges this might also entail a loss of LG privileges. Therefore, the MCC was seen as a natural ally in protecting group interests and these two groups constitute a powerful force in the internal policy-making of the church.

These two groups are also astute enough to realize that, despite internal criticisms, the most popular and successful activities in the church are not those of an overtly religious nature. They justified this emphasis on social activities on three counts. First, given the extensive membership of these two groups, it was obviously meeting an internal demand for overtly social activities. Secondly, there were alternative mid-week activities for the more religiously minded. Thirdly, those most actively committed to these groups were also the more actively committed elsewhere in the life of the church. This latter point had considerable foundation, whether one looks at the diaconate, church cleaning and maintenance, running the kitchen in the church hall or organizing and staffing the various events such as the Summer Fayre, church picnic, etc., that are annual features of the church's calendar. Understandably, this has meant that the minister, whatever his perceptions of these groups and their activities, has had to proceed cautiously in order to avoid alienating their personnel.

The Young People's Fellowship, described by the minister as 'basically going nowhere', is essentially a chaotic replication of the activities of their parents. Numbering only seven teenagers, there has been no attempt to develop this group into an inclusive youth club that might draw in outsiders. It is overseen by the minister (primarily because he is the only young man within the congregation) who commented: 'It keeps them off the streets and they are a close bunch of kids, so I suppose you can say it establishes some sort of group solidarity. It probably keeps them in the church too, if only out of habit.' The minister thinks that, if they stay together as a group into adulthood, it is likely that they will continue attending the church. On the other hand, they are as likely to move away for educational or occupational reasons. Significantly, there was nothing to suggest any level of religiosity in this group, however faint, and it would appear that they are the culmination of post-war trends in the internal culture of the church.

In contrast, the constituency of very elderly women among the congregation demonstrated a far more overt religiosity and this group provides some continuity with the past history and previously evangelical principles of the church. The natural home for these older members is the Sisterhood, a group with an average attendance of seventeen women that meets weekly for the singing of Sankey hymns and to hear an uplifting religious message. There is little doubt that these women are very ambivalent about the activities of the social clubs, viewing them as a diminishment of the church's original religious ethos. Indeed, Sisterhood members had successfully rejected efforts by the previous minister to dilute the religious content of their meetings and to make it more 'social' in character.

They tend to socialize exclusively with others in this group, which constitutes an identifiably separate social network in which the weekly Sisterhood meeting and home visits from the minister and other members of the Sisterhood are a key mechanism in the transmission of information. Despite this social marginality, they are very aware of the problems facing the church (more so than many deacons) and had an intelligent grasp of the specific areas in which the church was failing and a strong desire to see the church continue in the future. However, by reason of age and infirmity and lacking any representation within the diaconate, they are not in a position to influence policy within the church or indeed to contribute much at all to the general life of the congregation. (They are, though, regarded with affection by all members.)

Interestingly, and despite its evangelical leanings, the Sisterhood has little or no personal contact with the more religiously orientated members of either the Bible Study group or the Prayer Fellowship. Despite their implicit support for any activity that might raise the level of spiritual consciousness within the congregation, members of the Sisterhood do not attend these meetings and the reasons for this are unclear. However, given the fact that these meetings are relatively new innovations and are not patronized by the majority of the congregation, it may be that they see these groups as the natural province of younger newcomers. While this may be a reflection of age differences, the more likely explanation lies in the 'outsider' status of most members of those groups. Relations among the Sisterhood are close but very formal and I was told that it might take twenty years or more before an individual would be accepted enough to be addressed by their first name. Clearly, social acceptance is only grudgingly advanced and is a process that takes much time.

Membership of the Bible Study group and the Prayer Fellowship is inter-changeable and constitutes a very small grouping within the congregation, with numbers attending rarely exceeding twelve persons and the minister. The membership of these groups is predominantly female (with one male attending) and members (with the exception of one new recruit) are all transfers from other congregations. It has something of a siege mentality, not least because members of this group are aware that these overtly religious activities are viewed with some ambivalence by those in the congregation who view any overt demonstration of religious enthusiasm as highly unusual behaviour. Naturally, the minister sees these members as valuable allies and the potential nucleus of any project of spiritual renewal within the congregation. With this in mind, he has managed to manœuvre three of these individuals (one formerly a deacon elsewhere) on to the diaconate. However, other deacons are conspicuous by their absence at these meetings, reflecting their personal indifference to such activities. While some members of this group have evangelical sympathies this is by no means true of all and what unites this disparate group of individuals is the shared conviction that activities such as Bible study and organized prayer should be central to congregational life. Despite this conviction, these members intimated that, in the general life of the church, they had to hold their cards pretty close to their chest as far as any expressions of overt religiosity were concerned. In contrast, these meetings appeared to be a discreet forum for individuals to discuss religious matters openly and express their religiosity in overt public forms, albeit within an intimate group. Furthermore, the 'official' status of these activities and the presence of the minister at these meetings afforded some degree of legitimization in the eyes of other members.

Attitudes within this small group to the other members were mixed but the absence from these activities of so many (and named deacons in particular) was seen as a general indicator of the low levels of spirituality within the congregation. In the same vein, unfavourable comparisons were often made between thriving local evangelical churches that were experiencing growth (and where it was assumed that activities such as Bible study and prayer meetings would be the norm) and their own (to them) apparently moribund church. Indeed, by adopting this alternative frame of reference, these particu-lar members were able both to counteract their sense of marginality within their own congregation and affirm what to them was their own crucial con-tribution to the life of the church. Moreover, the experience of these outside groups also constituted a sign of hope (however faint) that if they remained faithful in these activities within their own congregation others might follow, bringing the possibility of renewal and growth nearer. Be that as it may, the presence of these subgroups both provides natural allies for the minister in his vision for renewal and alleviates some of the tensions that have grown within the congregation in recent years. However, any vision of congregational renewal is in the final instance dependent on both the goodwill of the majority of the congregation and a willingness to change – two attributes that have been in short supply in recent decades.

RESISTANCE TO CHANGE

Change requires the setting of goals and planning requires leadership. Conversely, resistance to change also requires leadership. Within the context of this congregation, the power to effect or resist change lies within the sets of relations that inform the leadership structure and, in turn, their relations with the congregation. As noted above, the form of church polity favoured by Baptists entails a leadership structure that includes both minister and deacons and a distribution of powers, and where these are in tension, also informal parties. This section will explore some of these relations and issues, from the perspectives of the minister and the members.

Opinions among the members about their new minister are mixed and reflect a number of tensions present within the congregation. In the time he has been with the church he has gained both the respect and the affection of the majority of the congregation, although opinions vary among members as to his strengths and weaknesses. Baptist churches are generally renowned for the quality of their preaching and understandably this is a central concern for some members. His preaching was characterized by some as lacking *hwyl* (an emotional and powerful sermon style that is distinctly Welsh). Others found the content of his preaching 'too deep', while some saw this as a strong point. His personal manner is seen as reserved and yet many cited his excellent communication skills, particularly in pastoral situations. Some members have taken his quiet and even diffident manner as an indication of weakness, others commented upon his inner strength and even stubbornness. Some see him as too diplomatic and accommodating towards the diaconate while others see him as bent on collision with them. Despite this contradictory picture, none of these assessments can be said to be untrue. His natural reserve is a reflection of a very private person and it is unsurprising that the majority of the congregation who only see him on Sundays should know little about him. More importantly, these opinions reflect deeper currents within the life of the church and differences of opinion about which direction the church should be taking for the future. There is also a growing general appreciation among members of his pastoral skills and the hard work and long hours that he puts in and this has been translated into a desire to see the church flourish again for his sake.

The minister himself has a number of concerns about the probable future of the church. The congregation is ageing rapidly, with most now on retirement-level incomes, and this has financial implications for the present and the future. At the moment the congregation is barely able to meet his stipend and the diaconate has not fully grasped the future implications of this. In part, he sees this lack of forward thinking by the deacons as an endemic part of a church culture characterized by a thirty-year legacy of complacency. He is aware through his contacts with local ministers that many other congregations in the area are thriving while his congregation is declining:

> I don't know what the secret is. I'm always baffled by the fact that the church is still going and I'm not sure what has sustained us. I think there is a very strong loyalty to the church without it meaning that you've got that faith and it's church as a social institution with whatever extras that brings you, the circle of friends you know, the things that our lot get up to. We've got a ladies group who do productions three or four times a year, concerts. So they're meeting a social need and I'm sure that is one of the things that has kept us going. But as a spiritual reality, I'm not sure that there's a great deal to it, you know *faith*. I mean, I talk about faith to them now and they look at me as if I'm coming from another planet. You know *discipleship*. We've [just] done a series on discipleship. It was met with *utter* blankness as a response. (Emphases in the original transcript.)

These ministerial frustrations are compounded by the lukewarm responses of some deacons to any changes designed to raise the spiritual life of the congregation or to address the question of numerical decline:

> I can identify who the most resistant deacons are and as a result have to very careful in the way we handle it. I think they are aware, I think it does concern them but it probably concerns them more that they would have to actually *change* to address the problem and turn it around. At the moment, the complacency thing, I think at the moment there is still a lot of that complacency. Financially we are struggling and the difficulty is that there is a little bit of capital resource and it could easily be used to sustain a minister for years still. I think come that point [when the money runs out] some of the deacons feel 'Well it won't be my concern because I'll be ninety by then'. There's a short-termism there. I think at the moment we're losing by deaths and we're not replacing them and there will come a time when full-time ministry cannot be supported. I can't help feeling that we're near that point and once the minister's gone I think that decline sets in very quickly. But I haven't reached the point of the answers because really, there's nobody else who is asking the questions with me. I mean, I came here aware of some of the problems and I also came here aware that there is time and potential if together we can fundamentally recognize

our place before God and say 'what would you have us do with all that you have given us'. I haven't seen much progress down that road since I've got here. It's not for me to just live in hope. It's got to be a shared thing. (Emphasis in the original transcript.)

These frustrations mainly centre on the longer established deacons. On the one hand, they want to see him expand the scope of his pastoral ministry, but are unwilling to shoulder some of his other responsibilities in order to free up his time for more visiting. On the other hand, they are unwilling to shoulder some of the burden of visiting themselves, with requests in this direction meeting point-blank refusals. These problems are compounded by a marked lack of urgency on the part of older deacons when faced with any decision-making processes. The minister has tried to set up dedicated training days for deacons and a Baptist Union training package has been disseminated among them. However, there is a marked lack of enthusiasm for these initiatives among the long-established members of the diaconate and, in the minister's own words, he 'is concerned about where their ultimate loyalties lie'. The minister views these older deacons, particularly the males, as both highly resistant to change and also lacking in the basic qualities and level of enthusiasm commensurate with the office and duties of deacon. With this problem in mind and, as noted above, a handful of new deacons have recently been appointed from among those members who are relative newcomers to the church. In contrast to their longer established counterparts they are both conscientious in their duties and enthusiastic in their support for the minister and his vision for the church. However, their fellows see them as very junior members of the diaconate, and it is the older deacons who continue to dominate the government of the church.

There are twelve deacons, five men and seven women, and it is the men who tend to dominate discussion within meetings. Four long-serving deacons with forceful personalities dominate the diaconate and newcomers have described this situation as, variously, an 'inner circle' and 'leading lights with too much revolving around them'. One commented, 'it's wheels within wheels, with a couple of them, they've served so long they don't think anyone else can do it'. While there is no formal distinction between long-serving and new deacons, the latter feel somewhat marginalized, not least because of this lack of transparency in the diaconate's workings. Often they do not get to hear of business matters until after they have been dealt with by this inner circle and they do not always understand what is going on in meetings due to these behind the scenes machinations. Indeed, criticism of these individuals appeared near universal within the church and came from all quarters – the minister, long-term members and newcomers.

A certain level of criticism is to be expected of those who manage affairs and conflicts of personality, ingrained attitudes and internal politicking are staples of any set of social relations. However, the level of complaints, the consistency of criticisms and the fact that critics were drawn from all sections of the congregation suggests that there were deep underlying problems that were detrimental to both the present life and future prospects of the church. While some distinction was made between new deacons and those older deacons who were seen as most resistant to change, congregational concerns were summed up in a number of key phrases, as the diaconate was described as 'died in the wool', 'stick in the mud' and 'secretive'. Female members were also particularly critical of the gender ratio of male to female deacons, arguing that this did not accurately reflect the wider congregational profile.

Nearly everyone mentioned the financial position of the church and what appeared to be a failure on the part of the diaconate to recognize that this was reaching crisis point. One newly elected deacon commented: 'They [the diaconate] are not concerned with finances or getting new people in. You think that they would realize that the only way we are going to be able to improve finances is by getting new people in, younger people who are earning.' Other members had suggested a number of potential fundraising activities, including the possibility of hiring out the hall to outside organizations and raising money through jumble sales, but deacons had refused point blank to countenance changes in this direction. (The general mindset of these deacons might be summed up by the comments of one individual who suggested that 'jumble sales might attract undesirables and gypsies'.) Indeed, older deacons appeared reluctant to recognize that there was anything untoward in the financial life of the church. While there might have been a few problems with the previous incumbent, as far as they were concerned this chapter had been closed. In contrast, new deacons pointed to the diaconate's aversion to any forward planning and their refusal to reorganize church finances in an ordered way, a failing that they felt was at the heart of the church's problems.

As we have seen, another major sticking point was the presence of a number of long-standing groups from within the congregation that used the church buildings for mid-week activities. The fact that older deacons were also intimately involved both as members and organizers of these groups had in the opinion of some members resulted in the well-being of these groups being conflated with the overall well-being of the church. Deacons were accused of 'setting their own agendas', the implication being that a large part of their energies was directed towards blocking any initiatives or innovations that might affect the prestige and power of long-standing groups. It appeared to many that the needs of these organizations were routinely given priority over other activities in the church and this did seem to be borne out in practice.

For example, the privileges of the Men's Contact Club and the Ladies Guild are jealously guarded and any attempts to increase the use of the church hall have been blocked even to the extent of 'keeping nights free just in case they need to use the hall'. More worryingly for the minister and many members, when plans were made for a special mid-week service to celebrate Holy Week, deacons refused to cancel a meeting of the Men's Contact Club which was scheduled for the same night in the same building. Understandably, the fact that the deacons were happy to privilege a slide show of the holiday snaps of one of the deacons over a service commemorating the holiest week of the year was seen by some members as disturbing evidence of how far the church had drifted away from its original vision. Other members pointed to the fact that the meetings of the Ladies Guild and the Bible Study group were held at the same time on the same night. One member who suggested that 'the deacons seem to want to run the church as a little social club for the benefit of the congregation' aptly summed up these critical sentiments. Certainly, there seemed to be little or no attempt on the part of deacons to make contact with the local unchurched population or to initiate any activities designed to bring newcomers in.

As noted above, the absence of these same deacons from the Bible study and prayer fellowship was a bone of contention with members of these groups. One person, commenting on the low turnout for these activities said 'How can you expect others to come if even the deacons can't be bothered to attend?' Members who had at some time had personal experience of other Baptist congregations were particularly critical of the prevailing ethos of the diaconate. They saw little sign among the established deacons of deep religious commitment, citing this as the main reason why they 'lacked vision' and appeared unconcerned about the future well-being of the church. These same deacons were also seen as conservative, resistant to change and ignorant of even the most basic duties attached to the role of deacon. Unfavourable comparisons were also made with those deacons of other local churches who had stepped in to help during the last interregnum and 'who could preach a sermon as well as a minister'.

Even those long-term members who were uninterested in these matters were highly vocal about what they saw as the secretive way in which the diaconate went about its business and its reluctance to communicate with the general congregation. Many members commented unfavourably about the diaconate's role in the events that led to termination of the previous minister's contract and the secrecy surrounding the whole episode. Members talked of 'being kept in the dark for a long time' over the financial mismanagement and one member succinctly summed up these sentiments:

We [the congregation] were the last to know. They only held a meeting when it was obvious that they couldn't keep a lid on it anymore. They had known about this for months but they didn't tell us until they had already decided he had to go. There was no consultation. It was just that *they* had decided. They only tell us things when they are absolutely necessary and even then they only tell us as much as *they* think we need to know. (Emphases in the original transcript.)

While these criticisms probably overstate the level of intentionality in the diaconate's deliberations, they nevertheless point to an internal culture of caution and conservatism. Furthermore, in talking to senior deacons it was clear that they at least felt that they had a fund of experience and level of expertise in running the church that should be deferred to by others. Again, although it was nowhere made explicit, there was also a sense that newer deacons were not expected to contribute much to policy decisions. These were traditionally the provinces of long-serving deacons and the minister and the newer deacons themselves recognized that they had been appointed largely, in the words of one, 'to do the donkey work'.

In terms of the management of internal politics, while the minister sees these new deacons as allies, he is concerned not to alienate the long-serving deacons, not least because this group is where the real power in the church resides. This necessitates a cautious approach, not least because there is a real danger that if he does not tread softly, individual egos may be hurt and some very active members of the congregation may vote with their feet. This creates very real difficulties for him, because in the past, where he has lost arguments in meetings of the diaconate, he has not been able to appeal directly to the congregation. For example, while the annual general meeting of the church offers an open forum for discussion of issues, it is not seen as appropriate for the minister and deacons to be seen to be publicly at odds with each other over policy matters. For the sake of appearances, then, a façade of unity must be maintained in front of the congregation. In practice, this favours the most conservative elements of the diaconate and it is here that the real balance of power resides.

INVISIBILITY

Compared to many congregations in Wales this particular church may appear to be relatively healthy both in terms of numbers (which are still in three figures) and its continued ability to maintain a full-time minister. However, this is more indicative of its history than its current health and if this church was a human patient one could characterize its state of health as a cause for concern. Like many churches in Wales it has experienced a constant trajectory of numerical decline throughout the past three decades. This decline has been fuelled by a number of factors.

Like many congregations in Wales there is a significant over-representation of older people and a marked under-representation of younger people. Factors that have contributed to this situation include the movement out of the district of the children of members, the failure to retain those who stay in the district and the failure to recruit new members locally in sufficient numbers to offset losses. This is not a recipe for growth and decline begins to be fuelled by the cumulative effects of deaths within an ageing congregation. Within the national context, and as the authors of the 1995 Welsh Churches Survey suggest, 'In the normal course of events, where this issue is not addressed, the eventual demise of the congregations concerned is unavoidable' (Bible Society, 1997: 48).

Given the evidence from elsewhere in Wales, Maestref Baptist Church is not unusual in experiencing the effects of the first two phenomena, as all churches are subject to some extent to the vagaries of mortality and the effects of a mobile society. However, other congregations in the district appear to have been able to offset what we might term this natural loss through the retention and recruitment of younger worshippers in sufficient numbers. While there has been some very limited recruitment in the case of this church it has not been in sufficient numbers to guarantee the future health of the congregation. More seriously, and despite visible successes in the past with retention, it now appears unable to retain the children of existing members, even when they remain in the district.

Part of this failure can be explained in terms of external circumstances. When the congregation was originally founded in 1913 it was because of the felt need for a Baptist presence in the locality, not least because there were no Baptist churches within easy walking distance. Now car ownership is widespread, there are five Baptist congregations all within less than fifteen minutes driving distance. In effect, Maestref Baptist Church has lost its local monopoly and is in competition with these other congregations. In many cases these competing congregations can offer aspects of corporate worship – all-age congregations, modern forms of liturgy, traditional evangelical preaching – that Maestref cannot compete with. Furthermore, Baptists in Swansea appear to have moved away from a communitarian model, where local people worshipped in their local church, to something akin to 'niche marketing' and 'the circulation of saints'. What we now see is the exercise of choice and some congregations reacting to this by offering different packages, often aimed at specific age and class groups and theological dispositions, and accordingly attracting worshippers from a wide geographical area. In contrast, Maestref Baptist Church appears to have been left behind in these developments and is still firmly based on a localized communitarian model.

This failure to adapt to a transformed religious marketplace is exacerbated by the atomized nature of the surrounding community and a lack of established social networks that might connect the church with its surrounding population. The actual location of the church, hidden away in a side street, does not help to raise its visibility and it is likely that many of the surrounding community are either unaware or only dimly aware of the presence of this church. These problems are not, in theory, insurmountable. In a locality where there is a distinct lack of community sentiment, and a significant number of individuals have moved into the area for retirement purposes, there are potential opportunities for recruitment. Furthermore, as Jenkins (1999: 131) suggests, it may be possible to identify a generational cycle where people are more likely to take up churchgoing in later life. Certainly, in the case of this congregation, which is largely made up of retired persons and which offers many associational activities with a proven attraction for older people, in principle there is much to attract the older worshipper. While there have been isolated successes in recruiting worshippers from this age group, this has not happened to the extent that it might have done, suggesting that Jenkins's thesis is not easily applicable to atomized middle-class communities. In terms of recruiting younger members, these successes have been even more limited. To answer why this is so we need to examine those cultural factors that may be inhibiting recruitment and retention.

'Invisibility' is not merely the effect of the physical location of buildings. Throughout its history the congregation has maintained a low profile in the community. Initially, the pre-war identity of the congregation, with a moral universe that encompassed total abstention from tobacco and alcohol, high levels of both formal and informal social control and a world-view that advocated separation from the world, would have been offputting to many individuals who did not share these sentiments. These same cultural traits would also have insulated the congregation from outside frames of reference as well as the local unchurched community. While these conditions were conducive to the retention of members' children, ensuring the continued post-war internal reproduction of the congregation, they were not conducive to recruitment from the surrounding 'catchment' community. The post-war years might be characterized as a period when the congregation underwent a progressive process of 'internal secularization'. This transformation of the internal culture, whereby a distinctly religious normative structure was progressively replaced by a focus on secular social activities, should, in theory, have lessened the cultural distance between the congregation and local people. However, what limited recruitment there was came primarily from individuals marrying existing church members and, invariably, these individuals were already members of other local churches. In terms of genuinely opening up the church to local people, the post-war years must be judged a failure.

These social activities, largely orientated as they were to the needs and desires of the congregation, and coupled with no real attempt to promote these activities to outsiders, have done little to allay the impression of this being a closed church community. Furthermore, there is little to distinguish much of this activity from secular recreational activities going on elsewhere, which begs the question, if there is little or no difference, what distinct characteristics associated with the congregation are powerful enough to influence individuals to join the church? Even in the case of the Ladies Guild, which over the years has managed to attract a few local women, none of these individuals have joined the church. The upshot of this is that there is no clear positioning of the church in terms of either the religious or recreational marketplaces. The high profile of 'social' activities is unlikely to attract the more religiously minded, while individuals who are not so minded are likely to be uncomfortable with the more overtly religious aspects of congregational life.

Over the years this internal culture has solidified into a distinctive congregational identity that is jealously guarded and preserved by key members of the congregation. Furthermore, it is a culture with few attractions for young adults. The authors of the Welsh Churches Survey argue that a major cultural issue facing the Welsh churches if they are to survive into the twenty-first century is 'how to genuinely open up our churches to young adults and their children' (Bible Society, 1997: 48). In the case of Maestref Baptist Church, a church polity where power nominally rests with the congregation, while in reality being concentrated within the diaconate, has restricted the sphere of opportunity for the minister to initiate change. Things remain largely the same and look likely to continue to do so unless the minister can muster enough support within the congregation to match that of the habitualists who dominate internal politics and policy.

Despite his best efforts, the situation at present remains one of 'drift' and this is reflected in the difficulties he has encountered in persuading the diaconate to consider the merits of forward planning in order to set even modest goals for numerical growth. Until now, the only real strategy for growth has been internal reproduction and this has demonstrably failed. While there have been some transfers into the congregation over the years, this avenue of recruitment has been largely unlooked for and certainly unplanned, and has been too low to offset the losses incurred over the years. A further unintended consequence of this over-reliance on internal reproduction has been the ossifying of congregational culture. Significantly, it is only among that section of the congregation who view themselves as 'outsiders' that we find the type of fresh perspectives that might equip the congregation for the future, but these individuals are at present too few to make a difference. The best that they have managed is to colonize those marginalized areas of church life to which the majority appear indifferent. The upshot is a church culture that on the one hand emphasizes its openness and friendliness to newcomers while on the other hand, and by virtue of its social and cultural homogeneity, appears rather like a closed shop to outsiders. This cohesiveness, worthy though it is, has led to high levels of frustration among those within the congregation who see it as an impermeable boundary holding the church back from engaging meaningfully with the surrounding unchurched population.

Impact on the local community is minimal. While schools work raises the profile of the minister in the community, it is not translated into churchgoing. Youth work is restricted to the children of members of the congregation, as is the Sunday school, with a few exceptions. The Brownie pack draws exclusively from children of the congregation and neighbouring churches. Public events such as the Ladies Guild concerts are mainly for internal consumption and at best only attract other local churchgoers. The same can be said for annual events such as the Christmas and Summer Fayres. Even the location of the church buildings contributes to a sense of local invisibility.

For the congregation, this low profile raises two dilemmas. On the one hand, there is a general recognition (even among the most intransigent members) that there is an impending financial crisis just over the horizon and that it is serious enough to threaten the future existence of their church. All are agreed, in principle anyway, that what is needed is an influx of newcomers who are young enough to be still active in the occupational sphere and able to make a significant contribution to church finances. Furthermore, new recruits of this type would significantly lower the average congregational age, offsetting losses through deaths. On the other hand, it is likely that any movement in this direction would inevitably lead to changes in the internal culture of the church. For many members this would be highly problematic.

The few recruits to the congregation are both more religiously orientated than most existing members and more open to innovation and it is likely that, if there was further recruitment, new members would be more likely to fit this profile. Clearly, any significant influx of newcomers of this type would provide valuable support for those who desire the renewal of congregational life. Given the fact that the most popular activities within the church are geared towards the needs of existing members and have little or no religious content, it is likely that this would be the first focus for change. In effect, the distinct identity of the church and the existing hegemony that organizations such as the MCC and LG exercise would be threatened. On an individual level, in a climate of renewal it is likely that long-term members would be encouraged in the direction of personal spiritual growth, something that many existing members have shown little interest in or enthusiasm for until now. Indeed, given the entrenched church culture, it is unlikely that long-term members would welcome either initiative with any fervour.

FACING THE FUTURE

Despite its negative connotations, it is this culture that has also held the congregation together through a general climate of difficult times for many mainstream churches. Older worshippers are now the mainstays of churches throughout Wales (Bible Society, 1997: 16–17) and without this faithfulness it is likely that statistics of church decline would be far greater. However, this has come at a cost, particularly among those denominations over-represented by older people and which constitute 89 per cent of churches in Wales (Bible Society, 1997: 16). This cost is expressed among many congregations in a failure to adapt to the changing circumstances in which the churches now find themselves. In this climate, how far older age congregations are prepared to change remains open to question, but if attitudes within Maestref Baptist Church are indicative of the wider picture, the prognosis is not good.

Without doubt, this is an insular congregation, but members are aware, however dimly, of the collective challenges that face them if they are to survive in the long term. While there is recognition that the congregational culture will have to change in order to attract and retain younger worshippers and particularly young families, the general feeling for many appears to be 'not in my lifetime'. The majority of members appear to be happy with business as usual, mainly because they see this as a holding exercise, leaving open the possibility of necessary changes in the future. In a congregation almost exclusively composed of retired persons, the prospect of innovation can be comfortably projected into the future to a time when the majority of members will no longer be affected by it. By putting off change now, members can continue to enjoy things much as they have always known them. As such, the agenda for the future is being set by the over-sixties, a group whose main characteristic is looking back rather than forward.

At present, even within a climate of ministerial dependency, the minister appears powerless to impose his own authority to the degree he would like and this is largely due to the stranglehold on church life that the present diaconate retains. Unless this situation changes the likely outcome is that he will move on to a more receptive congregation. This could have serious ramifications, not least because many newcomers cite his presence as the main reason why they joined the church or continue to remain in the church. Whether they would consider staying or whether they would move to a more innovative congregation remains an open question. In the longer term, how far the current financial position of the church would allow them to call another minister is also open to question. Given the overwhelming body of evidence from elsewhere in Swansea, it is highly likely that the permanent loss of ministerial leadership would significantly accelerate congregational decline.

Any prognosis as to the future of this congregation must be pessimistic. The financial position of the church is unlikely to improve. Internal reproduction is a failed strategy. Recruitment strategies are conspicuous by their absence. There is little, other than the presence of the Sunday school, to recommend the church to young families. Indeed, the lack of open social networks between the congregation and the community and the strong sense of internal identity have both created something of an impermeable boundary that is unlikely to aid any potential future recruitment. Wider congregational frames of reference largely encompass other churches in the same position as them and while members are aware that other local churches appear to have few problems in attracting new worshippers they do not appear to understand why. The tragedy for this congregation is that it has not been able to capitalize on the higher than average rates of churchgoing that characterize the district. In opting for a strategy of maintenance rather than mission it has unwittingly strengthened those internal characteristics that have made it so difficult to recruit locally.

The internal difficulties have been compounded by the general climate of secularization. The events described have been played out in a growing climate of indifference towards organized religion and this is exemplified by the attitudes of the local community. Whereas, even into the 1960s, personal and familial identification with Christianity remained a recognized marker of social respectability, from then on this was decreasingly so. An increasingly mobile population and the growth of competing leisure activities, coupled with the lower profile of the churches as they became increasingly divorced from the daily lives of ordinary people, fuelled the growing privatization of religion. In the case of Baptist churches nationally, this progressive privatization was also accompanied in the early 1970s by a decisive reversal of the trend towards increasing theological liberalism and a movement towards a more overt evangelicalism. Those churches that had previously opted for an identity mainly predicated on social functions increasingly appeared out of step with this normative sea change and ill equipped for the future. Maestref Baptist Church appears to have been left behind in a time warp and all that remains are the vestiges of sociability. Privatization and structural differentiation have also brought competition as churches have moved from being local social institutions embedded in communities to free-standing institutions. Clearly, the majority of this congregation have failed even to recognize this change, let alone adapt to it. Increasingly divorced from their local community, yet unable to position themselves effectively within the wider religious marketplace, the eventual demise of the church will probably pass unnoticed and unmourned.

7

Setting Goals for Growth

On the basis of the evidence for religious decline presented so far, it might be fair to say that the future health of organized religion in Wales would appear to be in some doubt. The majority of churches are both ageing and having difficulty in coming to terms with significant social and cultural changes within Welsh society. Clearly, the widespread habit of regular churchgoing that used to characterize the Welsh people is now a thing of the past and many denominations are struggling to survive in the face of falling memberships and widespread public indifference towards organized religion. The health of these denominations, while not totally dependent on the health of their individual congregations, is nevertheless dependent on the good health of the majority of their constituent congregations. Viewed in this way, the prognosis for the denominations is not good. A majority of congregations are shrinking and in terms of their relative demographic profile they are becoming increasingly unrepresentative of the Welsh population at large. While the denominations continue to try to resist these trends, many congregations are increasingly turning inwards at the same time as the generational cycle that had previously sustained these churches through internal reproduction has progressively broken down. For many congregations this failure to recruit new members or to retain the children of existing members in sufficient numbers puts their long-term survival in doubt. Clearly, many external factors that are largely beyond the control of the churches are affecting their capacity to reproduce themselves. However, it is just as clear that factors internal to the life of churches are also inhibiting growth in many cases.

In the last chapter we saw one example of the type of congregational culture that reflects the experience and needs of an older generation of churchgoers. Looking backwards rather than forwards and inwards rather than outwards, it exemplifies the almost total privatization and marginalization of organized religion in contemporary Welsh society. The disparate concerns that motivated and drove that congregation are not concerns that generally engage members of the broader community and to all intents and purposes this congregation is an irrelevancy to its surrounding population.

In chapter 5 we also saw another intensely conservative congregation but one, by virtue of its situation in a stable long-established working-class community and its inclusive orientation, which still retains some relevancy among elements of its surrounding population. In this case, the presence of the type of long-standing and intersecting social networks that used to characterize so many Welsh communities has helped to maintain a continuing visible presence in the locality.

In both cases this conservatism and resistance to change, while not in itself a recipe for meaningful growth, has nevertheless helped to sustain these congregations in the face of an increasingly secularized society. However, at best these might be seen as strategies of maintenance rather than of mission and, as we saw in the case studies in chapter 4, the eventual outcome of these trends for individual congregations if they remain unchecked is presumably eventual extinction. The crucial question then for the churches is whether organized religion has any sustainable future in the face of widespread and deep societal change.

The short answer is a qualified yes. In a climate where churches are closing and denominations are struggling to halt numerical decline, what we are seeing is not so much the eclipse of religion as the demise of certain religious institutions that are failing to adapt to the present social climate. Furthermore, as the authors of the 1995 Welsh Churches Survey point out, this is a natural process. They suggest that there is a natural turnover of churches and groups of churches 'according to their ability to meet the spiritual needs of the communities in which, and for which, they exist' (Bible Society, 1997: 46). Typically, they are formed as a response to certain social and cultural conditions, they grow and mature and then (if they fail to successfully adapt to further changing conditions) they gradually decline as their original remit becomes progressively undermined by changing social and cultural conditions. It is at this point that new religious groups emerge in response to societal change and the cycle begins again.

For the above authors, it is the growing emergence of the 'new' churches and groups, progressive in tenor, emphasizing mission over maintenance and often non-aligned, which best represent this evolutionary trend. While this is still a minority sector of the Welsh religious economy, these churches are more likely to be in a growth situation or to express clear intentions for growth. The authors of the above survey also suggest that the health of congregations can be effectively measured by their intentions to plant other churches:

> The intention to plant another congregation is an interesting indicator of potential church growth. Seriously contemplating an additional congregation suggests confidence in the wellbeing and continued development of the existing congregation. Also the planting of an additional congregation is a relatively

straightforward and unambiguous measure of growth . . . intentions to church plant were mostly held by new and non-aligned churches . . . and by Pentecostals. (Bible Society, 1997: 31)

One such church is the subject of this case study. A progressive and growing non-aligned church, in many ways it exemplifies the template for congregational health and growth held up by these authors. However, as we shall see, in other ways it also exemplifies many of the problems that churches are experiencing in trying to reconnect with a general population that appears increasingly distanced from the world of organized religion.

WESTSIDE EVANGELICAL CHURCH

Westside Evangelical Church (not its real name) is an independent Christian fellowship situated in the same district of Swansea as our previous case study. Located on the edge of the district's lone local authority housing estate, it is also a stone's throw away from some of the most expensive housing in the district. The original church building, dating from 1971, is small and architecturally unimpressive, seating 160 worshippers. Due to sustained numerical growth in recent years this building is no longer capable of accommodating the entire congregation, which now averages 300 people and meets for Sunday morning worship in a nearby comprehensive school.

This church had the fastest growth rate of any of the Swansea churches surveyed by myself in 1995. Formally constituted as a church in 1986 with twenty-eight members, by 1995 membership had risen to 105, representing an impressive growth rate of 275 per cent. Growth during this period was at a steady rate and has continued in this way. In the ten-month period between my surveying this church and commencing fieldwork membership had risen by a further 21 per cent to 127 persons. This is by any yardstick an impressive rate of increase and one that has consistently exceeded the church's own expectations. For example, in 1992, the church leadership made a projection of future membership to 1997 based on 10 per cent growth. This figure was achieved eighteen months in advance of its target date and membership growth has since continued to outstrip projections significantly.

Average attendance for Sunday worship is in the order of 354 persons, with 213 adult worshippers and 83 children and young people up to the age of 19 years in the morning and 59 worshippers (mostly double attendance) in the evening. In line with the growth in membership, the growth in attendance during the 1986–95 period was an impressive 128 per cent and underlines this church's success in attracting worshippers to its services. However, 60 per cent of the congregation are recorded as transfers (mainly from other evangelical churches) and only 15 per cent of the congregation are recorded as joining through the overt recruitment activities of the church. Notwithstanding this imbalance, and in the light of the current religious climate, this is a not inconsiderable achievement. Furthermore, the church also attracts many students from the nearby university although these tend to stay for no more than the three years of their university life. As the latter point suggests, this is an all-age congregation: 37 per cent of worshippers are aged 16 years and under; 18 per cent are aged between 16 and 25 years; 23 per cent are aged between 26 and 44 years; 13 per cent are aged between 45 and 64 years and 9 per cent are aged 65 years or over. The ratio of males to females is 5:6 and it is clear that this demographic profile differs markedly from the average Welsh congregational profile (Bible Society, 1997: 15–18).

The church is organized along the lines of a gathered congregation and while it was for a time a member of the Federation of Independent Evangelical Churches (FIEC) it is now independent of any formal associational structures. Leadership is constituted and shared through a team of five elders, two of which are employed full-time by the church. The most senior is designated 'pastoral elder', a position roughly analogous to that of a minister and he officiates at weddings and funerals and is the public face of the congregation in their dealings with other churches. The occupational background of the leadership team is in business and industry, where most were senior managers, and this experience is reflected in the organizational life of the church. The team functions rather like a board of directors and is responsible both for long-term planning as well as the overall oversight of the spiritual life of the church. While members of the leadership team distance themselves from the everyday running of the church, their doors are always open to members of the congregation if they have pastoral problems and the distance between leadership and congregation in personal and pastoral terms is minimal. Preaching duties and worship leadership are often devolved to other members, particularly the deacons, and this accords with the low-key leadership style that characterizes this church. There are four deacons and they function as a second line of management responsible for the practical day-to-day running of affairs material and financial and reporting back to the eldership. Promotion to eldership is invariably preceded by a period of time spent as a deacon, although not all deacons become elders. There is no free election of elders or deacons as such and individuals are invited to take office by the leadership and this is then formally ratified by the membership. In theory the membership could reject candidates but in practice this does not happen as candidates are individuals generally recognized throughout the congregation as having the proven spiritual and organizational qualities necessary for leadership.

The congregation is divided into a cell structure for mid-week activities and there are thirteen housegroups, each of which meets weekly and draws its membership from a distinct and fairly circumscribed locality. All members (and many attenders) belong to one of these local groups, which function to bond disparate groups of people together and to teach basic Christian discipleship. Members of the leadership team commented that in their view these housegroups constitute the real heart of the congregation and are the cornerstone of a church ethos of fostering individual personal development as well as corporate numerical growth. Housegroup leaders also constitute a line management structure (although housegroup leaders may also be elders or deacons) but their primary concern is with teaching and pastoral care rather than the general organizational life of the church. Leadership of this type is seen as a necessary training for eventual translation to the office of deacon and each group has a leadership team of two and the senior leader trains the junior. All housegroup members are encouraged to see themselves as potential leaders and leadership at this level is flexible and tends to change quite frequently. In contrast, elders and deacons once appointed tend to stay in office permanently.

This careful nurturing of those with potential leadership qualities and clear avenues of promotion to leadership positions contrasts markedly with the fairly *ad hoc* approach to the election of church officers that characterized the previous case study. Clearly, church office in this congregation is seen in the light of taking on board ministerial responsibility and all that that entails in terms of 'vocation' and not merely the temporary elevation to a rotating office where office holders are primarily engaged in purely administrative and organizational activities. Because leaders emerge from within the congregation rather than being appointed from outside, the distance between leaders and laity is not great. Furthermore, in terms of 'ownership' the fact that it is the congregation itself that provides the resources for leadership, both ensures a steady stream of new leaders and, within the context of a team ministry, some continuity.

Many activities are devolved to semi-autonomous groups within the congregation who report back to the deacons. For example, those groups that provide stewards, music and sound and lighting for church services are largely left to their own devices and organize themselves. A Sunday school with five age-banded classes meets in the local comprehensive school and there are also a number of well-attended subsidiary activities coordinated by semi-autonomous groups, including a mother and toddlers group, after-school clubs and activities for senior citizens, all of which are based on church premises. There are also a number of programmes for new believers, although these tend to be bought in packages (such as Alpha), and these are rigorously monitored. It is not unusual for these to be replaced if the leadership feel their effectiveness is waning. Regular open meetings provide members with a forum for discussion about all major decisions or proposed new directions in the life of the church. Overall, little is left to chance in both the spiritual and organizational departments. There appears to be little overt tension between the ethos of personal spirituality encouraged by the church and the highly evolved nature of the organizational structures that closely resemble those of any modern business enterprise and which draws from the leadership's personal experiences of working within modern secular organizational frameworks. One deacon defined this approach as 'just sanctified common-sense really . . . there's nothing wrong with organizing ourselves along business like lines as long as the Spirit isn't shut out of the process. We have to balance the two really.'

The church is structured in such a way that performance can be easily monitored and changes made if necessary. Leadership at all stages is accountable, both to other members of the leadership team and to the congregation. Accountability, in the sense of recourse to denominational norms and leadership structures, is of course absent and this could be seen as a potential problem for members. The abuse of authority is not unknown in some independent churches and, if this happens, the individual has nowhere to go other than to the internal leadership if they wish to voice concerns and, if these are not addressed, nowhere to go but out of the church. However, in this case, the absence of any external regulatory or mediating authority appears to be offset by the extremely open access members and attenders have to the leadership.

The public face of the church is the main Sunday service and this is designed, in the words of one worship leader, to be as 'unchurchy as possible'. The school hall in which the congregation meets is invariably full at least half an hour before the service begins, which lends itself to a sense of occasion, but the atmosphere is relaxed and people wear bright casual clothes. There is a lot of social interaction before the service and one of the reasons why people arrive early is to take advantage of this. Music is supplied by an eight-piece band and is almost exclusively in the modern Christian idiom of songwriters like Graham Kendrick. Song-books are available but most people read the words as they are projected onto walls, allowing for a greater feeling of freedom during worship. Some people raise their hands during worship (in the charismatic manner) but generally worship is restrained and there is no incorporation of more overt neo-Pentecostal practices such as glossolalia. Preaching is relaxed and cogent and people listen attentively. Services are quite long (about ninety minutes) but there is no sense that they are being artificially drawn out and, as before the service, people tend to remain for a further half hour chatting animatedly to each other. Unusually for an evangelical milieu, in all the services that I observed there was never any attempt to pressure the congregation and the prevailing atmosphere was intimate, warm, reasonable and relaxed, with none of the triumphalism that characterizes much 'new' church worship.

Sunday evening services were much less well attended, averaging about sixty persons, mostly long-term members with a noticeably higher overall age profile. These services are considerably more traditional in character, with conventional hymns sometimes being sung and a noticeable Brethren influence permeates proceedings, particularly in the monthly communion services. These services followed the Brethren pattern of long periods of silence interspersed with appropriate readings, slowly building up to the act of communion. Interestingly, there were visible parallels with liturgical practice in eucharistically orientated churches and a practising Anglican communicant would not have felt out of place there. Certainly, these services constituted an interesting counterpoint to normal Free Church practice, where the celebration of communion is often treated as an afterthought to the main business, which is preaching.

Relations with other local churches are somewhat strained. One elder commented that locally their church was seen as 'a wild card . . . people are always suspicious of rapid growth'. With the exception of two local Anglican churches, cooperation or even contact with other local churches ranges from minimal to non-existent (despite the fact that it was this church that supplied the majority of preachers for Maestref Baptist Church during its interregnum). This state of affairs appears to reflect both antipathy towards this church's overt evangelicalism and suspicions about its phenomenal growth rate. However, some elements (but not all) of the Westside congregation also appeared generally ambivalent about the status of non-evangelical Christians and congregations. In common with many other evangelical churches in the city, it has nothing to do with the local council of churches (CYTUN) which is deemed theologically suspect, although it does associate informally with other like-minded 'new' churches.

ORIGINS AND RECENT HISTORY

Although the church was formally constituted in 1986, its origins go back to the late 1960s at a time when much new housing, including the present local authority housing estate, was being built in the district. Many young families moved into the area and subsequently a large city centre independent Baptist church began a small Sunday school based in one of the local schools. In 1971 a hall was erected on the edge of the local authority estate to house both the Sunday school and a newly constituted women's group, although the status of the hall continued to be that of a satellite of the main city centre congregation. Regular monthly services for worship commenced in 1979 under the direction of a deacon who lived in the district (and who subsequently became pastoral elder) and in 1980 these became weekly affairs. At this time the work was very small and lacked a clear direction, but those involved felt that there was some potential for a permanent independent church to be established. In pursuance of this vision a steering group was appointed in 1983 to see the proto-church through to autonomy and in March 1986 twenty-one members (joined by seven local evangelicals) transferred from the mother church with a parting gift of £2,000 and Westside Evangelical Church was formally constituted. The current pastoral elder was inducted in 1987 and the first mid-week housegroups were set up in 1989.

Initially growth was very slow. Only two more people joined the congregation in the first year of its formal existence and it was not until 1988 that the first adult baptism took place. However, 1988 was to prove a significant year. In common with many other evangelical churches the congregation was heavily involved with the organization of the inter-denominational *Tell Wales* mission (itself part of a number of initiatives associated with the UK-wide 'Decade of evangelism'). While the mission itself was not particularly successful in evangelistic terms, it did bring disparate groups together and new friendships were forged in this milieu. Many local Brethren fellowships were also involved and a small group of younger Brethren leaders who had become increasingly dissatisfied with what they saw as the entrenched conservatism of their own churches were sufficiently impressed by the experience of working with members of Westside church to seek new horizons. Fourteen of them made the decision to transfer to Westside, eventually selling up to move into the district. They brought with them the best of the Brethren tradition of deep personal spirituality coupled with an openness to innovation and a desire to leave behind the more narrow sectarian elements of their previous church experience. From the beginning they were active in the life of the church and they went on to constitute a significant presence among the Westside leadership.

It was this influx of new blood and ideas that laid the foundations for much of the present character and policy orientation of Westside church, as did the relative failure of the *Tell Wales* mission. The resounding lack of public response nationally to this project convinced many of those involved of the futility of large-scale evangelistic missions carried out in a post-Christian environment. In this context, and after much discussion, the enlarged membership of Westside church opted for a new model of mission. This model saw the future of the church as lying in small independent congregations opting to live in local communities rather than merely travelling in for activities and with a remit proactively to plant other small local churches.

The first stage of this process was realized when these new members sold their houses in other parts of the city in order to move into the district. Things moved quickly from here. They worked with their ex-Baptist colleagues to pursue this vision, and membership had doubled by 1990, while Sunday services were regularly attracting as many as 230 worshippers of all ages.

In comparison with general churchgoing trends in Swansea this was very much a success story and the profile of the congregation among Swansea evangelicals grew accordingly. The church also began to attract students from a nearby university and this led indirectly to a more innovative approach in worship, drawing from elements of charismatic practice, particularly in relation to music. At the same time the housegroup structure was firmed up (after initial reservations from some of the more conservative members) and the church began to take an interest in setting up local community projects catering for retired persons and young families.

However, notwithstanding the respectable growth rates and increased internal activity, by 1992 the leadership felt that the congregation was beginning to stagnate and, indeed, that something of an internal crisis was developing. While the congregation was growing steadily, this came to be perceived as a problem, not least because of the leadership's reservations about a 'big church' model. The upshot of this was that they began actively to consider the prospect of another church plant. The thinking behind this stemmed from the conviction that big churches actively inhibited personal growth and active individual involvement in the life of the church. It was felt that the challenge of establishing a new congregation would prove beneficial to all those involved. With a view to taking this forward, in the summer of 1992 an internal report was produced providing both an audit of the congregation's activities and a detailed assessment of the religious needs of neighbouring communities.

This concentrated period of reflection and reassessment culminated in the production of a formal 'vision statement' that established a clear set of new aims and objectives for the church. Numerical growth as an end in itself was rejected in favour of an emphasis on 'fellowship, teaching and personal development and building relationships and growing together'. Priority was also given to providing an introduction to worship practices for the unchurched and a firm grounding in the basics of the Christian faith, as well as resourcing established members for mission and church planting. While none of the above policies were particularly remarkable in themselves, the mission statement went further in that it committed the congregation to what the leadership termed a 'hospital' role. Simply, this was a commitment to take in individuals from other (invariably hardline) evangelical churches who had experienced difficulties in their former fellowships, giving them breathing space (and often counselling) to resolve their difficulties and then encouraging them to return to their church of origin.

This in itself was a radical departure from normal practice among evangelical churches in Swansea. While cases of insensitivity and heavy-handedness by church leaderships in Swansea are not widespread they do exist and in the final instance people can and do vote with their feet. While not all transfers are for this reason, local evangelical churches have shown little compunction in taking in 'refugees' from other evangelical churches and attempting both to retain and to integrate them into their own congregations. In effect, this is seen as just another means of numerical growth. In contrast, Westside Church appears to have rejected such opportunist strategies of recruitment, opting instead for an approach that eschews the idea of competition in favour of a wider vision that encompasses the whole church in Swansea. Furthermore, in a highly competitive church environment where success is all to often measured in terms of numerical growth, this church stands out in its rejection of the principle of growth for growth's sake. As with the 1988 influx of new members from Brethren churches, the creation of this inclusive vision statement was another defining moment for the congregation. However, and paradoxically, the decisive rejection of the 'big church' model also heralded a period of sustained numerical growth and the congregation grew rapidly. Reflecting this surge in recruitment, another full-time elder was appointed in 1994 and the number of house-groups grew from three to nine. The most visible indicator of this rapid growth was the decision to move Sunday morning worship to a nearby com-prehensive school as the existing building was no longer able to accom-modate comfortably an expanding congregation.

In 1994, the church briefly flirted with what came to be known as the 'Toronto Blessing', a variant on the Pentecostal practice of glossolalia, characterized by unusual physical manifestations including uncontrollable laughter and weeping, apparent intoxication and out-of-the-body ex-periences. Introduced to the church mainly by the students and young people in the congregation it looked for a time as if the church might be swept along this particular current. This period coincided with the establishing of links with some of those charismatic fellowships in the city that had welcomed the Toronto Blessing and the eventual incorporation of these like-minded congregations in a loose umbrella organization named 'The Church Together' (which resulted in the FIEC finally severing its links with the congregation). However, the congregation never wholeheartedly grasped the nettle of the Toronto Blessing (reflecting the initial provenance of many older members in non-charismatic conservative congregations) and the moment passed. Worship services settled into their current format, utilizing the musical elements and liturgical informality associated with charismatic worship while forgoing public manifestations of ecstatic practices. By 1996, the church had moved on again. The current leadership structure of five elders and four deacons was now firmly in place and Easter Sunday 1996 saw the opening of the first church plant in a neighbouring community and plans being formulated for a second plant.

THE CONGREGATION

The social composition of the congregation is overwhelmingly that of the affluent middle class. It is a genuine all-age congregation in that all ages are represented, although those in the 16 to 45 age band tend to be over-represented and older people under-represented. The typical pattern of attendance is of married couples and this is reflected in a ratio of 5 males to every 6 females. Most men are employed in a professional capacity and their partners tend not to be in full-time paid employment. Those women who do work for a living tend to be employed in the caring professions as teachers, nurses, social workers and counsellors. Many in the congregation are people of English origin, who have moved to Swansea at the behest of their employers who are often national and multinational companies, and are highly mobile. Invariably, they also have a prior background within evangelical Christianity and most have sampled a number of churches in Swansea before settling in Westside.

People cited a number of reasons for joining this church. Some English people who joined this church did so because it most closely approximated their previous church experience and these individuals tended to have their origins in the southern counties of England, where Alpha-type churches are strong. Others (often from the north or west of England) joined for precisely the opposite reason. Typically they had been brought up in hyper-conservative evangelical churches and were seeking to break away from fundamentalism. This latter group was particularly interesting in that they tended to cite their own changed social circumstances as the main catalyst for this move. University education and a geographically mobile lifestyle had enabled them to relinquish more easily their former ties with fundamentalist groups. Furthermore, the conservative mindset of their former religious upbringing was often compared unfavourably with the intellectual flexibility required in their occupational sphere, although their commitment to evangelicalism (albeit in a more liberal form) remained strong. These latter sentiments were also echoed by many of those members who were natives of Swansea. While they retained great affection for the churches that they had been brought up in, nevertheless they were critical of their innate conservatism.

One ex-Brethren member, active both in his former congregation and now in Westside, commented that he had initially felt very guilty about leaving a struggling church:

> The Brethren way of doing things was just too restrictive . . . you know we tried to change things but it just wasn't possible in that environment. We were working with youngsters then and having some success but we couldn't integrate them into the church, not in a million years . . . The Gospel Halls were set up to give freedom from church strictures and now they just replicate them . . . [Westside] was a totally different experience.

Another commented that older members were setting the policy agenda in Gospel Halls and that there was an unwillingness on their part to embrace the type of changes that younger members were pushing for. This had led to many actively involved married couples voting with their feet. Indeed, a regular and ongoing stream of transfers has followed the initial 1988 influx of ex-Brethren from Gospel Halls. This movement has been facilitated by the presence of social networks that link ex-Brethren members now in Westside with friends and family members who remain within the Gospel Halls. These linkages and the maintenance of social contact over the years have allowed those still in the Brethren movement to make comparisons with their existing church experience while the existence of family and old friends within the Westside congregation has made the act of transfer easier.

Brethren spirituality is measured by the level of active membership and many of these transfers had been among the most active workers in their old churches. It is unsurprising therefore that they constitute some of the most active members in their new church setting. Understandably, this core of active members also draws heavily on that cohort of ex-Baptists that were instrumental in founding the church. Despite their shared commitment to the well-being of the church, both ex-Baptists and ex-Brethren constitute definite and recognizable subgroupings within the congregation, complete with their own internal social networks. To a certain extent, the pattern of informal socializing still tends to cohere around prior denominational affiliations and these patterns are reinforced by the almost daily face-to-face contacts these more active members have as they work together in various church activities.

In latter years there has also been an influx of individuals drawn from the wider evangelical community. Some characterize themselves as psychologically or emotionally 'damaged' in some way by their prior church experiences. Others were merely dissatisfied with the 'coldness' of their previous fellowships or were seeking something better. While there was no single reason why individuals were drawn to the church, a warm caring local church ethos, sound doctrine, proven success in recruitment, lively worship, the availability of counselling and the 'hands off' approach of church leaders, were all cited as features that had initially attracted evangelicals disaffected from their previous churches. Understandably, the level of commitment of these individuals tends to be uneven, in many cases reflecting negative experiences elsewhere.

Mention should also be made of the many retired people in the district who are tangentially attached to the church. In contrast to the rest of the congregation, these individuals are likely to be residents of the local council estates or domiciled in residential homes. A group of elderly women are stalwarts of the mid-week Ladies Fellowship, while many more retired people (of both sexes) are regulars of the church-run luncheon club. Church members also visit residential homes in the district and the pastoral elder is a familiar face among the older residents of the district. This contact with these residents is primarily an aspect of the church's desire to be seen as a community church and not too much is expected of these people in terms of potential recruitment. While a few individuals have chosen to become members, most limit their involvement and the current leadership appears happy with this state of affairs. That is not to say that the leadership is happy with levels of commitment elsewhere in the church. There are many worshippers who attend services regularly but have yet to immerse themselves fully in the organizational life of the church.

CORE MEMBERS

The most active members tend to be those individuals drawn from Baptist and Brethren backgrounds. Typically, they have been immersed in evangelical Christianity since childhood and are confident in their Christian identity. They also tend to be active 'doers' rather than passive recipients, with a highly developed sense of personal responsibility to the corporate life of the church. Sociologically, they constitute a distinct and differentiated core grouping within the church and perceive themselves as such. Consequently, some individuals on the periphery of the congregation see these internal networks of active members as a negative factor. They are seen as closed social networks, constituting 'cliques' that are too close to a leadership that is drawn exclusively from the same networks. One ex-worshipper commented:

> It was alright there but I wasn't getting *in* . . . I wasn't getting to know anybody in any depth. There was a lot on offer there but I didn't feel attended to when I was in need. If you talked to the common or garden Christian there, someone

who wasn't in a leadership role . . . well there's quite a lot of unrest there because they don't feel touched by other people. There's a hierarchical type of successful leaders with their wives and children, and they *are* nice people . . . but the people there are untouched by them. The church has got bigger and bigger but it's quite evident that you've got these groups there. [Westside] is a safe place to be but the people are really locked into themselves. I was there for a year but not one person invited me around for a coffee. There is counselling, there are housegroups, but you remain untouched by people for common friendship. Everybody seems locked into themselves . . . and lots of groups and subgroups. The people who came from the Brethren. The group who came from the evangelicals . . . and so on . . . and they're stuck together. (Emphases in the original transcript.)

While there was some recognition by active members that they might be seen in this way by relative newcomers, this was largely thought of as something related to the large size of the congregation rather than deliber-ate social closure. Long-term members felt that it was unremarkable that they would seek to retain long-standing friendships and also perfectly nat-ural (given the many daily activities they were involved in) that they should have a high level of face-to-face contact with other active members.

Indeed, these active members commented positively on what they saw as their ability to utilize their closeness with the leadership to adopt a criti-cal stance where necessary and to influence policy decisions. For example, a move by ex-Baptists to convince the leadership to become more respon-sive to the concerns of the congregation was cited as one instance of this capacity to influence leaders, as was the successful resistance by ex-Brethren members to the Toronto Blessing. One founder member com-mented:

There was something of an authoritarian stance for a couple of years. Since we've been growing more elders have been made and we suddenly found we were being presented with things, and you see to people like myself, this is not how we felt things should be done, not scripturally and not in past experience. We were told that the elders had decided this and there really was no discussion of this. It went down well with younger members but older members resisted this and eventually the leadership agreed to a survey of the congregation. It came back strongly that the congregation should have more say in the direction the church was moving and things are now put to the church. Church members are now getting more say in how we do it. I think that was really something of a major issue.

What is interesting about this particular vignette is that it clearly demon-strates a continuity with Baptist thinking about the question of internal democracy and that the leadership felt constrained to take account of these concerns. In contrast, the following vignette is very much the product of a Brethren background:

> We had some involvement with the Toronto Blessing but a lot of us were never very happy with it. A meeting was organized with other churches and it was billed as a prayer meeting. We expected a prayer meeting and this was a deception in many respects as it was nothing to do with that at all. There was music going all the time and a chap telling people they were going to fall down and as people were falling down I thought to my self 'this cannot be right'. Some of the young people were very dissatisfied with our church after their experience of the Toronto Blessing. It was almost like they needed their weekly 'fix' for a while. But the older people didn't get so involved.

Clearly, there are some tensions associated with different religious traditions but at the same time active members tended to see these events as episodes in the life of the church that had been successfully negotiated with no lasting damage to the collective ethos. Furthermore, in the case of what is still relatively a new church, its identity (by necessity) has been forged within the context of diverse understandings of congregational polity. While younger members came in for some criticism because of their perceived theological naivety, older members appeared relaxed with this, emphasizing the importance of ensuring that the church retained its inclusive orientation and that it did not fall into extremes.

Active members appeared more concerned about the fact that, although they constituted a minority within the congregation, the extent of their involvement in the practical life of the church far outweighs their small numbers. One commented:

> It's disappointing for us in a way. When the church was small, a fair amount of people were very actively involved but now it is still largely those same people. But I think wherever you go, you will always have a periphery of people, because I do think that there are people who just don't want to do anything. I know that sometimes it looks as if it is working so well that people feel that they have nothing to offer because its such a well oiled machine, but we need to try and invite people on board really.

Clearly, in terms of the problem of engendering active commitment within congregations, some things remain the same despite the very different settings that we have encountered so far. In this, evangelical congregations appear little different from their mainstream counterparts. In the same way, despite their dissatisfactions, these active members were keen to emphasize the personal satisfactions of active engagement and the positive benefits of the socially cohesive nature of the work groups into which they are organized.

However, active members were in many ways the least effective in terms of personal evangelism. There is a general recognition throughout the congregation that it is transfer growth rather than recruitment from the ranks of the unchurched that is responsible for the rapid growth of the church. While there is little doubt that members are committed to the idea of personal evangelism, in practice they are presented with few opportunities for meaningful engagement with those whom they desire to recruit. For active members, the strength of the internal networks to which they belong and the large expenditure of time on church activities leave little space for nurturing the type of external relationships necessary to reach the surrounding unchurched population. As one member commented:

> Most of our friends are in the church or go to other churches and as you get older it becomes more difficult to make new friends doesn't it? I mean I'm not a member of a sports club or anything, I don't play bowls or tennis, so its difficult really.

This lack of sustained contact with the surrounding community is not uncommon in evangelical churches and for older Christians it is sometimes very hard to break out of this self-imposed straitjacket in order to reach the unchurched. Paradoxically, it is those less active members on the periphery of the congregation who have proved rather more successful in this respect.

PERIPHERY

Those individuals who might be characterized as being on the periphery of the congregation demonstrate a number of shared characteristics. They are in the majority, they tend to be younger than the core of active members and are more likely to adopt a passive role. Whereas the concerns of active members tended to focus on the direction in which the church was going, these individuals appeared rather more concerned with a privatized individual spirituality. Many individuals suggested that their decision to affiliate themselves with Westside was primarily because it was seen as the 'best' environment available locally in which to achieve spiritual growth. This instrumental orientation to church allegiance suggests that many on the periphery see their involvement with the church in functional rather than affective terms (although it would be too simplistic to state that there were no affective bonds to the church). In some cases this reluctance to invest too much emotional capital in a new church situation is very understandable. Where psychological and emotional damage had been inflicted by other churches in the past, individuals will naturally be wary about investing too much of themselves for fear of history repeating itself. Nevertheless, many of these individuals were also keen to stress that they saw Westside as a warm and welcoming family church and an environment in which they felt 'safe' and 'at home'.

While some on the periphery choose to only attend the main worship service many are also involved with the housegroups. These groups have a clear integrative function in that they help to establish affective bonds with others in the church. However, there is a danger (recognized by the leadership) that these affective bonds will stretch no further than individual subgroups. There was some evidence to support this contention, both from the main worship service where subgroup members tended to cluster together and from individual friendship patterns that often centred on particular housegroups. On the other hand, given the large size of the congregation and the fact that housegroup members are invariably also close neighbours, it is likely that these groups constitute the best vehicle for engendering a sense of belonging. It is also the case that the teaching content of housegroup sessions tends to emphasize the promotion of personal spirituality and individual discipleship, thus reinforcing a privatized religiosity. This privatized religiosity is a near constant feature among those on the periphery and constitutes an antithesis to the models of Brethren spirituality where personal spiritual growth is directly equated with increased active group involvement.

Peripheral members are also more likely to move house frequently, as a result of the need to relocate at their employers' bidding. Mobility reduces the level and frequency of face-to-face contact with families and old friends and movement tends to be between faceless suburban housing estates where the privatized lifestyle is the dominant cultural form. In essence this is a mobile lifestyle where social bonds are continually being broken and remade and where social networks are of necessity temporary in their nature. All this creates a climate that is arguably detrimental to the establishment of close (and certainly long-term) church involvement as it has customarily been understood. These trends are also exacerbated by high occupational costs. Many males on the periphery are in occupations where they have a high level of responsibility and this is reflected in a culture of long working hours. Free time is at a premium and what little there is must be divided between the nuclear family and the church. Younger evangelicals in this position have increasingly been led to question the customary evangelical shibboleths of regular church attendance, formal church membership, Sabbatarianism and even the traditionally sharp distinction between the church and the world.

Increasingly, church life has to accommodate itself to the life of the nuclear family rather than the other way round. If time is at a premium, families will not feel guilty about missing church to take their family to the beach. If they attend on Sunday it will be the morning service only, leaving space and time for family activities. Housegroups may be attended if they are sufficiently local (and if a babysitter can be found) but weekday activities on church premises are unlikely to be attended. The general approach is optional and individuals appear happy to 'buy into' only as much as they feel they are able to afford in terms of time. Conversely, a transitory lifestyle opens up new possibilities for social networks. Those on the periphery differed from older active members in that their personal networks were more likely to cut across the church–world dichotomy. Moving to a new city particularly meant making new friends and these friendships were just as likely to be drawn from work colleagues or neighbours as they were from religious circles. Indeed, family and social life appeared as influenced by the secular middle-class values of materialism as by traditional evangelical values.

In the course of visiting people's homes it was clear that, in common with many in the district, they lacked for nothing materially. The obvious levels of affluence on display appeared to reflect the predominance of material values rather than the frugality and lack of display customarily associated with evangelical households. Interestingly, this lack of distanciation between church members and their neighbours opened up distinct possibilities for evangelization. Given that, on the surface, there was little to differentiate church people from their unchurched neighbours and friends, these same friends felt relatively comfortable with them. Indeed, while the church as a whole has been exploring the possibilities of what it terms 'friendship evangelism' (that is, networking), it has often been those on the periphery who have been in the best position to establish themselves in undifferentiated social networks. One young mother of three, married to a busy executive, commented:

> It's a one to one thing. People in Swansea are so friendly and we have a lot of unchurched friends now. The neighbours were very kind to us when we moved here and we've made some strong friendships, and the great thing is they all take an interest. I don't push things at them but we've never made a secret of the fact that we are churchgoers. Usually *they're* the ones that ask questions, they're really curious as to why we attend church. Some have even come along to things [in the church] when I've asked them. Some haven't too, but that's alright. When we were in Cardiff we had only church friends there but here it's not . . . moving to a new city we had to start new friendships, it was a new start. I play badminton every week with four mums from the school and one of them has started to come to the housegroup. We have dinner parties with the neighbours. Yes, I do think that social networks are important to reach people . . . we just didn't have that in Cardiff. (Emphasis in the original transcript.)

In common with many on the periphery, despite her continued ideological commitment to evangelicism and practical commitment to evangelization, and despite rating Westside very highly as a church, she expressed no desire to move from the periphery although she had been a highly active member of her previous church.

A thoughtful woman, she saw this not so much as a response to finding herself in a new social situation but as part of an ongoing lifestyle trajectory. Her biography included being brought up in a 'strict' evangelical church, then moving into an innovatory church but still within a closed Christian social network and finally moving into her present Christian lifestyle. For her and her family this was seen in terms of their 'liberation from church culture' and very much the product of the opportunities opened up by increased mobility and the changes in their social and economic status. Tellingly, she was highly resistant to the thought of returning to her previous patterns of church allegiance. More generally, for those on the periphery one of the major attractions of this church was the semi-permeable nature of boundaries and the fact that individuals were as free to leave (without censure) as they were to join. For many evangelicals this was a new experience and the relaxed nature and light hand of leadership was in distinct contrast to the insular and doctrinaire nature of their previous church experiences.

LOCAL COMMUNITY RELATIONS

Welsh evangelicals are not, by and large, noted for their commitment to social action. The concept of a 'social gospel' is still regarded by the overwhelming majority with suspicion and as something associated with liberal mainstream churches. In contrast, for most of the twentieth century evangelicals have customarily chosen to place their emphasis on the individual rather than on the collectivity and to work towards the conversion of individuals in order cumulatively to change society. While this may still have worked as a strategy in the 1904–5 Welsh Revival (if very briefly), since then it has looked increasingly threadbare. In terms of relations with their surrounding communities, in many cases these relations are almost non-existent and even where churches do seek to provide amenities for local people, invariably this is seen merely as the means to an end, namely the religious conversion of individuals. Understandably, for the unchurched, while they may wish to avail themselves of services that churches might provide, they are wary of the baggage that comes with them. In practice, therefore, evangelical churches tend to stand apart from their surrounding populations. Westside church differs from this norm in that it describes itself as a 'community church' that, in the words of its mission statement, actively seeks 'the general wellbeing of people within the community'. Unusually, therefore, for an evangelical church in Swansea, Westside has a fringe of local people who avail themselves of a number of services provided by the church and among whom the church operates in a pastoral role without necessarily seeking to recruit them.

Elderly people constitute one significant group on the fringe of the congregation and they are enthusiastic users of services. There has been a thriving Ladies Fellowship for many years and this predates both the formal constitution of the church and its transformation into a 'community church'. In many ways this is the most typically 'religious' activity and one that most traditional evangelicals could identify with. Drawing its membership exclusively from elderly residents of the local authority housing estate, it seeks to cater for the spiritual needs of women who can no longer easily attend their churches and chapels of origin. While evangelically orientated it is also ecumenical in spirit, in that its personnel represent many Free Church denominations. This group, numbering anything from twenty to fifty individuals, meets weekly for worship and, unlike the main Sunday morning service, it is very traditional in style, reflecting the cultural preferences of its users. Church leaders are clear that this is not a feeder into the main church but an autonomous activity with a remit to provide religious and social fellowship to those unable to attend a church regularly elsewhere. No demands are made on these people and none are expected. The church also provides a similar service for residents of a large local nursing home. In more recent years a weekly luncheon club has been established, with meals served in the church building, and this is invariably fully subscribed. The church also sponsors 'Tea and Talk', a weekly social get-together for retired men and women, and this is again very popular with local residents.

These activities provide the basic context in which pastoral care is provided. Westside provides the only Nonconformist presence actually based in the local authority estate (there is also an Anglican church) and the pastoral elder is seen by many local people as the resident Free Church minister. In this role he is often called upon by local families (and residential homes) to conduct funerals or to make home visits. There is also a limited amount of informal cooperation with the local Anglican priest in pastoral matters and something of a recognized division of labour between them. In the past they have, at the request of local families, jointly officiated at funerals of residents known to both of them. Indeed, in recent years, the inclusive Anglican approach to pastoral ministry within the community has been highly influential on the way that Westside church has developed its own approach to local community relations and, despite some continuing internal tensions (detailed below), it now actively seeks to conform to this model.

The church is also heavily involved in providing services for the other end of the age spectrum. A mother and toddler group, 'Chatterbox', was established in 1990 both to provide a service to members of the congregation and (more contentiously) to facilitate 'friendship evangelism'. With the latter thought uppermost it was originally envisaged as having a clientele equally drawn from church members and local families, but in recent years it has come to be numerically dominated by the latter group. This, and the fact that it never really fulfilled its potential as an evangelistic vehicle, have raised questions both about its continued future and, indeed, a lively debate as to what the end purpose of this activity should be. Clearly, despite the emerging 'community church' ethos, there remains some tension between those in the congregation who see this type of activity as only justified if it is an effective vehicle for recruitment and those who wish to see the church contributing to the general well-being of the local community.

These tensions are less apparent in youth work. There is a thriving Sunday school and two mid-week after-school clubs ('Rock Solid' and 'Trainers') and the children of church members and those of local families are represented in these activities in approximately equal proportions. Work with young people is carried out with a high degree of professionalism, which is unsurprising given that the congregation contains thirty members of the teaching profession. In line with the managerial ethos that pervades much of the organizational life of the church, performance is constantly reviewed and nothing is left to chance. With the exception of 'Trainers' (a youth group for younger children), all teaching materials are derived from bought-in packages. These are constantly under scrutiny as to their effectiveness and when new packages come on to the market, they are monitored and assessed for their potential suitability to the church's needs. For example, the Sunday school has successfully utilized the SALT package and, while there are five age-banded classes that all study the same subject on any given Sunday, the style of presentation and substantive content differs by age group. 'Rock Solid', a youth group for older children, utilizes a package based on PSE programmes in state schools. This is therefore familiar to the children from their school experience, although as one youth leader (himself a PSE teacher) noted, the particular 'fun' element in Rock Solid broke down the traditional teacher–student barrier in a way that was not possible in schools. 'Trainers' was a more impromptu affair, with material devised by its two leaders, and did not appear to hold the children's attention to the same degree as professionally designed packages. The general consensus among these youth workers appeared to be that in buying in tried and tested packages the church was able to avail itself of a level of expertise not usually available in the average congregation, with some guarantee that materials are suitable for particular age groups.

Many on the fringe of the church tend to remain there and there is little evidence to support any alternative reading. In the case of work with children from unchurched families (who are nearly all drawn from the local authority estate), while their parents appear happy for their children to participate in these activities, they do not themselves have any substantive contact with the church. In the same way, the overwhelming majority of the mothers that use Chatterbox do not show any apparent interest in the fuller life of the church. In the case of the elderly, while they are happy to avail themselves of the various services and activities provided by the church, they remain outside the main life of the congregation. Nevertheless, this fringe is a concrete entity with a life of its own, sustained both by a network of local social relations and this church's willingness to engage with the local community in a relatively altruistic and inclusive manner. Some tensions relating to this activity on the fringe remain apparent, not least among those in the congregation who still see any engagement with the local community in terms of a payback in very narrow evangelistic terms. However, it is also clear that there have been significant departures from the customary evangelical practice of being concerned exclusively with the actual or prospective members of the gathered church.

MANAGING CHANGE

In part, this willingness to change has its origins in a leadership willing to take risks and a congregation who are willing to share this vision, albeit to differing degrees of enthusiasm. One striking aspect of all this is the marked lack of visible dissension or factionalism within the congregation, something that any long-term observer of Swansea evangelicals would find quite unusual. Welsh evangelicals are noted both for their conservatism and for their schismatic tendencies and yet there are few signs of internal dissension over policy matters. It is difficult to arrive at a simple explanation for this.

Clearly, this is not a utopian community and the congregation has not reached any level of cohesiveness that might automatically preclude dissent. Nevertheless, the presence of a number of intersecting social networks within the church based on kinship and long-standing friendships serves to tie in individuals from both leadership and congregation. The upshot is a lack of internal distanciation between leadership and laity. Individuals have open access to the leadership and can expect to have their concerns seriously listened to. The personnel of housegroups changes quite regularly and individuals are encouraged to change groups every few years. Most long-term members who I talked to had been in two or three groups during the course of their time in the church. While the ostensible reason for this is that individuals and groups 'do not get stale', one might note that this practice also inhibits the emergence of factions or centres of dissension. (Schism needs a schismatic *group* and it is very difficult for these to coalesce within this particular organizational structure.) Furthermore, individuals are free to leave the group at any time without censure and, indeed, the leadership actively encourages this if it is felt to be in the interests of the individual or individuals concerned. Both factors act as something of a safety valve preventing internal pressures from building up.

Moreover, there is an absence of the culture of fear that has characterized internal relations in some evangelical churches in the past. Leadership is carried out with a light hand and, as one leader commented, 'we give people permission to make mistakes'. In part, this enlightened attitude is informed by a number of scandals relating to the abuse of power and heavy-handed attempts at social control (known then as 'heavy shepherding') that rocked the UK charismatic community in the 1980s (Walker, 1985: Chambers, 1997). In more recent times, a similar scandal has adversely affected at least one high-profile Swansea church. Consequently the leadership is very aware that they are publicly accountable not just to the congregation but also within the wider Christian community.

SOME LEADERSHIP CONCERNS

Despite the widespread impression that evangelical congregations are somehow different from their mainstream counterparts, in many of their essentials this is clearly not the case and while this congregation differs from our previous cases in terms of its success in recruitment, leadership concerns tend to mirror those found elsewhere. For the casual observer, it is all too easy to assume that the enthusiasm and active participation of worshippers in the flagship Sunday morning services is translated into other areas of church life. However, the leadership cited many of the same problems with motivating their congregations to take on more responsibilities that we have encountered in the case studies of mainstream congregations. In common with those groups we have what appears to be a very committed core of long-term members active in organizing and maintaining congregational activities while the majority adopt a more passive stance. (Indeed, whatever the nature of activities, the same faces seemed to crop up again and again.) Where Westside leaders differed from their mainstream counterparts is that they tended to see this as a negative outcome of the very rapid growth of the church in recent years. One leader commented that:

> In a big church it's easy for people to *think* that everything is being done. In a small church they can see the need. It's also a question of commitment. You know we've had a lot of growth recently but that's left us with an awful lot of

people on the periphery so to speak. We don't push people into membership and we've got about three times as many attenders and people who've got some connection to the church. I just see some of these as incapable of real commitment. They're not membership material and until they show the commitment we don't press them about membership and we don't come the heavy hand with people. (Emphasis in the original transcript.)

This state of affairs was contrasted with that of a recent church plant in a neighbouring district:

We've just planted a new congregation up there and I think we saw something quite significant. The first Sunday that we were there we saw people putting away chairs, engaging in conversation or giving out books when in [Westside] they would have just sat down or been like statues in services not participating whatever. I think the church is just too big to mobilize all its members, so in the planting, where you've got a core of thirty to forty adults, its been quite significant to see that *that* person is now mobilized whereas before, after two years, they never did anything . . . just because of the size. (Emphasis in the original transcript.)

Clearly, there is much in these observations about congregational size but just as clearly and as we have seen above, many of those on the periphery who have a long history of involvement in evangelical churches are deliberately choosing to limit the type and degree of their involvement. While this is in part an effect of the increased mobility of individuals, it may also indicate a significant shift in the way that younger evangelicals relate to their churches. Tellingly, leadership concerns also focused on the future of younger elements in the congregation:

We're concerned that the young people are not developing their talents in the direction of leadership in the way that we've anticipated. They have not lived up to expectations. They are not using their abilities. There's no excitement about the development of the church. We've tried appointing younger men as housegroup leaders but that's not developed in the way that we thought it would. It *is* a failure and it's something we need to look at. (Emphasis in the original transcript.)

However, despite these concerns, there was also a hard-headed recognition that outside factors such as an occupational culture of long hours and family commitments often left individuals with very little time for church activities.

As a church with a conversionist ethos, evangelism has a high profile and this was a major leadership concern. The fact that so much of the congregation's recent growth has been through transfers from other evangelical churches rather than the product of conversions is seen as a far from ideal state of affairs, although there were differing interpretations among the leadership as to why this was so. Younger leaders were concerned that the congregation was too middle-class in terms of composition and culture and that the church had failed to make any significant inroads into the evangelization of the adjacent local authority housing estate. Indeed, only one new member had been recruited from this estate in recent years. More senior leaders were rather less concerned about class and took the position that it was 'like attracting like'. The positioning of the church in the religious economy was analogous with niche-marketing principles and they were comfortable with the idea that Westside was a middle-class church attracting middle-class people. (Similar to the 'homogeneous unit principle' of McGraven and Wagner (1990) that states that new groups of converts should be socially homogeneous and that hopes to integrate them into a socially different congregation should be modest.) The social and cultural characteristics of potential recruits aside, all the leadership were agreed that customary evangelistic practices lacked impact and were, in the words of one leader, 'largely a waste of time and effort'. (For example, a recent mailing to 6,000 local homes garnered two enquiries, both from Christians.) Sunday services and special events were not seen as having any impact locally and, as one leader noted, 'very few people come in off the street to any service'.

An internally generated analysis of why people joined the church suggested that prospective recruits tended to seek out the church themselves or came in through pre-existing social networks. However, while networking was seen as the best potential strategy for recruitment, there seemed to be little agreement as to how networks that incorporated both churched and unchurched individuals might be realized. Indeed, it was universally recognized that most people in the congregation socialized exclusively with other 'born again' Christians and that for cultural and social reasons this state of affairs was unlikely to alter overnight. Nevertheless, as I noted above, some individuals have, by dint of establishing new friendships (often in the workplace), managed to overcome these barriers, although these have tended to be the product of individual initiatives rather than group efforts. Indeed, this is the nub of the problem for Westside. There was much talk among both the leadership and laity about the need to be 'relevant' to the local population, but little agreement as to what this might mean in real terms. While some of the reasons why people joined had been identified, the congregation appeared to be unable to formulate a viable group strategy that would transcend the *ad hoc* nature of recruitment. In essence, the growth reported so far was largely the result of the efforts of individuals and could not be said to stem from any formal planned evangelistic strategy by the church.

RELATIONS WITH OTHER EVANGELICAL CHURCHES

In an earlier description of Swansea evangelicals in chapter 3, we saw a disputative and competitive evangelical culture characterized by bitterness and conflict. Westside church has tried to remain aloof from these disputes and to build bridges where it can. In the brief outline of the recent history of the church we saw some limited cooperation with like-minded churches and the church also provides office space and some support to evangelical charities. While the church briefly aligned itself with the charismatic community, it stepped back from a fuller identification with this grouping, preferring instead to forge a middle way.

Despite (or possibly because of) this moderate stance, relations with conservative evangelicals and their churches are not good. The church's tenuous link with the charismatic community had led to them being labelled a 'Toronto Blessing' church and the church's adoption of the Alpha course has also been viewed very negatively in some conservative quarters. Clearly, this is guilt by association, as Westside is not a charismatic church, but the effects have been real enough, including the church's expulsion from the conservative FIEC and the withdrawal of recognition from the Evangelical Movement of Wales. Closer to home there have been a number of evangelically sponsored press campaigns against the church that have done little to dispel the atmosphere of mistrust and mutual animosity among evangelicals in the city.

These letter-writing campaigns in the local press have mainly concentrated on attacking personalities in the Westside leadership team (or those closely associated with them) and the direction in which the church is going. One such campaign was sparked by the leadership's decision (prompted by the membership) to initiate an internal survey of members to ascertain what they wanted from the church. This fairly innocuous response to the call from their congregation for greater internal democracy was interpreted by prominent local conservatives as an example of 'unbiblical practices' and the leadership was accordingly roundly condemned by this party. By listening to and acting on the concerns of their congregation, the leadership were apparently guilty of undermining the natural order of authority and the role of exhortational preaching, although another interpretation might be that some evangelical leaders in the city felt threatened personally by this exercise in congregational democracy.

Be that as it may, this emphasis on listening and responding is part and parcel of the leadership's desire to locate their church in the middle ground. Leaders often referred to Westside as a 'middle of the road church', although in evangelical parlance this is more to do with successfully striking a balance between conservatives and radicals within the congregation. If anything (and despite public criticism to the contrary), and as the congregation's very brief dalliance with charismatic practices demonstrates, this balance actually appears to favour the conservatives in the congregation. Viewed in this light, the leadership and long-term members are fairly sanguine about attacks from outside critics and this has not blunted their desire to continue operating as an innovatory church.

SETTING GOALS FOR GROWTH

Westside is an interesting church both from the perspective of church growth and in terms of its relationship with evangelical culture and customary practice. It appears to have found a highly successful formula for sustained recruitment while at the same time it has chosen not to go down the 'big church' road in the way that successful evangelical churches in other Welsh cities have done. The model that Westside church has sought to follow since its inception is that of a locally based and relatively inclusive church; not too large, and committed both to the personal development and well-being of its congregation and to an ongoing programme of church planting. In terms of the thoughts of the authors of the 1995 Welsh Churches Survey on the links between congregational health and the intention to church plant, clearly Westside church is at the cutting edge of contemporary church culture and well placed to make the transition into this new century.

Nevertheless, in terms of setting goals for growth these are framed by a number of contradictory factors. This church is relatively unconcerned about numerical growth (or at least growth for growth's sake) and yet in less than a decade the size of the congregation has grown phenomenally compared to many other churches in the city. It does not have a particularly distinctive evangelical identity, neither holding to the extremes of doctrinaire biblical fundamentalism nor immersing itself in charismatic experientialism. Yet this 'middle way' attracts recruits from both these types of church and all points in between. Moreover, it has managed to model itself as a relatively inclusive church within an ideological framework (evangelicalism) that is customarily associated with exclusivism. Indeed, it appears to be successfully managing to move away from sectarianism and towards the mainstream without compromising either its commitment to evangelicalism or its independence and without falling into protodenominationalism. Consequently, it does not look or behave like a sectarian grouping but nor does it much resemble a mainstream Free Church. It falls somewhere else, recognizably drawing from the Welsh Congregational tradition but looking forward rather than backward.

While there are dangers in trying to be all things to all people, nevertheless it would appear that much of the attraction of Westside church lies in its growing reputation for taking the middle way. Its lack of extremism and overt social control by leaders and the sense of safety and genuine care for those in its orbit that it engenders are clearly powerful pull factors. At the same time, the dissatisfactions of younger evangelicals with the state of the local evangelical sector and the resistance to innovation and adaptation to changing social conditions in some quarters have emerged as significant push factors. The presence of pre-existing social networks linking members of the congregation to the wider evangelical community have also played a significant role in generating discourses around these issues, raising awareness about Westside church generally and in some cases facilitating the act of transfer into the church.

Westside church is also linked with a more general movement associated with many who took part in the *Tell Wales* mission to attempt to reconnect with the idea of community and a return to the local church ethos. This communitarian ideal is not particularly novel, in that it has been the mainstay of the 'new' churches' thinking for three decades now. However, the reality of this model of 'community' among these particular churches has often been the creation of tightly closed groups with little or no outside controls. This sectarian mentality has on occasions in the past led to excesses of social control and, in some cases, much emotional and psychological damage to individuals. Even so, it should also be recognized that this movement has been fuelled by the desire of many Christians for a more 'real' spiritual experience in religious groups that are not afraid to make waves and which are prepared to challenge people's lives and religious experience. Westside church offers this dimension of religious and social experience for those who desire it but within an environment that is perceived as safe and secure. For certain Christians, this combination of activism *and* security represents a powerful combination that may go a long way to explaining the high level of transfers into the church.

However, this apparently successful church has singularly failed to make much of an impact (certainly in terms of direct recruitment) among the surrounding unchurched community. While there are groups, notably the elderly and the young, who inhabit the fringes of the church, the majority of the local population appears indifferent to the presence of the church in the district. For a church whose identity is firmly based on the principle of personal conversion and whose success is measured in those terms, it would be easy (if somewhat simplistic) to lay the blame for this indifference on the general effects of 'secularization'. While the effects of general secularization should not be underestimated, there are also some localized factors that need to be taken into consideration. The moving of the main Sunday service to the local comprehensive school has somewhat reduced the church's local visibility but there is no evidence that this has affected levels of local recruitment either way. A far more pertinent factor relates to the question of the closed nature of the social networks that members of the congregation belong to. With a few exceptions, these are generally restricted to within the congregation and between other churchgoers in the city and the surrounding hinterlands. Exceptions to this pattern tend to be found within the periphery of the church (young families newly arrived in the city, students, members of sporting associations) and among those individuals who have managed to make friendships within the occupational sphere, but the general pattern still remains fairly fixed.

A recurrent theme throughout all the case studies has been the erosion of customary understandings of the nature of community. As the meaning of community has changed and as organized religion has become progressively privatized, this has become a growing problem within many churches. For evangelical churches this has often been compounded by a world-rejecting philosophy that can, if left unchecked, result in a ghetto mentality with fairly obvious consequences as regards sustained interaction with those outside the fold. This general culture of closure is exacerbated in the case of this church by the presence of a number of internal social networks based on former church allegiances. While it is clear that they are not consciously based on any principle of exclusion, in practice, membership of these networks, with all its benefits and satisfactions and common points of autobiographical reference, can inhibit members from looking to establish friendships outside the networks. However, both the Westside leadership and some members are astute enough to identify this as a problem and to recognize that this culture of closure needs to change if more meaningful contact with the local community is to be achieved. In practice this means the encouragement of new undifferentiated social networks that reflect the social and cultural composition of the local community. In terms of potential recruitment, sociological conversion process models (Richardson and Stewart, 1977; Stark and Bainbridge: 1985) suggest that most recruits come into religious groups along social networks. In the case of Westside church, this has to a certain extent been true of recruitment both by transfer and personal conversion. The leadership has a common-sense understanding of how these processes work. They also appear to have the will to change but it remains to be seen whether the congregation (particularly its older members) can overcome both the weight of evangelical tradition and their natural inclination to stay with those they know and who they can intimately relate to.

Notwithstanding these impediments, it is unlikely that the current growth rate will be substantially impaired in the future. This is because the church is structured and organized for growth even if at present this is primarily transfer growth. Westside operates within a religious economy and, as within any economic framework, the presence of factors such as efficient use of resources and effective organizational structures informed by careful and objective planning is a precondition for success. Moreover, church leaders (as in so many cases elsewhere) are not weighed down with routine administrative responsibilities and are thus free to concentrate on policy formulation and the bigger picture. In terms of effective human resource management, the church draws its inspiration as much from modern management techniques as it does from customary practices. There are clear avenues of 'promotion' and a wide availability of 'training opportunities' to ensure the smooth and successful internal reproduction of personnel capable of both leading the church as it is and new ventures such as church plants.

There is also a clear strategy in place that offers direction for the future, church planting, and on the basis of the limited evidence available from the first church plant this may resolve some of the motivational problems that have exercised the leadership in recent years. The small church model should reduce the sense of distanciation between core and periphery and existing social networks will be shaken up. Within the smaller fellowships that will grow out of the original church, newcomers should find it easier to penetrate into the social life of these new congregations. Moreover, these new fellowships, being in effect new social networks, are likely (at least in their initial stages) to be more fluid and permeable and thus less closed off from the local community. This has been the case with the first church plant and there is no reason why these experiences should not be reproduced in successive moves in this direction.

There is then a clear set of organizational imperatives underpinning and driving the life of this church forward. As is evident from the previous case studies and the wider picture of religious life in Wales captured in the 1995 Welsh Churches Survey, this in marked contrast to the experience of most churches and what passes as organization and resource management for so many congregations. If the last case study exemplified some of the negative consequences of what we might term the internal secularization of congregations, this case study offers a very different and positive perspective on a similar theme. The occupational provenance of the leadership team, many of whom have held responsible managerial positions in industry and commerce, has clearly influenced their approach to church organization. Indeed, it would appear natural to most people that they should seek to utilize this experience if possible within the context of church life. However, as the evidence of conservative evangelical criticism of the leadership demonstrates, some individuals and groups persist in seeing this as anathema within a religious context. (Although why seventeenth- or eighteenth-century models of church polity are 'more scriptural' never seems to be satisfactorily explained.) Be that as it may, sociologically it is true that organizational imperatives remain much the same whether in a business enterprise, a football club or a church. There appears to be no reason why lessons learnt in one organizational environment are not transferable to another.

Arguably, it is possible in large part to link the successes of this church, both in terms of numerical growth and in its perception of a duty of care to its congregation, to its organizational structure. In contrast, most congregations merely muddle through and this shows itself in a culture of complacency and inevitably, if unchecked, in numerical decline. Certainly, among the declining churches that we have come across in these pages, any coherent strategies for growth or even the ability to engage in short-term planning are largely conspicuous by their absence. Indeed, the rapid decline of organized religion in Wales in the latter part of the last century is largely due to the wholesale adoption by individual congregations of strategies of maintenance over mission. In the face of widespread secularization, this has guaranteed nothing but the continued erosion of the place of the churches in Welsh society. There is a lack of vision for the future. In contrast, innovatory churches such as this are achieving at least some partial successes in resisting the currents of secularization, even if they are swimming against the tide. They demonstrate what can be done, despite the difficulties inherent in a secularized society, given the vision and the will. Furthermore, this church offers us a possible template, not only of how to achieve success in recruitment but also of what many churches may come to look like as the present century progresses.

There has been no shortage of writers prepared to hazard their opinion on what the church of the future might look like. From Wilson through Wallis to Bruce, one strand of opinion suggests that in a highly secularized environment, world-rejecting sectarian groupings (fundamentalists) are best placed to resist the currents of secularization and to survive and flourish within what will presumably be a very arid religious landscape. Others of a more postmodern bent suggest that religion will of necessity become less organized and more free-standing. The authority of institutions will continue to be progressively eroded and religion will come to be largely the province of individual judgement and more syncretic in character.

If Westside church is one face of the future for organized religion in Wales, this raises some interesting theoretical questions. Clearly, the success of Westside church (and others like it) in recruiting new members is based upon its relatively moderate evangelical stance and its hands-off approach to social control. On the evidence presented above, many evangelicals in Swansea (particularly the younger generation) appear to be retreating from fundamentalism, not rushing towards it. Indeed, there appears to be something of a cultural shift among individual evangelicals who are more likely to question customary authority and less likely to commit themselves wholeheartedly to membership of religious organizations. Religion has become more a matter of choice and the relationship between secular and religious values is in many cases becoming blurred. Individual evangelicals are coming to question many of the shibboleths of evangelicalism and its world-rejecting ethos, while remaining committed to evangelicalism as an ideology. Clearly, the nature of evangelicalism is changing while the form remains.

In terms of congregational identity, the experience of Westside is indicative of a significant shift away from sectarianism and this is reflected in a syncretic identity forged out of a synthesis of different evangelical traditions and increasingly informed by practice elsewhere in the Christian church. It is also clear from Westside's experience that there is a continuing place for organized religion. People still wish to associate together meaningfully in churches (if increasingly on their own terms and according to their own judgement) and, indeed, there appears to be a move towards and a demand for a more inclusive community-based church model among many evangelicals. At the same time, Westside exemplifies a move away from denominationalism and the growing preference for independent and non-aligned status among new churches, freeing them to innovate and adapt to contemporary social and cultural conditions. None of this looks much like Bruce's thesis or indeed that of the postmodernists, although clearly currents and trends associated with 'postmodernity' are (to a limited extent) informing the social transformation of evangelical religion in this part of the world. Whether the organization of churches along the lines of Westside will become the norm in Wales is still a matter of conjecture. With their independent status they are better placed than many to adapt and survive in a post-Christian environment and, if the mainstream denominations continue to decline at their present rate, then the profile of these new churches within the Welsh religious economy will continue to grow, if only by default. However, they will not suit everyone and the challenge for the mainstream, therefore, is to look at and learn from the innovatory practices and forms of organization that the new churches have pioneered.

8

Understanding Church Growth and Decline

Religious institutions in Wales are all struggling in their various ways to make sense of the transformed social and cultural environment in which they are forced to operate. Religion has moved from the centre of communal life to a marginal position. At the same time the customary meanings that the Welsh have attached to the notion of community are increasingly undergoing a transformation and these two processes, the decline of the social significance of religion and the decline of community, are linked. Nevertheless, organized religion continues to persist, albeit under very difficult conditions. There are some instances of successful adaptation by groups and this is reflected in pockets of growth even within a wider social and cultural landscape of decline. As we have seen from previous chapters, many of the factors that inhibit or promote congregational growth are essentially local in provenance, even if they reflect wider societal currents. These factors are complex, but nevertheless recognizable patterns may be discerned and these give us some basis for a more analytic approach to the problems facing the churches in what is increasingly a post-Christian landscape.

Church growth and decline is clearly a social process, but in recent years it has often been treated more as the effect of another process, secularization, than as something worthy of investigation in its own right. While that particular approach has some merit for the social theorist who wishes to explore and capture the broad span of social change as it affects religion, it throws little light on the social processes within the religious domain triggered by secularization. Nor can it provide explanations of the very different responses to broader social changes by the religious constituency. If sociology is about anything, it is about reflecting the idea that human behaviour is the product of community life and that people's behaviour cannot be reduced to individual properties. Social life and its achievements are dependent on both intersubjective meaning (that is, ideas about the world derived from shared experiences) and the ongoing practical experience of putting those ideas into operation (praxis) as well as being subject to wider structural constraints such as 'secularization'. Clearly, religion does not exist in a vacuum but is the product of human group life and should be treated in a spirit of enquiry that seeks to situate theory in the actualities of lived social life.

In this spirit the research that informs this particular volume began its life as an attempt by one sociologist to answer two related questions. The first question was related to the visible decline of organized religion in Wales in the twentieth century. Simply, how was it that a population previously noted for religiosity had become so extensively divorced from its religious institutions and what are the implications for these institutions as they face the future? The second question related to the secularization paradigm. Simply, how useful or not was this idea in terms of its practical application to the problems of church growth and decline?

In terms of the first question, historians in Wales have done much to further our understanding of the historical processes underlying the progressive secularization of Welsh society. However, the more recent past remains relatively uncharted and there has been little or no discussion of events in the latter part of the twentieth century, a crucial period in terms of the disengagement and marginalization of religious institutions in Wales. Moreover, these processes are certainly not exhausted yet and there may be more twists and turns in the narrative as it continues to unfold. Although general religious decline appears to be a fact of life in contemporary Wales, the process has always been uneven and the future remains (at least notionally) open-ended. In terms of the second question, there are now so many variants of the secularization thesis, often presented in highly abstracted forms, that it is, to use a colloquialism, becoming increasingly difficult to see the wood for the trees. Some sociologists interpret contemporary religious phenomena as expressions of continued secularization while others see these phenomena as proof of the irrelevance of this thesis. Moreover, this is a debate that has become increasingly self-referential, with an over-emphasis on the merits of competing theories as opposed to a more grounded approach.

I have sought to approach the problem differently. Much of what we know about the transformation of religion in Welsh society in the twentieth century comes from a series of community studies carried out by anthropologists and sociologists in the middle part of the century. These have not only provided valuable snapshots of changing communities and lost lifestyles but have contributed to our understanding of the wider nature of social change in Welsh society without which we cannot fully understand the nature of change within the religious sphere. In this spirit I have limited my enquiries to one geographical area, south-west Wales, which seems to me to best encapsulate various features of Welsh life. This is a region where English-speaking Wales meets Welsh-speaking Wales and where historically urban and rural communities have existed in close proximity. That said, there is no one 'typical' region in Wales, which is why I have also sought to concentrate my enquiries on the experience of actual congregations in order to begin to understand the various processes that are affecting the churches and chapels of Wales. This approach carries its own risks, and as Davies *et al.* (1991: 282) have suggested, there is inevitably some tension between seeking to rise above the local and anecdotal while at the same time recognizing the crucial importance of local factors on congregational life. My rationale therefore has been to describe and account for the changes affecting congregations in a local setting while at the same time working towards a more generalizable understanding of decline and growth of religious groups.

THE CHURCHES AND SOCIO-ECONOMIC AND CULTURAL CHANGE

It is clear that the marked economic and social changes that have taken place in Swansea have been reflected in the life of the churches and chapels of the city and its surrounding hinterland. In addition to the decline of religion as a socially significant force, three visible major changes have affected social life:

(1)   the disappearance of much of the traditional industrial base;
(2)   the marked decline of the Welsh language in influence and everyday use;
(3)   the exponential growth of the city.

All these factors have to varying degrees impacted on the relations between the churches and chapels and their social environment. This is most apparent in what was historically the strongest sector of Welsh religious life, Nonconformity. The decline of industry has undercut the socio-economic base of Nonconformity, while the general decline of the Welsh language has undercut the cultural base of a significant sector of Nonconformity, the Welsh-medium chapels. At the same time, the growth of the city and related population movement have emphatically altered the traditional religious ecology of the area.

In sociological and socio-geographic terms Swansea is best characterized as a loose collection of discrete localities or 'urban villages', reflecting past patterns of industrial activity and existing within a larger structural framework, the city (Rosser and Harris, 1965: 42). The changes outlined above have all significantly contributed to the decline of both the real and imagined local community, and, in turn, those customary patterns of religious life associated with the local communities of Swansea. In the past religion was embedded in the local community and its cultural, social and economic structures and referentially tied to particular places and buildings. Today, these neighbour-hoods, while they still constitute sites of common residence, no longer reflect the shared experience of living, working and engaging in shared leisure activities that were typical of the communities of Swansea.

The transformation of the labour and housing markets has weakened the occupational and residential bases of the traditional working class, leading to the progressive erosion of a distinctive working-class culture that was visibly connected to the churches and chapels. While these buildings remain, they now function primarily as witnesses to the past. Swansea has also seen expansion in its western environs and the emergence of a substantial suburban fringe not centred on historic villages, while at the same time the customary areas of residence to the east are increasingly run down and economically marginalized. Significant numbers of that section of the local population most likely to attend churches and chapels have moved or are moving out of traditional working-class locales and into suburban settings. Moreover, this exodus is as much a move in social terms (up into the middle class) as it is a geographical movement. Some have continued with churchgoing, some have not, but all have, by virtue of their changed social circumstances and physical location, adopted a privatized lifestyle at odds with their previous experience of life in solidaristic communities.

At the same time, the populations of traditional working-class areas have fragmented socially and culturally, undermining both local social solidarity and church–community relations and eroding customary bases for local identifications. A sense of local identity is dependent not only on sharing geographical space but on the shared meanings of what it is to be born and brought up in a bounded locality and the long-standing social connections and networks that give flesh to the idea of 'community'. In many communities an influx of younger families drawn by the presence of affordable housing has led to further erosion of long-standing social networks and a growing discontinuity between the population of the churches and chapels and their surrounding communities. Moreover, in many cases these new-comers demonstrate little desire to establish any long-term roots, typically moving on to better housing as their financial circumstances improve. In terms of the maintenance of a collective sense of local identity, this situation is exacerbated even further in the case of those English-speaking families moving into traditionally Welsh-speaking locales. These population movements have left those churches and chapels that are predicated upon a strong sense of continuous local identity high and dry. In consequence, these churches and chapels are now left in a position whereby they increasingly appear to have little cultural or social relevance to their surrounding catchment populations (a situation not helped by the difference in the average age of congregations and that of the general population). Understandably in these changed circumstances, churches and chapels are experiencing marked difficulties in terms of recruitment and outreach into their local populations.

Churches and chapels in the suburban fringe also find themselves in a similar position as regards outreach and recruitment, although for different reasons. Whereas the older part of the city is characterized by the steady erosion of communitarian social networks and the progressive atomization of populations, the suburban population of western Swansea has always been characterized by an atomized social structure and a virtual absence of shared local social networks. While there are generally not so marked differences in age or cultural dispositions between churchgoers and their surrounding communities, this cultural similarity is based primarily on the shared experience of an affluent privatized middle-class lifestyle. The aggregated effects of this lifestyle can be seen in the sparsity of community facilities, reflecting both the lack of active social solidarity and a weak sense of community consciousness. Leisure pursuits tend to be centred on city-centre facilities and churches tend to be relatively disconnected from the lives of their unchurched neighbours. Among a highly mobile population shared local networks tend to be weak and very limited in scope. Indeed, it is only among the churches and their social networks (and possibly the local schools) that anything approximating to the idea of community might be found. However, despite the possibilities inherent in the fact that congregations themselves constitute 'communities of association', the churches remain largely disengaged from the general population.

Clearly, there are marked social, cultural and economic differences between these social environments in which churches and chapels operate. We might also say that social changes within the environments in which churches operate have significantly affected the relations between the religious and general populations. While these changes do not themselves constitute a definite process of 'secularization', nevertheless they are characteristic of those modern Western societies that are becoming increasingly and visibly secularized. However, it is also clear from the evidence that, notwithstanding these social environmental differences, some church types have adapted better to these changing conditions than their competitors operating in the same districts. Clearly, some churches continue to maintain a viable presence in districts where churchgoers are thin on the ground while other churches are struggling to survive even in areas with a relatively high rate of churchgoing. It is to this aspect of the religious economy that I now turn.

A PROVISIONAL CHURCH TYPOLOGY

The religious ecology of Swansea encompasses a wide variety of churches and church groups with varying institutional structures and ideological orientations. Nevertheless, religious institutions might be classified into two rudimentary types[1] for the purposes of my analysis. These are:

1. *Communal institutions*

These are the long-established churches and denominations that filled the late nineteenth- and early twentieth-century religious landscape. They are represented by the Church in Wales, the Roman Catholic Church and the historic Free Church connections. The latter can be further subdivided into Welsh- and English-speaking connections. These groups were the product of a time period when religion was a normative institution and eligibility can be either ascriptive or voluntaristic, although in both cases there are likely to be formal procedures for full admission. Typically, these groups customarily operated with a close identification with community but under conditions of secularization have tended to become progressively differentiated from society.

2. *Associational institutions*

These are churches (both independent and connectional) that have progressively established themselves throughout the twentieth century. Predominantly English-speaking, often sectarian in nature and overwhelmingly evangelical in their theology, these groups include the Christian Brethren, Pentecostals and neo-Pentecostals and many independent congregations. These groups are the product of the increasing trend towards voluntarism in religious allegiance, and associational eligibility is invariably marked by some test of religious commitment. Structurally, these groups tend to be differentiated from society from their inception.

Of necessity this is a rudimentary classification, not least because there is some crossover between the two types. A significant number of independent congregations represent congregations that have broken at some point with the historic Free Church connections, while some of those connections (such as the United Reformed Church) are relatively new creations. Moreover, many evangelicals and evangelical congregations are to be found within the historic churches and denominations. Nevertheless, as a *provisional* classification it provides the basis for the following discussion that will highlight the significant variations in the rate of decline between these two categories of religious institutions.

As a rule of thumb, the associational type churches have experienced a much slower rate of decline than their communal type counterparts and in some individual cases there is even growth. This is not altogether unsurprising, given their active commitment to proselytization and their sectarian nature. As tightly bounded groups they appear rather more successful in the retention of their younger members than the more loosely bounded communal type churches. Furthermore, it is axiomatic that the historic churches and denominations, by virtue of the fact that they have had a longer history as institutions, are more vulnerable to changes in church life and institutional decay.

However, there are also significant variations in the rate and extent of decline *within* these broad categories as well as *between* them. In general, among those historical churches and connections that have customarily exhibited a close relationship with community, the Anglicans and Roman Catholics have not experienced decline to the same degree as their Free Church counterparts. Indeed, marked decline in that quarter has seen the Church in Wales emerge by default as the largest single religious grouping in Swansea. Among the Free Churches a very different story unfolds. The Welsh-speaking churches have progressively lost support as their natural constituency has faded away and (with one or two special exceptions) most of their congregations in Swansea have either ceased to exist or are now facing what looks like imminent extinction. The English-speaking sector has held up rather better, but only relative to their Welsh-speaking counterparts, and it continues to experience a general decline in its fortunes. Among the associational type churches the only real areas of growth are among the 'new', associational, churches and some city-centre Pentecostal congregations. In contrast, older established groups (notably the Brethren and the Pentecostals) are beginning to experience many of the problems associated with mainstream Free Churches, although not yet to the same extent or degree.

In summary, while these two typologies enable us to see a very rudimentary pattern they, of necessity, provide us with a very incomplete picture. Religious institutions operate within a much wider social and cultural environment and there are a number of factors relating to this environment that also need to be taken into consideration if we are to more fully understand these processes and their implications for the futures of these institutions.

CHURCH GROWTH AND DECLINE: ECOLOGICAL, SOCIAL AND CULTURAL FACTORS

It is abundantly clear by now that geographical factors have had a significant influence on the religious ecology of Swansea and that this is related to other factors such as class, culture and social mobility. An increasingly mobile society has lessened the ties of church membership, fuelled transfers and is partially responsible for the emergence of a floating population of worshippers who flit from congregation to congregation. Among the churches this has created winners and losers. While these trends have had a negative impact on some congregations clearly it has benefited others, although the resulting higher levels of attendance in some churches have also been accompanied by a parallel decline in commitment to formal membership. Given that individual congregational growth (particularly among associational type churches) appears highly dependent on transfers from other congregations, this inevitably raises uncomfortable questions for the future. Clearly, much of this transfer growth has negative implications for those churches that are losing members to other churches. However, of more significance is the fact that this movement is within a fixed (and declining) religious constituency. If this constituency continues to decline numerically (and there is no reason to suppose that it will not, at least in the short term) then the potential gains in terms of recruitment through transfers are also likely to lessen.

Viewed in this light it would appear imperative for churches to seek once again to engage with and recruit from the general population if they are to reverse these trends. However, this is obviously easier said than done. In working-class districts the progressive westward drift of churchgoers into the suburbs and their resultant movement up into the middle class has led to the disembedding of organized religion from its traditional working-class frames of reference. Religion is no longer visibly part of that culture in the ways that it used to be and churches and chapels are increasingly divorced from their local populations. Furthermore, there are far too many places of worship relative to current local demand. Therefore the returns from any putative recruitment strategies in these communities are likely to be slim. Over in the suburbs, the lack of long-standing community structures and the ubiquity of the privatized lifestyle, while very different factors, have led to similar problems. In general, churches in these districts have not been able to engage with their local populations to any significant degree. Accordingly, the pool of potential new recruits is mainly restricted to existing churchgoers who happen to move into the district and are seeking a new church to attend or car-owning individuals from other districts who wish to transfer their religious allegiances. The problem is perhaps most acute in the newer housing developments that have sprung up around the city. These estates are less likely to have any formal religious provision nearby and in many cases lack even the most basic social networks and sense of community. The average age of residents tends to be somewhat lower than that of more established residential areas and anecdotal evidence from those few Christian groups working in these estates suggests a widespread indifference to organized religion.

Whether this is indifference towards religion or merely towards religious institutions is unclear and requires further research. What is clearer is that there are a number of factors relating to the internal organization and culture of churches that are affecting their capacity for mission. Contrasting systems of financial accountability between the churches and denominations can inhibit or enable mission. Where congregations are solely responsible for the financial upkeep of their church, including the payment of ministers, affluent middle-class congregations clearly have an advantage over poorer congregations. This is something that also helps to explain the increasingly middle-class profile of organized religion in Wales. Leaderless congregations are unlikely to be effective in the sphere of mission and indeed, as we have seen in a number of cases, marked numerical decline follows on quickly from the loss of a minister. However, it should also be borne in mind that, while the absence of ministerial leadership exacerbates numerical decline, this absence usually results from a drop in adult congregational numbers to a point where they can no longer pay for leadership.

Those churches that have a centrally funded ministry are in a rather more advantageous position and this is most clearly exemplified within the Church in Wales, which is out-performing the other historic mainstream denominations in terms of numerical strength. Certainly, the experience of the Anglican churches in the city where every parish has an incumbent minister suggests that the role of the parish priest in halting or reversing decline is of crucial importance. However, the experience of those Free Churches that do have a centrally paid ministry (notably the Presbyterians and the Methodists) is mixed at best. Nationally, numerical decline within these denominations has placed strains on this system and their human resources are increasingly over-stretched. Indeed, for many congregations the presence of a paid minister is no guarantee of their long-term survival. In many cases Free Church ministers are spread very thinly, with oversight of multiple congregations, effectively reducing their role to that of preaching and teaching and their status to that of an occasional visitor. Clearly, this is not a recipe for the type of sustained engagement with local communities that might reconnect the churches with the people. Indeed, how far the Anglicans can continue to maintain their inclusive national parochial system in the face of their own growing financial difficulties and the falling levels of clergy recruitment remains to be seen.

There also appears to be a correlation between the length of time a congregation has been established locally and levels of decline. Over the years long-established congregations have a tendency to get set in their ways, a trend that is exacerbated by ageing memberships. All too often they can appear to their surrounding local populations to be both culturally irrelevant and socially exclusive, leading to their marginalization within those communities that should be their lifeblood. In contrast newer churches and congregations, by virtue of their recent provenance, do not have the weight of tradition and customary practice to contend with. The language question succinctly highlights this problem as many Welsh-speaking churches are in a very disadvantageous position in relation to their surrounding local populations who have over the years become predominantly English-speaking.

These observations apply most strongly to independent and semi-independent congregations who tend to have a distinct localized identity and hard boundaries. Conversely, in those congregations whose identity is partially informed by the cultural and organizational characteristics of a central institutional structure the picture is somewhat different. For example, among the Anglican churches, an institutional principle of hierarchical authority structures and open inclusive pastoral ministry all serve to promote a wider sense of identity within which congregations can negotiate their relations with their catchment populations. Among those other communal churches that do not practise an inclusive pastoral ministry, opportunities to engage with local populations are rather more limited. Moreover, while their respective denominational connections constitute a point of reference, hierarchical authority structures tend to be looser. This opens up the danger of congregations losing sight of the wider picture and socially and culturally closing in on themselves. Again, the upshot is local marginalization.

In trying to identify those factors that are affecting church growth and decline obviously we cannot ignore the effects of increased competition between religious groups. The idea of competition necessarily leads us into a consideration of the place of churches and chapels within the religious economy of Swansea and the positioning of that economy within the wider social and cultural environment. For the purposes of this analysis, religious groups in Swansea can be said to have two distinct constituencies. The first and most important constituency is to be found within the churchgoing population of the city and their churches and chapels. This constitutes the religious economy of the area. Even where religious institutions have been subject to privatization and marginalization and despite appearances to the contrary, this religious economy does not exist in a vacuum. It is situated within the second, wider constituency that is the general population of the city and the surrounding hinterland. While in the real world there is no concrete distinction between these groups, for the purposes of this analysis, these constituencies will be dealt with separately, with a discussion of the churches and their social environment following on from this section.

As the high level of transfer activity between some churches indicates, the existing churchgoing community constitutes an important resource for church growth. Self-evidently, transfer activity of this magnitude also points to competition between churches. While simple geographical mobility accounts for some of this activity, this is by no means the whole story. Swansea churchgoers are also by nature a conservative constituency and as mainstream churches have become more liberal in doctrine and preaching there has been some movement of individuals from communal type to associational type churches. More recently, with the arrival of the new churches and the growing profile of neo-Pentecostalism and the challenges that this has thrown up among conservative evangelical congregations, there has been much movement in both directions within this sector of the religious economy. Clearly there are high levels of competition between associational type churches and, we might assume from the ways in which congregations position themselves theologically within this environment, some rudimentary 'marketing' of different churches. Conversely, there is far less overt competition among the historic communal churches. In general, congregations in this sector are rather less concerned with matters of doctrine and more concerned with matters of practice. Among the Free Churches many of their congregations appear to be preserved in a form of cultural aspic, making it difficult for remaining ministers to initiate the necessary changes that might enable their congregations to compete in the modern religious marketplace. Perceived by many outside the churches as socially exclusive and culturally irrelevant, there is little to attract newcomers to these congregations. Unsurprisingly, this is the sector of the religious economy that is most visibly declining.

In contrast, Anglican churches appear to have benefited somewhat from this climate of competition. If many communal type churches increasingly resemble clubs for the religiously and socially minded, it could be argued that the social cachet that is still associated with the Church in Wales is a powerful attraction for the upwardly mobile churchgoing individual. Certainly in the immediate past, many upwardly mobile chapelgoers who have made the move to the suburbs have marked their parvenu status by becoming churchgoers. Moreover, the perceived stability and sense of historic continuity of the Church in Wales are attractive features both to the conservative minded and those with a liking for tradition. In contrast, because of its particular institutional nature, the Roman Catholic Church has a fixed constituency, referentially tied to the church by ties of blood as much as belief and transfers in from the Protestant churches are extremely rare.

Clearly, religious institutions are increasingly operating in an environment that does not easily lend itself to their purposes, even if it is clear that many churches are also partially responsible for their own progressive marginalization. In summary, there appear to be a number of recurrent factors informing patterns of church growth and decline in Swansea. These are:

(1)   the effects of social and geographical mobility;
(2)   the effects of disembedding from customary social and cultural frames of reference;
(3)   the financial health of congregations;
(4)   the nature of the churches' cultural and social relations with their surrounding populations;
(5)   the effects of competition between the churches.

While all these factors are germane to the health of the churches and chapels, this is by no means an exhaustive list of factors that inform church growth and decline. We now need to consider in more detail the social environment that these religious institutions operate in and how secularization has impacted on the relationship between the churches and the general population of Swansea.

THE CHURCHES AND THEIR SOCIAL ENVIRONMENT

The overall trajectory of religious decline in south-west Wales as it played itself out in the late twentieth century suggests a growing disengagement of religious institutions from their surrounding social environment. This is most clearly illustrated in areas of relatively new housing where any sense of community is largely absent and where individuals appear increasingly indifferent to organized religion. While this indifference suggests that a lack of any strong religious belief (or indeed, any belief at all) on the part of individuals is inhibiting recruitment, belief is only part of the equation. Religious affiliation is often as much a social disposition as a religious one and both Bernice Martin (1992) and Robin Gill (1994) suggest that for many individuals a sense of belonging is as important as belief.

In these cases, it is the perceived social benefits of belonging to a church that initially draw individuals or families into church or chapel attendance and is only then followed by the maturation of religious belief. It follows that a set of social relations linking churches to their surrounding catchment community is essential if this process is to happen. In pursuing this line of argument, the most obvious explanation for the decline of churchgoing based on the survey evidence for Swansea is not so much 'secularization' as the increasing lack of shared social networks in many communities. Certainly, it is clear from the evidence presented so far that where networks that link churches to a catchment population exist (however weak or attenuated) recruitment is facilitated by these links. Conversely, where they are absent decline inevitably follows.

Clearly, this is one explanation for the continued buoyancy of Anglican congregations relative to other mainstream churches in the city. Simply, with their tradition of inclusive parish ministry reaching into the surrounding population they appear better placed to retain some localized social significance. We might also assume that this is more the case in long-standing traditional communities than in those newer areas of residence that lack the necessary social networks for sustained engagement. However, if this is the case, there is then the problem of explaining why suburban churches and chapels operating in these atomized neighbourhoods are doing rather better than their counterparts elsewhere in the city.

If we take the situation in the western suburbs first, a number of related factors emerge. Population movement is one. This is most clearly illustrated in the experience of suburban Anglican and Roman Catholic congregations, where their growth is largely a result of in-migration over a long period of time from the traditional eastern areas of residence. However, things are not so clear-cut within the Free Church sector and it is among these churches that the key to understanding the patterns of growth and decline in the suburbs might be found.

Survey returns revealed that declining Free Church congregations were overwhelmingly non-evangelical in orientation and that any significant growth was to be found among evangelical congregations. This suggests that, among the Free Churches, theological orientations are an important variable. Certainly, evangelical congregations are self-evidently committed to the idea of mission and active proselytization. Be that as it may, this is at best a partial explanation of success in recruitment, as successful evangelistic outreach requires a receptive population *that can be reached*, implying a network process (Lofland and Stark, 1965; Heirich, 1977; Richardson and Stewart, 1977; Stark and Bainbridge, 1980; Welch, 1981). As we have seen, however, there is a general absence of established social networks in the suburbs. Furthermore, if evangelicalism was the only operational variable, it could be expected that evangelical congregations would flourish wherever they were located in the city, something that is not borne out in the survey data.

It is the presence or absence of concrete social networks linking churches to a pool of potential recruits that appears to be a much stronger variable. In the case of communal type Free Churches operating in the suburban fringe, their lack of success is understandable in the light of their weak links with the surrounding population. Associational type churches in the district are also confronted with the same problem of operating in an immediate social environment where social networks rarely stretch beyond family and immediate neighbours. It follows that any success in recruitment (other than those partial successes in accessing these limited networks) is primarily the result of operations within a *different* type of social environment. Given that most of their recruits are transfers from other congregations, it is clear that this operational environment must be the wider religious community of Swansea. It is here that we find complex networks of social relationships linking individuals, families and congregations that are not particularly tied to geography but which, by virtue of their shared identification with evangelicalism, might be characterized as a 'community'. Access to these social networks is one key to understanding congregational growth in this sector of the churches, although these are clearly not localized networks but 'inter-subjective' networks that link like-minded individuals who possess a shared social and cultural experience.

In contrast, declining Free Churches appear unwilling or unable to establish the wider frame of reference necessary for them to extend their relations with others in the religious community in order to benefit from transfer growth. (The nearest these churches come to this is in the forced closures of some churches and their merging with other congregations.) Furthermore, as the case studies suggest, internal congregational cultures and the question of identity can inhibit or enable growth. The suburban churches represent discrete communities within a wider social environment and all congregations, to a greater or lesser degree, have boundaries that differentiate them from the wider population. Clearly, the nature of these boundaries and their strength or weakness are important factors in outreach (Douglas, 1996). Perhaps this is stating the obvious, but in terms of engaging with those living in the immediate neighbourhood, congregations with an outward-looking orientation self-evidently appear to be in a better position than those that direct their gaze inwards. However, in practice, within a suburban setting this means adopting strategies and providing services that are most likely to appeal to a middle-class constituency. Furthermore, success is dependent on some measure of social and cultural congruence between local churched and unchurched populations.

Clearly, the most successful congregations are those that have sought to hedge their bets and engage both with their local surrounding community *and* the wider community of churchgoers in Swansea. In contrast, where churches have over the years increasingly adopted an inward-looking orientation, with their activities directed exclusively towards existing members, then the appeal of those churches remains largely with members. Within this context intimations of decline tend to become a self-fulfilling prophecy and more so where congregations are also ageing. In these cases, congregational activities almost inevitably tend to be increasingly orientated towards the upper age group, making these churches unattractive to younger age groups. This can result in a failure not only to recruit outsiders but also to retain younger individuals and families.

In terms of retention, if this culture is too strong all too often younger members will either move to the margins of the congregation, attending infrequently, or they will leave. More generally, where the life of a congregation is progressively directed inward, this creates a dense group structure that also tends to inhibit recruitment by virtue of its cohesiveness. The upshot is that, while churches may employ a rhetoric of hospitality and see themselves as a welcoming congregation, prospective recruits will see a tightly bounded group and draw their own conclusions. Moreover, where a church is orientated towards satisfying the needs of existing members, it is unlikely to explore the types of liturgical or organizational changes that might appeal to a wider constituency. This can all too often result in a situation where the appeal of a congregation to prospective newcomers is limited to those individuals who most closely match the cultural and social profile of the existing congregation.

Moving away from the problems of suburban churches, it is clear that the social and cultural environment of the eastern part of the city is very different and this poses alternative challenges for the churches. The majority of places of worship in the city are (for historical reasons) located in the eastern districts and therefore competition between churches is greater, in the sense that there are more places of worship relative to local populations. It follows that congregations are much smaller, leading to a general perception of greater religious decline within these districts. However, the over-provision of places of worship is more a symptom than a cause of decline. More obviously, congregations in these eastern districts have declined as existing members have died or moved away and they have not been replaced with new blood.

This constitutes a failure to replicate on two counts. The majority of congregations have failed to reproduce themselves through *autogenous* growth (growth accruing from the recruitment of members' children) or through *allogenous* growth (growth accruing from the recruitment of non-members or their children). The failure to recruit internally is primarily the result of the processes of social and geographical mobility outlined above. The failure to recruit externally is more complex. Clearly, factors such as the decline of traditional industries and the decline of the Welsh language have contributed to religious decline in much the same way as they have contributed to the decline of social cohesion and voluntary association in working-class localities in general. Furthermore, small, ageing congregations have few resources with which to engage in mission. However, this is not the whole story. The ways in which congregations in these districts perceive their individual and shared situations is also an important factor in how they respond to their local difficulties.

For many declining congregations, particularly those with no professional leadership, the processes that have led to their numerical decline appear to them to be unrelenting and totally outside their control. Many individual members are at a loss to explain the social and cultural transformations that have affected organized religion in their lifetimes and their typical response is to continue what they have always done in the hope that conditions might change for the better. This entails little more than maintaining the Sunday worship service until such time as there are no members left or the building becomes unfit for further use. For those congregations with a dozen members or fewer, that time is not far away. Typically, these congregations are small, ageing, insular and without effective leadership, and they constitute an overwhelming majority of congregations in these older districts.

However, there are some exceptional congregations that, despite the problems of operating within this environment, can point to some limited success in resisting these processes. For these congregations, typically larger in size, with an age range more representative of their surrounding population and invariably with professional leadership of some sort, while confidence in the future is muted, it is not entirely absent. A larger congregation, better cared for buildings and the presence of a priest or minister all help congregations to maintain both a sense of continuity and a sense of social significance (real or imagined) within the communities in which they operate. In this respect, confidence in the continued future presence of their congregation is greater among Anglicans and Roman Catholics who assume, rightly or wrongly, that in at least the immediate future their respective church authorities will continue to subsidize financially a church presence in the locality. Within these churches the role of the incumbent cleric is crucial for the maintenance of this confidence. In the eyes of the congregation their priest both acts as an advocate and mediator between the congregation and the institutional hierarchy and provides leadership and direction for the future. For the surrounding community, the continued presence of clergy in their locality is also a source of confidence that their local religious institutions will continue to maintain a presence and remain a resource for local people.

Be that as it may, if we are to understand their situation more fully these relations with the wider local community need to be taken into consideration. Both autogenous and allogenous growth are self-evidently network-dependent. Within these long-standing communities, while their social composition and character has radically changed, some traces of traditional social networks are still present. These may be *vestigial* networks (composed of *individuals*, not visibly apparent to the observer and of little remaining social significance) or *truncated* networks (composed of a few remaining long-established *families* and still retaining local social status and cultural significance). In terms of the relationship between these networks and the churches and chapels there appears to be some correspondence between the health of congregations and the types of network that they have access to.

Vestigial networks are invariably the provinces of elderly inhabitants who remain resident after their families have long moved away. In this they correspond most closely to the demographic and cultural profile of small declining congregations. Indeed, the personnel of these vestigial networks and ageing small congregations are often interchangeable, tied together as they are by long-standing social relations fashioned in a tightly circumscribed locale. They have little or no local social contact outside their immediate networks and age group and this is the world of day centres, luncheon clubs and afternoon tea in the parlour. While limited allogenous growth is possible within this situational context (given the high level of social and cultural congruence) it is not a long-term solution to decline. In contrast, congregations whose members are part of or who have access to truncated social networks can still hope to pursue both allogenous and autogenous growth strategies based on their social relationship with families and friends. While they cannot hope to reach *all* in the wider local community they can potentially reach *some* of that community. While this proposition holds for all types of churches, the crucial question is whether congregations with access to truncated social networks are willing to motivate themselves in the area of active recruitment. The evidence suggests a qualified 'yes' although strategies for engaging with these catchment populations will differ somewhat by church type and in their degree of success or failure.

Self-evidently, in any district marked by pervasive religious decline, all churches will find it difficult to operate effective missions. Among those communal type churches with some access to truncated networks, while they may reject the idea of aggressive evangelism, they are acutely aware of the need to recruit new members if they are not to experience the fate of many surrounding churches. In general, 'mission' is interpreted as the establishing of closer relations with those individuals and families who lie within the immediate social orbit of the congregation. However, while this may raise the profile of the congregation locally and improve the quality of life within the community, it does not in itself necessarily lead to any significant congregational growth. Associational type churches, by virtue of their distinctive theology, are manifestly committed to overt evangelization. However, in practice, there are two factors that actively inhibit local recruitment among these churches. First, aggressive evangelization does not always resonate within the type of social environment in which these churches find themselves.

In general, and human nature being what it is, people do not like to be told that they are sinners whose likely final destination is the fiery pit. Truncated social networks, based as they are on sets of close relations and a long-standing sense of familiarity and mutuality, do not lend themselves to this type of approach (a prophet often being without honour on their own home patch). Secondly, and much more significantly, these congregations are more likely to find themselves in competition with larger, often city-centre, evangelical congregations. This competition is a constant drain on the remaining human resources that these congregations can deploy and there is the constant danger that any new recruits, once converted, will also join this exodus.

What unites all these churches, communal and associational, is their apparent inability to make any significant inroads into the wider local community that exists outside their immediate social networks or to attract floating churchgoers living elsewhere in the city in their direction. Consequently, these churches tend to have a more localized orientation, with the ever-present possibility that they will turn inwards and abandon mission for maintenance. Furthermore, the types of social networks that remain open to them are also declining in size and significance and constitute at best a finite resource for potential recruitment. Once these are gone, the future looks bleak for the remaining churches and chapels in these traditional working-class localities.

Table 1. Social environmental factors in church growth and decline

	Social ecology I	*Social ecology 2*	*Religious ecology*
Environmental factors favouring decline	Low degree of cultural/social fit between churches and catchment population	Absence of social networks linking churches to catchment population	Over-provision of places of worship/high level of competition
Environmental factors favouring growth	High degree of cultural/social fit between churches and catchment population	Presence of social networks linking churches to catchment population	Under-provision of places of worship/low level of competition

It is evident that a number of recurrent factors are impacting on religious institutions in Swansea and these are both internal factors related to the institutional characteristics of the churches and external factors related to the environments in which they operate. However, while distinctions such as whether churches belong to the religious mainstream or the evangelical sphere and the length of time they have been operating are germane to the argument, their success or failure is not entirely conditional on these factors. Clearly, the local environments that churches operate within are an important variable and these explain the significant variations *within* as well as *between* church types. The presence or absence of varied types of social networks that might facilitate contact with surrounding communities and potential recruits appears to be an important factor in the health of religious groups. However, the mere presence of a pool of potential contacts and recruits does not in itself mean very much unless we also consider the dispositions of congregations. In this light, the collective meanings that congregations apply to the social situation in which they find themselves also appear to be a key variable in whether they opt for a collective strategy of maintenance or mission.

CHURCHES AND MISSION IN LATE MODERN SOCIETY

It is clear from the previous discussion that the starting point for any under-standing of individual church growth or decline is to be found in the nature of the sets of relations between congregations and their surrounding social environment. Clearly, these relations change over time. As we have seen, Welsh religion has grown out of and was dependent on a complex and very localized set of social and economic conditions. Deindustrialization and related cultural transformations, notably the decline of the local community, have led to the progressive disembedding of religious institutions from their host communities. The rapid growth of the city, in terms of new housing and accompanying geographical and social mobility, has further exacerbated this process of disembedding. Moreover, this has resulted in the building of more places of worship elsewhere, supplementing those already existing and resulting in an over-provision of places of worship that in turn leads to more competition. The result of these twin processes of disembedding and over-provision is a change in what we might term the customary equilibrium of religious institutions, leading to both their visible general decline and in-creased levels of competition within the religious economy.

At this stage (and with the idea of mission in mind) it might be instructive to pause and consider what basic irreducible conditions must be fulfilled if there is to be any possibility of individuals aligning themselves with or joining a religious institution. First, it is axiomatic that there needs to be some system of religious ideas, a recognizable faith that individuals can choose to believe in and that these ideas need to be institutionalized in a recognizable social form. That is, they need to be embodied in the common life of members of a social group, recruitment being to *groups* and not to systems of ideas. In terms of potential recruitment, there also needs to be some element of prior religious socialization (in order to explain why individuals are willing to adopt a religious problem-solving perspective over any other problem-solving perspective) and concrete networks linking religious institutions to individuals and groups. Clearly, the effectiveness of recruitment strategies will be influenced by both the mode of communication of a religious message and the degree and type of prior socialization.

Beck (1992; Beck *et al.*, 1994) and Giddens (1991, 1994) have emphasized the importance of trust and risk (which are universal aspects of human social interaction) in understanding late modernity. In Beck's discussion of 'risk societies' (1992) he suggests that there has been a significant shift in the relationship between trust and risk under conditions of late modernity. Participation in traditional face-to-face relationships was characterized by high levels of trust and lower levels of risk, whereas Beck's version of modernity is characterized by a shift from these high-trust/low-risk relationships to their opposite, low-trust/high-risk relationships. Giddens (1991) suggests that within a high-risk/low-trust society it is clear that affinitive relations (however constituted) are at a premium, not least because they constitute an important remaining site of trust. Beck (1992) argues that personal assessments of risk and its obverse trust are now pervasive elements of all social action and, as Rose (1996) suggests, these have now supplanted those ties of tradition and traditional certainty that underpinned religious life in the past. As Stark and Bainbridge (1987) have argued, acceptance of a religious ideology or the decision to affiliate to a religious group will entail both 'costs' and 'benefits' to the individual and it is likely that they will weigh these up (however imperfectly) before acting. In this vein, we might say that the decision to affiliate to a religious group also constitutes a 'risk' (however great or small) and is dependent on its obverse 'trust'.

It follows that primary group affiliations such as the family constitute a strong influence on church affiliation, given that there are high levels of trust and low levels of risk (Gautier and Singelmann, 1997: 5). However, this was no means entirely the case in Swansea. The presence of so much transfer activity between churches and the growing trend whereby some individuals sought out religious groups at marked variance with their childhood experience also need to be taken into account. Nonetheless, there does appear to be a link between prior religious socialization and subsequent openness to religion. (For example, some evangelical converts disparaged the validity of their childhood experience in 'dead' (that is, non-evangelical) churches, but this early religious socialization nevertheless constituted part of their spiritual biography.) Moreover, Stark and Bainbridge (1985) argue that prior affinitive relations are a crucial component of subsequent religious affiliation and that acceptance of a religious ideology (belief) and religious affiliation (practice) are each dependent upon a degree of trust and that trust is largely derived from existing social relations.

However, if we accept Anthony Giddens's (1991) contention that the sphere of trust has progressively moved away from primary affiliations such as the family to new sites derived from personal relationships of friendship and intimacy, then this raises some interesting questions. In this light, Gautier and Singelmann's contention that prior *familial* religious affiliation is the primary indicator of subsequent religious affiliation either appears too strong a statement or, as is more likely, suggests that in a climate of transformed social relations as typified in Giddens's portrait of late modernity, the religious imperative must grow weaker. This may be the case, but it must also be recognized that, even in Giddens's formulation of late modernity, there is a recognition that the past and the present are not discrete phenomena but that they overlap. It follows that environments of trust derived from primary familial affiliation can still exist in tandem with transformed environments of trust based on personal intimacy.

Within Stark and Bainbridge's formulation, *either* environment can be a route into religion and what is important is the level of trust derived from personal associations of whatever type (which suggests a network principle). In contrast, they suggest that *any* commitment to religious belief and practice, entailing as it does some 'costs' and 'benefits', also constitutes a significant risk. As a rule of thumb, therefore, the higher the degree of risk in affiliating with an organization the higher the level of trust necessary to consider joining it.

SOCIAL CLOSURE, CULTURAL IDENTITY AND SOCIAL NETWORKS

I now need to turn to a consideration of religious institutions and their internal characteristics. Churches variously constitute *populations, institutions* and *cultures*. As such they are both religious institutions and social groups. Religious values and social values represent two aspects of congregational life and two potential continua along which groups relate to their social environment and where group action might be predicted. In religious terms, all congregations are situated somewhere between the polar opposites of a world-rejecting or a world-affirming orientation. In social terms, congregations may be to varying degrees open or closed. Both continua represent aspects of the institutional interaction of congregations with their surrounding environment and its values and also constitute potential boundaries.

This notion of boundaries can be expressed in terms of relations of *high tension* and *low tension* with the surrounding social environment (Chambers, 1997: 149–50). For example, sectarian groupings holding a strong set of beliefs that are out of step with societal norms *and* a distinctive lifestyle that marks them out from their surrounding social surroundings might be said to exhibit high tension with society. Conversely, an inclusive state church with a liberal outlook might be said to be in low tension with society. However, there may also be a number of dimensions to the high tension–low tension continuum. For example, a congregation may be in low tension with secular ideologies and formally open, while practising social exclusion along lines of class or ethnicity. There are, therefore, a number of possible permutations of belief and practice that will influence the effectiveness of congregations in terms of mission.

Demographic and cultural factors are also undeniably relevant to putative recruitment. It follows that, where the age characteristics and social and cultural attributes of congregations and their potential catchment populations exhibit the greatest degree of similarity, then it is most likely that those populations will be receptive to recruitment. Again, where the institutional characteristics of churches exhibit a high degree of similarity with surrounding institutions, this better enables catchment populations to make the transition to attendance and, potentially, membership.

This can be illustrated in two ways. Where there is a recent tradition of local social involvement in the churches, then the cultural distance between congregations and their surrounding populations is lessened, facilitating relations and opening up the possibility of successful mission. These conditions are likely to benefit congregations seeking older members. Where religious institutions have sought to adapt themselves structurally to changing organizational imperatives in the wider world, they are again likely to be in a better position as regards recruitment, although in this case this is likely to benefit congregations seeking younger members. These examples are certainly not exhaustive and there are any number of potential factors, not least class, ethnicity, gender or subcultural characteristics, that will also be germane to this argument. Simply, where the social structure and cultural characteristics of any church approximate or match those of their surrounding population, then the distance is minimized, facilitating both retention and recruitment of members. Following McGraven and Wagner (1990: 69–71) this might be termed the 'homogeneous unit principle', whereby the distance between social and cultural barriers is minimized to such a degree that the transition into church life is made relatively painless. Clearly, then, social and cultural congruence (or not) with a potential catchment population is an important factor in church growth or decline, as is the broader question of identity and identities.

Identity is derived primarily from lived human experience and this experience is to be located within the mundane sets of social relations (networks) that individuals and groups are attached to (Bourdieu, 1977). Clearly, the type of relatively homogeneous communities that used to be based upon a strong sense of collective identity and shared situation are less present in society than they were in the recent past. Identity has progressively become 'decentred', both in terms of classificatory structures derived from local social structures (that is, traditional geographically circumscribed communities) and in terms of the boundaries derived from those erstwhile communitarian structures (Lash and Urry, 1987). Typically, individuals and groups have to live both with this sense of inhabiting an increasingly fragmented social world and with the problem of how to fashion a satisfactory identity from multiple points of reference. Understandably, collective identities are now most likely to be mediated through relations of intimacy derived from relatively compact sets of social relations (Giddens, 1991). It follows that, under these conditions, churches can no longer take their potential catchment populations for granted. They need to identify those networks of individuals and groups in the community that most closely match their own collective social and cultural characteristics and seek either to establish or to exploit existing relations to a degree where the level of trust outweighs perceptions of risk. Clearly, where congregations are unable or unwilling to utilize these networks they will decline both numerically and in general social significance.

In the case of Swansea, while in terms of supply there is clearly still an abundant religious provision in terms of places of worship, congregational growth is only apparent among those churches with social and cultural links into communities that best meet the minimum conditions for religious allegiance. These are communities where social networks linking internal congregational networks to external networks exist and where there is evidence of some cultural congruence generated through prior religious socialization. In practice, this can mean physically bounded local populations *or* affective communities that have no clear geographical boundaries. It follows that congregational growth is least likely to be found within those social environments situated in traditional working-class locales. These are districts where customary shared social networks have been subject to attrition, where there is little remaining social or cultural congruence between churchgoers and non-churchgoers (most noticeable in terms of age) and where there is a marked over-provision of places of worship. Given that these processes are not new, the majority of local people in these districts have not received any meaningful prior religious socialization and certainly not to the degree necessary for receptivity to the idea of regular churchgoing. Moreover, recruitment strategies are necessarily highly dependent on existing relations between churchgoers, their families and friends and it follows from this that new recruitment (such as it is) is largely to be found among the diminishing pool of long-term residents. In contrast, over in the western suburbs there is a fairly strong social and cultural congruence between churchgoers and non-churchgoers, particularly in terms of age, but the atomized nature of these communities and the absence of strong social networks largely negate this. This last factor is clearly significant in the light of the experience of those suburban congregations that are growing.

If we identify where and among whom these successful recruitment strategies are finding fruit then it becomes apparent that these congregations are successfully tapping into social networks that draw their strength from the wider religious constituency. It follows that those churches that are benefiting from transfer growth have identified a catchment community with a high degree of social and cultural congruence and one that can be reached along pre-existing social networks. Moreover, this activity is carried out within the context of a physical environment where there are fewer places of worship. Churches appear fuller and, therefore, ostensibly more 'successful' and that in itself is a significant factor in attracting recruits from other congregations.

At the risk of stating the obvious, in the final instance recruitment and retention is dependent on action. This implies both the setting of goals (recruitment and retention strategies) and a level of internal resources sufficient to make such action possible. Within the sphere of declining congregations two patterns are visible. There are those congregations that desire to implement church growth strategies but who lack the internal resources to make this possible. These are elderly congregations with very limited human and financial resources. Alternatively, there are those congregations who prefer to target their remaining resources on the promotion of internal activities over external outreach and again this is characteristic of older congregations. In practice, most elderly congregations fall somewhere in between. In both cases these church populations have become resigned to their position, viewing matters as largely out of their control, and understandably they tend to adopt a fatalistic attitude to their continued numerical decline, preferring instead to concentrate their energies inwards. In contrast, congregations with the will and the resources to engage in mission have seen some (if in most cases very restricted) growth. While this growth is clearly limited by localized social environmental factors, nevertheless, it is evident that effective action is possible. Moreover, growing churches recognize that organized religion has experienced major reversals in terms of its loss of social significance and rapid numerical decline, but nonetheless they remain cautiously optimistic about their individual futures.

UNDERSTANDING CHURCH GROWTH AND DECLINE

The argument advanced in this book has been that the success or failure of religious groups is *primarily* dependent, not on some abstract process characterized as 'secularization', but on the rather more immediate environmental conditions and considerations that impact on congregations. This is not to argue that secularization does not exist. Clearly, on any institutional measurement, modern European societies and Welsh society in particular are visibly less religious and therefore more secularized than they were in the past and the marked decline of religious institutions in Wales cannot be understood outside this event. While the history of modern Wales always was characterized by the periodic disengagement of churches and people and its counterpoint, religious revival, this balance appears now to be lost. It is now a century since the last great religious revival in Wales and, despite the occasional very localized resurgence in religious fervour, those days now appear as remote as the age of steam and the telegraph. What, then, does this presage for the future of Welsh religious institutions?

This study has not set out to explain religious change at the societal level. Nor has it sought to claim that one geographical area, Swansea, is 'typical' of the religious situation elsewhere in Wales. It has sought instead to examine, describe and account for the current social and cultural situation of that most basic of religious institutions, the individual congregation. Any macro-theory that seeks to account for religious decline at the societal level inevitably struggles to accommodate an explanation of those examples of religious institutions that are growing rather than declining. Invariably they end up filed under the heading 'exceptions that prove the rule'. Conversely, any macro-theory that seeks to explain the persistence of religious belief and practice invariably avoids or downplays the question of institutional decline, usually by relocating 'religion' somewhere else. While I do not wish to quarrel with either approach, I have sought to isolate and identify those factors that influence the decline or growth of local congregations and by extension different types of religious institution.

I would argue that it is here, among the mundane sets of relations that characterize human social life, that many (but not all) of the answers pertaining to the general decline of religion might be found. Moreover, it seems to me that the irreducible nature of religion (however defined) lies within small-scale human groups, their experiences and the ways in which these shape shared interpretations of the social world that they find themselves in and the ways in which they collectively accomplish that which we term 'religion'. As far as what I have to say on these matters is concerned, I would point to the data that inform this model of church growth and decline. Their plausibility rests with their effectiveness in explaining patterns of growth and decline in the localities studied. Its validity lies in its general-izability and testability and the latter remains open to further investigation by others.

That said, faith groups in Swansea are subject to much the same pressures and dilemmas that are the lot of any religious institution that seeks to chart its way within an increasingly secularized environment. In the broadest terms, and as far as the statistical evidence on a national level is concerned, the demographic and institutional patterns that characterize the churches and chapels of Swansea are recognizably similar to those recorded for their counterparts elsewhere in Wales (Bible Society, 1997). However, by focusing on particular narratives of growth and decline and the realities of contem-porary congregational life, a more nuanced picture emerges that can put flesh on the bones of dry statistics. In the ethnographies that have characterized much of this book we see that church growth and decline has a human face, even if much goes on behind closed doors. It should also be clear by now that congregations are not, by and large, homogeneous social groups and that, as in any social group, individual dispositions can vary significantly within the overall dynamics of congregational life. In visiting these varied congregations we have learned something of what it is like to lead a congregation where unremitting numerical decline is a fact of life and where leadership is carried out in a spirit of faith tempered with the hard realities of practical experience and diminishing resources. The counterpoint to this is the persistence of faith and we also see much evidence of that faithfulness in the stories that have emerged. Clearly, while Welsh religious institutions may be down, they are certainly not yet out. Nonetheless, in the prevailing climate of reli-gious indifference that characterizes Welsh society, any realistic prognosis for the future health of Welsh religious institutions must of necessity be circumspect.

In terms of mission, clearly there is much to be done from the perspective of the churches if they are to re-engage with Welsh society in any meaningful way and, as the evidence from chapters 4 and 6 suggests, there is no room for complacency or prevarication in this. It is no longer enough merely to ensure that 'the doors are kept open' or to 'carry on as we have always done'. The long-term survival of free-standing religious institutions is highly dependent on their ability to reinvent themselves anew for every generation. For many contemporary commentators it is now the evangelical churches that hold the keys to the kingdom and evangelicalism is widely touted as the answer to the malaise affecting the churches. However, as chapters 5 and 7 demon-strate, many of the evangelical nostrums for congregational health also leave something to be desired in terms of their effectiveness. Certainly, as chapter 5 clearly shows, congregations without a tradition of evangelicalism cannot be expected to jettison their customary group identifications without a fight and, as in that case, the upshot can often be the opposite to that which was originally intended. Moreover, as we saw in chapter 7, even in the most successful cases of congregational growth, evangelicalism appears to have little resonance outside its own core constituency. This is reflected in this case in the very marked imbalance between transfers into the congregation from other evangelical churches and recruitment from the general population.

I have deliberately not sought to impose the many variations of the secularization thesis on what I have to say and, for that reason, chapter 2 may appear somewhat disconnected from the rest of the text. My preference has been to let the data speak for themselves and for the reader to draw their own conclusions about the usefulness of the literature underpinning the secularization thesis. Nevertheless, it should be apparent to the reader that there are various themes that have emerged in the empirical chapters that resonate with developments in thinking about secularization. The best of these theoretical developments recognize that religious institutions are an integral part of society and should not be seen as over or against society. Clearly, any theory of religious change that does not recognize that abiding sociological principle cannot be anything other than sociologically deficient (Durkheim, 1995). What follows is a synthesis of those ideas that seem most relevant to the Welsh context.

The Christian church in Wales has a long and varied history and, during the time it has been in existence, the world has changed considerably. Christianity became progressively embedded in Welsh society and, indeed, for a long time was a prime constituent of society, influencing manners, morals and much more. However, human societies rarely remain in a state of stasis for long. Social changes of the same magnitude (if not the same type) that led to the rise of religion as a socially significant force in Wales have led to its progressive disembedding and disarticulation from the traditional social and cultural roots that ensured its status as a core Welsh institution. Customary religious institutions are by definition guardians of tradition but they are also subject to change both from without and within (Harris and Startup, 1999). There is then always some tension between their role as protectors of tradition and the need constantly to reinterpret their position in the light of new circumstances. In a society characterized by growing insecurity and the progressive disattachment of individuals and groups from customary social bonds and cultural understandings, *any* institution predicated on social solidarity is likely to suffer a marked loss of social significance (Beck *et al.*, 1994).

This applies as much to secular voluntary associations predicated on these lines as it does to the churches and *all* institutions of this type are progressively losing support and are struggling to maintain their organizational existence (Davie, 2000: 50–1). For traditional religious institutions in Wales there is now just this lack of continuity between organizational and social environmental boundaries and herein lies their problem. At the same time there has been a parallel shift in attitudes towards authority (Davie, 2000: 51). Clearly, this is a trend that does not sit well with organizations that seek to disseminate their values among the general population on the basis of either their customary power or the authority of the scriptures or both. In a post-Christian society, the claims that the churches make for themselves, in the sense of holding in trust for the people an immutable and divinely revealed body of religious knowledge about God and humanity (Kent, 1982: 1), are unlikely to find much purchase outside their declining core religious constituency.

Evidently, religious values are becoming (but have not yet become) marginalized, although as Davie suggests (ibid.) it is not clear if anything comparable is replacing them. It is just such a problem that Fevre (2000) has recently addressed and he pessimistically concludes that, increasingly, it is only the values of the marketplace that have any widespread purchase in Western societies. The growing lack of societal consensus about ethical and moral values does not bode well for institutions predicated on an unambiguous approach towards these matters. Moreover, as the theologian John Kent suggests, 'For a society that does not value itself, religion cannot exist on the strength of its value to society' (Kent, 1982: 2). Be that as it may, it is clear that religious institutions are progressively losing both authority and any cultural and social congruence with their general populations. With this in mind, the accounts of social and religious change that both Fenn (1972) and Luhmann (1987) have advanced appear increasingly plausible in the light of the growing structural differentiation of Western societies. Clearly, there is much more that can be said on the subject of secularization and many theorists are willing to take up the challenge. Not all theories relating to secularization, it seems to me, are particularly helpful in furthering our understanding of religious and social change. Moreover, as Bruce (2002) has recently argued, much of modern social theory is now so abstracted as to be untestable. However, it goes without saying that, without that literature and the people that produced it, this book would not have seen the light of day.

FACING THE FUTURE

As to the future of religion in Wales, clearly the prognosis for many religious groups is not good. Facing the future, some of these groups will be lost to history, others will undergo radical transformations, some will inevitably be forced to merge together and new institutions will emerge from their ashes.

It is highly unlikely that religious institutions in Wales can ever recover their historic hegemony within the working class and indeed that particular stereotype of the chapel – Nonconformist, Welsh-speaking and rooted in compact and cohesive communities characterized by long-standing patterns of residence – is fast vanishing. (As I write, in another sign of the times yet another nearby local chapel has closed its doors for the last time.) The new face of Welsh religion is increasingly middle-class in character and in its concerns and demonstrates little continuity with what has gone before.

'Suburban religion' is now arguably becoming the dominant mode of religious expression in many parts of Wales, even if the majority of places of worship are still to be found in rural areas. In those areas, which are also the least densely populated, continued rural depopulation and the haemorrhaging of young people to urban areas inside and outside Wales has progressively eroded the social salience of religion in the countryside. While religion persists in rural localities, it is mainly among the middle-aged and elderly and clearly its long-term future is problematic. At the same time continued in-migration of persons of English provenance raises many difficult questions for Welsh-speaking communities and their Welsh-medium religious institutions. Customary linguistic patterns are breaking down in the face of the progressive erosion of Welsh as a first language in rural areas, while at the same time the use of Welsh is increasingly becoming a status marker of a distinctive minority middle-class and urban population. This urban Welsh-language culture is primarily the province of those individuals professionally engaged in education, medicine and the media and their families and it remains very much a minority cultural expression within a heavily anglicized linguistic environment. Moreover, the parallels between the changing fortunes of religion and the Welsh language are striking. This is apparent in the shift in the centre of gravity of Welsh as a public language from its customary cultural location among the rural and urban working classes to its new life within the middle class. Moreover, its use in urban areas is essentially restricted to the home and classroom and again there are clear parallels with the privatization of religion. Significantly, this shift has not been accompanied by any noticeable revival in the fortunes of urban Welsh-medium churches and chapels.

Away from the countryside, it is likely that the 'new church' sector will continue to grow in visibility if only by default. Paradoxically, it is now within this sector of the religious economy that we find places of worship that are often full to overflowing and the most visible expressions of the type of religious fervour that used to characterize revivalist religion in Wales. However, despite these superficial similarities with the past this movement is firmly anglicized and middle-class in character and represents a further erosion of customary expressions of Welsh religiosity. Moreover, many of the personnel of these churches and their leaders are highly mobile English migrants and it is likely that these churches will continue to experience a fairly rapid turnover of adherents.

New varieties of religion of non-Christian provenance are also visibly emerging in those areas where ethnic minority groups are concentrated, notably, Cardiff, Newport and Swansea. Islam is the dominant faith group, reflecting its long history among the seafaring communities of those cities and in recent decades in-migration, primarily from Bangladesh, has added to the incremental growth in this religious sphere. While Islam exists in some tension with its surrounding social and cultural environment this is not a situation of its own choosing. On the one hand, Islamophobia and racism are ever-present realities, while younger Muslims are no less immune to the blandishments of a materialistic and secularized society. In recent years non-Christian faith group leaders in Wales have repeatedly expressed concerns about the attitudes of their young people towards faith matters and the fact that young Muslims, Hindus and Sikhs are in effect called to straddle two cultures (Thompson and Chambers, forthcoming a). Nevertheless, these same leaders were upbeat about the current health of their individual groups and their future prospects and this is reflected in the steady growth of non-Christian places of worship in Wales. Among these faith groups, it is likely that ethnic ties to religion will continue to exercise an influence on identification with religious institutions and religious affiliation and it may be that this will benefit these groups for some time to come. In 2002 the National Assembly for Wales established an Inter-Faith Council of Wales, chaired by the First Minister. For the first time this body brings together Christian and non-Christian faith groups in a quasi-political forum which recognizes the principle of formal participation of religious institutions in political affairs (Thompson and Chambers, forthcoming b).

None of the above suggests the imminent death of religion, even in a country that has become so rapidly secular in character. Moreover, let us not forget the contribution (for good or bad) that religious institutions have made to Welsh society and culture. Popular identification with religion and indigenous religious institutions were crucial factors in the emergence and consolidation of a distinctive Welsh 'national' identity and shaped the contours of both civic and cultural life. Faint echoes of this relationship persist but the tragedy for these institutions lies in the progressive disarticulation of national from religious identity and the resultant loss of the ability of those institutions to be able to lay claim to represent the collective spirit of the Welsh people. Wales is now an increasingly fragmented land of multiple identities, forged out of many diverse types of lived experience of which religion is only one dimension. The Wales of a 'Bible black' public morality and a way of life predicated upon a remarkably homogeneous and egalitarian social structure is now a thing of the past. Pluralism and diversity of experience are now the new watchwords and this is mirrored in the emergence of many competing varieties of national experiences and the reflection of these processes within an increasingly fragmented religious sphere. Nonetheless, the question of 'national' identity remains a pressing public issue, not least in the light of the lukewarm response of the Welsh people to political devolution and the establishment of the National Assembly for Wales. Moreover, rapid and pervasive social and economic change in Wales and the breakdown of a sense of community solidarity has raised many questions about the nature of community and public social bonds. How far current political thinking and public policy initiatives might serve to successfully address these issues remains an open question. Nonetheless, as the theologian and ecumenicalist Aled Edwards writes, in terms of issues such as social justice, social inclusion, equal opportunities and sustainable development, 'few Christians would quarrel with the Assembly's priorities as indicated in its policy statement *A Better Wales*' (Edwards, 2001: 60). It is here, within this new public discourse and the field of civil society, that religious institutions and values may yet have a continued role to play in reaffirming, through cooperation with other agencies, the principle of community and, ultimately, in shaping faith in the new Wales.

Notes

Chapter 1

[1] Elements of this discussion have previously appeared in a more detailed and theoretically informed account of Welsh religious history by this author (Chambers, 2003c).

[2] The focus of this volume is on the Christian religion and its institutions, reflecting their historical hegemony within Welsh society. However, there are other faith narratives present in Welsh history and for more information on non-Christian faith groups the reader is directed to Henriques 1993; Chambers, 2003a, d.

[3] As such, this book contributes to the burgeoning area of congregational studies, a relatively new academic discipline that seeks to locate religious belief and practice within the dynamics of congregational life. Its focus is on the study of local congregations as the primary expressions of institutional religion and as symbolic representatives of the Christian faith among the communities in which they are located. Since the groundbreaking publication of the *Handbook of Congregational Studies* (Carrol *et al.*, 1986) congregational studies have become firmly established in the United States and have emerged more recently in the United Kingdom with the publication of *Congregational Studies in the UK: Christianity in a Post-Christian Context* (Guest *et al.*, 2004). Some elements of the discussion contained in chap. 5 of this book are also to be found in a rather different form and emphasis in the author's chapter, 'The effects of evangelical renewal on congregational identities', in Guest *et al.*, 2004.

Chapter 2

[1] The title of this paper was 'God really is dead: a challenge to the silver liningists'. Subsequently published in 1996 in revised form in the *Journal of Contemporary Religion* 11/3: 261–75.

[2] Prof. C. C. Harris, in a private conversation, observed to me that most funerals now seem to function more as secularized memorial services highlighting the

positive achievements of the deceased rather than their original religious purpose of offering prayers for the souls of the departed in the face of their imminent judgement by God.

3 Although, as David Martin (1997) has recently commented, there are built-in limits to the potential spread of this sector.

4 A theme echoed by those radical theologians (Cox, 1965; Edwards, 1987; Bonhoeffer, 1993; Kung, 1995) who would seek to embrace the secularization of society for precisely these reasons.

5 Thus a definition of religion in institutional terms will lead to the delineation of the secularization process in institutional terms also.

6 However, another reading is possible. Both the partial vacation by religion of the political sphere and its decline as an apparatus of social control and welfare is not primarily a narrative about the decline of the social power of religious institutions but rather part of the narrative of nation-state formation (Calhoun, 1997). *All* institutions, not just religious, are subject and subservient to this process (Giddens, 1985, 1991; Billig, 1995). Further, religion can play a renewed role in the legitimization of the state (Waters, 1995; Casanova, 1994; Calhoun, 1997) as recent events in Poland, the former Yugoslavia and the former USSR demonstrate. (Martin warns that this type of case should not be seen as 'epiphenomenal i.e. *really* nationalism' (1991: 468)) Further, Martin (1991) argues that the type of argument that Wilson espouses is essentially Eurocentric. While the nation-state model is now universal, it can take many forms (Giddens, 1991) including a religiously orientated form (Robertson and Chirico, 1985; Lawrence, 1989; Martin, 1991; Robertson, 1991, 1992).

7 David L. Edwards (1987) suggests that Wilson places far too much emphasis on the decline of traditional institutional forms and points to many European examples of the renewal and re-engagement of historic churches and religious denominations. Edwards suggests that, rather than sectarian groupings becoming a dominant religious form, they will continue to recruit largely from the marginalized and those individuals effectively disengaged from society.

8 The title of his book is *The Invisible Religion.*

9 An indirect result of this is the creation of a religious marketplace where 'consumer preference' becomes increasingly important, something which Berger is ambivalent about (1967: 145–7).

10 Stark and Bainbridge do not explicitly align themselves to rational choice theory, preferring the characterization 'exchange theory' and they are usually placed within this category (Hamilton, 1995). However, a close reading of their theorizing in both (1995) and (1997), particularly the emphasis on individual evaluation, social networks and social exchange, suggests to this writer that this is a variation on rational choice theory.

Chapter 8

1   These ideal types draw loosely from Tönnies's (1955) distinction between *Gemeinschaft* and *Gesellschaft* and the related ideas of ascribed and achieved status as they relate to religious affiliation. While not novel, within the Welsh context these distinctions seem to me to best sum up the relationship between pre- and post-1904 Revival religious institutions and serve better than terms such as 'mainstream' and 'evangelical'.

Bibliography

Abell, P. (1996) 'Sociological theory and rational choice theory', in B. Turner (ed.), *The Blackwell Companion to Social Theory*. Oxford: Blackwell.

Anderson, B. (1991) *Imagined Communities*. London: Verso.

Arjomand, S. A. (1991) 'The emergence of Islamic political ideologies', in J. A. Beckford and T. Luckmann (eds), *The Changing Face of Religion*. London: Sage.

Beck, U. (1992) *Risk Society: Towards a New Modernity*. London: Sage.

Beck, U., Giddens, A. and Lash, S. (1994) *Reflexive Modernization*. Cambridge: Polity.

Beckford, J. A. (1989) *Religion and Advanced Industrial Society*. London: Routledge.

Beckford, J. A. (1992) 'Religion, modernity and postmodernity', in B. Wilson (ed.), *Religion: Contemporary Issues*. London: Bellew.

Berger, P. and Luckmann, T. (1967) *The Social Construction of Reality*. Harmondsworth: Penguin.

Berger, P. (1967) *The Sacred Canopy*. New York: Doubleday.

Berger, P. (1971) *A Rumour of Angels*. Harmondsworth: Penguin.

Berger, P. (1973) *The Social Reality of Religion*. Harmondsworth: Penguin.

Bible Society (1997) *Challenge to Change: Results of the 1995 Welsh Churches Survey*. Swindon: Bible Society.

Billig, M. (1995) *Banal Nationalism*. London: Sage.

Bonhoeffer, D. (1993) *Ethics*. London: SCM.

Bourdieu, P. (1977) *Outline of a Theory of Practice*. Cambridge: Cambridge University Press.

Brennan, T. (1954) *Social Change in South West Wales*. London: Watts.

Brierley, P. (1991) *Prospects for the Nineties: All England Trends and Tables from the English Church Census*. London: MARC.

Brierley, P. (2000) *The Tide is Running out*. London: Christian Research.

Brierley, P. (2001) *UKCH Religious Trends No. 3*. London: Christian Research.

Brierley, P. and Wraight, H. (eds) (1995) *UK Christian Handbook 1996/7 Edition*. London: Christian Research.

Briggs, A. (1983) *A Social History of England*. London: Wiedenfield & Nicolson.

Brown, C. G. (1992) 'A revisionist approach to religious change', in S. Bruce (ed.), *Religion and Modernization*. Oxford: Clarendon Press.

Bruce, S. (1992) 'Introduction', in S. Bruce (ed.), *Religion and Modernization*. Oxford: Clarendon Press.

Bruce, S. (1993) 'Religion and rational choice: a critique of economic explanations of religious behaviour', *Sociology of Religion*, 54: 193–205.

Bruce, S. (1996) *Religion in the Modern World: From Cathedrals to Cults*. Oxford: Oxford University Press.

Bruce, S. (1999) *Choice and Religion: A Critique of Rational Choice Theory*. Oxford: Oxford University Press.

Bruce, S. (2002) *God is Dead: Secularization in the West*. Oxford: Blackwell.

Calhoun, C. (1997) *Nationalism*. Buckingham: Open University Press.

Carrol, J. W., Dudley, C. S. and McKinney, W (eds) (1986) *The Handbook for Congregational Studies*. Nashville, TN: Abingdon Press.

Casanova, J. (1994) *Public Religions in the Modern World*. Chicago: University of Chicago Press.

Catholic Media Office (1996) *Cardiff Province Directory and Yearbook 1996*. Cardiff: Archdiocese of Cardiff.

Chadwick, O. (1975) *The Secularization of the European Mind in the Nineteenth Century*. Cambridge: Cambridge University Press.

Chambers, P. (1997) ' "On or off the bus": identity, belonging and schism. A case study of a neo-Pentecostal house church', in Hunt, S., Hamilton, M. and Walter, T. (eds) *Charismatic Christianity: Sociological Perspectives*. Basingstoke: Macmillan.

Chambers, P. (1999) 'Church growth and decline in Swansea' (unpubl. Ph.D. thesis, University of Wales).

Chambers, P. (2003a) 'Religious diversity in Wales', in C. Williams, N. Evans, and P. O'Leary (eds), *A Tolerant Nation? Exploring Ethnic Diversity in Wales*. Cardiff: University of Wales Press.

Chambers, P. (2003b) 'Secularization, human rights and sacred texts', unpubl. paper presented at the BSA Sociology of Religion Study Group Annual Conference Oxford, 12 April.

Chambers, P. (2003c) 'Social networks and religious identity: an historical example from Wales', in G. Davie, L. Woodhead, and P. Heelas (eds), *Predicting Religion: Christian, Secular and Alternative Futures*. Aldershot: Ashgate.

Chambers, P. (2003d) 'The long shadow: religion and identity', *Planet: The Welsh Internationalist*, 158: 85–90.

Chandler, J. (1997) 'Religion in Europe', in T. Spybey (ed.), *Britain in Europe*. London: Routledge.

Cohn, W. (1969) 'On the problem of religion in non-western cultures', *International Yearbook for the Sociology of Religion*, 5:7–19.

Cotton, I. (1995) *The Hallelujah Revolution: The Rise of the New Christians*. London: Little, Brown & Co.

Cox, H. (1965) *The Secular City*. London: SCM.

Craib, I. (1992) *Modern Social Theory: From Parsons to Habermas*. Hemel Hempstead: Harvester Wheatsheaf.

Currie, R., Gilbert, A. and Horsley, L. (1977) *Churches and Churchgoers: Patterns of Church Growth in the British Isles since 1700*. Oxford: Clarendon Press.

Davie, G. (1994) *Religion in Britain since 1945: Believing without Belonging*. Oxford: Blackwell.

Davie, G. (2000) *Religion in Modern Europe: A Memory Mutates*. Oxford: Oxford University Press.

Davies, D., Watkins, C., Winter, M., Pack, C., Seymour, S. and Short, C. (1991) *Church and Religion in Rural England*. Edinburgh: T. & T. Clark.

Davies, O. (1996) *Celtic Christianity in Medieval Wales*. Cardiff: University of Wales Press.

Davies, R. (1996) *Secret Sins: Sex, Violence and Society in Carmarthenshire 1870–1920*. Cardiff: University of Wales Press.

Dobbelaere, K. (1981) 'Secularization; a multi-dimensional concept', in *Current Sociology*, 29/2: 3–213.

Douglas, M. (1996) *Natural Symbols: Explorations in Cosmology, with a New Introduction*. London: Routledge.

Durkheim, E. (1995) *The Elementary Forms of the Religious Life*. New York: Free Press.

Edwards, A. (1990) 'People, Places and Prospects', in R. Jenkins and A. Edwards (eds), *One Step Forward? South and West Wales towards the Year 2000*. Llandysul: Gomer.

Edwards, A. (2001) *Transforming Democracy: A Christian Reflection on Welsh Devolution*. Bangor: Cyhoeddiadau'r Gair.

Edwards, D. L. (1987) *The Futures of Christianity*. London: Hodder & Stoughton.

Elster, J. (1989) *Nuts and Bolts for the Social Sciences*. Cambridge: Cambridge University Press.

Evans, C. (1987) *My People*. Bridgend: Seren.

Fenn, R. K. (1970) 'The process of secularization: a post-Parsonian view', *Journal for the Scientific Study of Religion*, 9/2: 117–36.

Fenn, R. K. (1972) 'Towards a new sociology of religion', *Journal for the Scientific Study of Religion*, 11/1: 16–32.

Fevre, R. W. (2000) *The Demoralization of Western Culture*. London: Continuum.

Finke, R. (1992) 'An unsecular America', in S. Bruce (ed.), *Religion and Modernization*. Oxford: Clarendon Press.

Fox, R. G. (1990) 'Hindu nationalism in the making, or the rise of the "Hindian" ', in R. G. Fox (ed.), *Nationalist Ideologies and the Production of National Cultures*. Washington, DC: American Anthropological Association.

Gautier, M. L. and Singelmann, J. (1997) 'Children's religious affiliation in Eastern Germany', *Journal of Contemporary Religion*, 12/1: 5–15.

Gellner, E. (1983) *Nations and Nationalism*. Oxford: Blackwell.

Giddens, A. (1985) *The Nation State and Violence*. Cambridge: Polity.

Giddens, A. (1991) *The Consequences of Modernity*. Cambridge: Polity.

Giddens, A. (1994) 'Living in a post-traditional society', in U. Beck, A. Giddens and S. Lash (eds), *Reflective Modernization*. Cambridge: Polity.

Gill, R. (1989) *Competing Convictions*. London: SCM.

Gill, R. (1992) 'Secularization and census data', in S. Bruce (ed.), *Religion and Modernization*. Oxford: Clarendon Press.

Gill, R. (1993) *The Myth of the Empty Church*. London: SCM.

Gill, R. (1994) *A Vision for Growth*. London: SPCK.

Glasner, P. (1977) *The Sociology of Secularization*. London: Routledge.

Guest, M., Tusting, K. and Woodhead, L. (eds), (2004) *Congregational Studies in the UK: Christianity in a Post-Christian Context*. Aldershot: Ashgate.

Hall, S. (1992) 'The Question of Cultural Identity', in S. Hall, D. Held and T. McGrew (eds), *Modernism and its Futures*. Cambridge: Polity.

Hamilton, M. (1995) *The Sociology of Religion: Theoretical and Comparative Perspectives*. London: Routledge.

Harris, C. (1990) 'Religion', in R. Jenkins and A. Edwards, (eds), *One Step Forward? South and West Wales towards the Year 2000*. Llandysul: Gomer.

Harris, C. and Startup, R. (1999) *The Church in Wales: The Sociology of a Traditional Institution*. Cardiff: University of Wales Press.

Hastings, A. (1991) *A History of English Christianity 1920–1990*. London: SCM.

Heirich, M. (1977) 'Change of heart: a test of some widely held theories about religious conversion', *American Journal of Sociology*, 83/3: 653–80.

Hempton, D. (1994) 'Religious life in industrial Britain 1830–1914', in S. Gilley and W. S. Sheils (eds), *A History of Religion in Britain*. Oxford: Blackwell.

Henriques, U. (ed.) (1993) *Jews of South Wales*. Cardiff: University of Wales Press.

Hill, C. (1991a) *Society and Puritanism in Pre-Revolutionary England*. Harmondsworth: Penguin.

Hill, C. (1991b) *The World Turned Upside Down: Radical Ideas during the English Revolution*. Harmondsworth: Penguin.

Holton, R. J. (1996) 'Classical social theory', in B. Turner (ed.), *The Blackwell Companion to Social Theory*. Oxford: Blackwell.

Hornsby-Smith, M. (1992) 'Recent transformations in English Catholicism: evidence of secularization?', in S. Bruce (ed.), *Religion and Modernization*. Oxford: Clarendon Press.

Howard, R. (1996) *The Rise and Fall of the Nine o'Clock Service*. London: Mowbray.

Hunt, S., Hamilton, M. and Walter, T. (eds), (1997) *Charismatic Christianity: Sociological Perspectives*. Basingstoke: Macmillan.

Hunt, S. J. (2002) *Religion in Western Society*. Basingstoke: Palgrave.

Iannaconne, L. R. (1992) 'Religious markets and the economics of religion', *Social Compass*, 39/1: 123–31.

Jenkins, G. H. (1978) *Literature, Religion and Society in Wales 1660–1730*. Cardiff: University of Wales Press.

Jenkins, G. H. (1988) 'The new enthusiasts', in T. Herbert and G. E. Jones (eds), *The Remaking of Wales in the Eighteenth Century*. Cardiff: University of Wales Press.

Jenkins, P. (1992) *A History of Modern Wales*. London: Longman.

Jenkins, T. (1999) *Religion in English Everyday Life*. New York: Berghahn.

Jones, V. (ed.) (1969) *The Church in a Mobile Society*. Llandybie: Christopher Davies.

Kent, J. H. S. (1982) *The End of the Line? The development of Christian theology in the last two centuries*. London: SCM.

Kim, A. E. (1996) 'Critical theory and the sociology of religion: a reassessment', *Social Compass*, 43/2: 267–83.

Kung, H. (1995) *Christianity: The Religious Situation of our Time*. London: SCM.

Lambert, W. R. (1988) 'Some working class attitudes towards organized religion in nineteenth-century Wales', in G. Parsons (ed.), *Religion in Victorian Britain*, vol. IV, *Interpretations*. Manchester: Manchester University Press.

Lash, S. and Urry, J. (1987) *The End of Organized Capitalism*. Cambridge: Polity.

Lawrence, B. (1989) *Defenders of God: The Fundamentalist Revolt against the Modern Age*. New York: Harper Row.

Lofland, J. and Stark, R. (1965) 'Becoming a worldsaver: a theory of conversion to a deviant perspective', *American Journal of Sociology*, 30/4: 862–75.

Luckmann, T. (1967) *The Invisible Religion: The Problem of Religion in Modern Society*. London: Macmillan.

Luckmann, T. (1983) *Life-World and Social Realities*. London: Heinemann.

Luckmann, T. (1996) 'The privatization of religion and morality', in P. Heelas, S. Lash and P. Morris (eds), *Detraditionalization: Critical Reflections on Authority and Identity*. Oxford: Blackwell.

Luhmann, N. (1974) 'Institutionalized religion in the perspective of functional sociology', *Concilium*, 1/10: 45–55.

Luhmann, N. (1987) 'The representation of society within society', *Current Sociology*, 35/2: 101–8.

McAllister, L. (2001) *Plaid Cymru: The Emergence of a Political Party*. Bridgend: Seren.

McGraven, D. A., and Wagner, C. P. (1990) *Understanding Church Growth*. Grand Rapids: Eerdmans.

McLeod, H. (1992) 'Secular cities? Berlin, London and New York in the later nineteenth and early twentieth centuries', in S. Bruce (ed.), *Religion and Modernization*. Oxford: Clarendon Press.

Martin, B. (1992) 'Church and culture', in W. Carr, P. Bates, D. Conner, J. Cox, G. James, C. Lewis, B. Martin, S. Platten, R. Reiss, T. Stevens and A. Tilby, *Say one for Me: The Church of England in the Next Decade*. London: SPCK.

Martin, D. (1967) *A Sociology of English Religion*. London: Heinemann.

Martin, D. (1969) *The Religious and the Secular: Studies in Secularization*. London: Routledge.

Martin, D. (1978) *A General Theory of Secularization*. Oxford: Blackwell.

Martin, D. (1991) 'The secularization issue: prospect and retrospect', *British Journal of Sociology*, 42/3: 465–74.

Martin, D. (1997) *Reflections on Sociology and Theology*. Oxford: Clarendon.

Martin, D. C. (1995) 'The choices of identity', *Social Identities*, 1/1: 5–20.

Mehl, R. (1970) *The Sociology of Protestantism*. London: SCM.

Mellor, P. A. and Shilling, C. (1997) *Re-forming the Body: Religion, Community and Modernity*. London: Sage.

Merton, R. (1957) *Social Theory and Social Structure*. Glencoe: Free Press.

Munson, J. (1991) *The Nonconformists: In Search of a Lost Culture*. London: SPCK.

Noll, M. A. (1992) *A History of Christianity in the United States and Canada*. London: SPCK.

O'Toole, R. (1996) 'Religion in Canada: its development and contemporary situation', *Social Compass*, 43/1: 119–34.

Parsons, T. (1960) *Structure and Process in Modern Societies*. New York: Free Press.

Parsons, T. (1966) *Societies: Evolutionary and Comparative Perspectives*. Englewood Cliffs, NJ: Prentice Hall.

Parsons, T. (1967) *Sociological Theory and Modern Society*. New York: Free Press.

Parsons, T. (1971) *The System of Modern Societies*. Englewood Cliffs, NJ: Prentice Hall.

Pope, R. (1998) *Building Jerusalem: Nonconformity, Labour and the Social Question in Wales, 1906–1939*. Cardiff: University of Wales Press.

Price, W. (1989) 'Church and society in Wales since the disestablishment', in P. Badham (ed.), *Religion, State and Society in Modern Britain*. Lampeter: Edwin Mellen.

Richardson, J. T., and Stewart, M. (1977) 'Conversion process models and the Jesus movement', *American Behavioral Scientist*, 20/6: 819–38.

Robertson, R. (1991) 'Globalization, politics and religion', in J. A. Beckford and
    T. Luckmann (eds), *The Changing Face of Religion*. London: Sage.
Robertson, R. (1992) *Globalization*. London: Sage.
Robertson, R. and Chirico, J. (1985) 'Humanity, globalization and worldwide
    religious resurgence: a theoretical exploration', *Sociological Analysis*, 46/3:
    219–42.
Robbins, K. (1994) 'Religion and community in Scotland and Wales since 1800', in
    S. Gilley and W. S. Sheils (eds), *A History of Religion in Britain*. Oxford: Blackwell.
Rose, N. (1996) 'Authority and the genealogy of subjectivity', in P. Heelas, S. Lash
    and P. Morris (eds), *Detraditionalization: Critical Reflections on Authority and
    Identity*. Oxford: Blackwell.
Rosser, C. and Harris, C. (1965) *The Family and Social Change*. London: Routledge.
Sacks, J. (1991) *The Persistence of Faith: Religion, Morality and Society in a Secular Age*.
    London: Wiedenfield & Nicolson.
Sharpe, E. (1983) *Understanding Religion*. London: Duckworth.
Shiner, L. (1967) 'The concept of secularization in empirical research', in
    K. Thompson and J. Tunstall (eds), *Sociological Perspectives: Readings in Sociology*.
    Harmondsworth: Penguin.
Stark, R. and Bainbridge, W. S. (1980) 'Networks of faith: interpersonal bonds and
    recruitment to cults and sects', *American Journal of Sociology*, 85/6: 1376–95.
Stark, R. and Bainbridge, W. S. (1985) *The Future of Religion: Secularization, Revival
    and Cult Formation*. Berkeley: University of California Press.
Stark, R. and Bainbridge, W. S. (1987) *A Theory of Religion*. New York: Peter Lang.
Stark, R. and Iannaccone, L. (1994) 'A supply-side reinterpretation of the "secular-
    ization" of Europe', *Journal for the Scientific Study of Religion*, 33/1: 230–52.
Symonds, A. (1990) 'Migration, communities and social change', in Jenkins, R. and
    Edwards, A. (eds), *One Step Forward? South and West Wales towards the year
    2000*. Llandysul: Gomer.
Thomas, K. (1971) *Religion and the Decline of Magic: Studies in Popular Beliefs in
    Sixteenth and Seventeenth Century England*. Harmondsworth: Penguin.
Thompson, A. and Chambers, P. (forthcoming a) 'Faith on the margins: organized
    religion and civil society', submitted to *Sociological Review*.
Thompson, A. and Chambers, P. (forthcoming b) 'Public religion and political
    change in Wales', *Sociology*.
Tomlinson, D. (1995) *The Post-Evangelical*. London: SPCK.
Tönnies, F. (1955) *Community and Association*. London: Routledge.
Towler, R. and Chamberlain, A. (1973) 'Common religion', in M. Hill (ed.) *A
    Sociological Yearbook of Religion*, vol. vi. London: SCM.
Turner, B. (1991) *Religion and Social Theory*. London: Sage.
Walker, A. (1985) *Restoring the Kingdom*. London: Hodder & Stoughton.
Walker, A. (1997) 'Thoroughly modern: sociological reflections on the Charismatic
    movement from the end of the twentieth century', in S. Hunt, M. Hamilton and
    T. Walter (eds), *Charismatic Christianity: Sociological Perspectives*. Basingstoke:
    Macmillan.
Waters, M. (1995) *Globalization*. London: Routledge.
Welch, K. (1981) 'An interpersonal influence model of traditional religious com-
    mitment', *Sociological Quarterly*, 22/4: 81–92.

Williams, G. (1994) 'Medieval Wales and the Reformation', in S. Gilley and W. J. Sheils (eds), *A History of Religion in Britain*. Oxford: Blackwell.

Williams, G. A. (1985) *When was Wales?* Harmondsworth: Penguin.

Williams, G. A. (1988) 'Beginnings of radicalism', in T. Herbert and G. E. Jones (eds), *The Remaking of Wales in the Eighteenth Century*. Cardiff: University of Wales Press.

Wilson, B. (1966) *Religion in a Secular Society*. London: Watts.

Wilson, B. (1982) *Religion in Sociological Perspective*. Oxford: Oxford University Press.

Wilson, B. (1992) 'Reflections on a many sided controversy', in S. Bruce (ed.), *Religion and Modernization*. Oxford: Clarendon Press.

Yeo, S. (1973) 'A contextual view of religious organization', in M. Hill (ed.) *A Sociological Yearbook of Religion in Britain*, vol. vi. London: SCM.

Index